STARVATION AND INDIA'S DEMOCRACY

Dan Banik

Routledge
Taylor & Francis Group

LONDON AND NEW YORK

First published 2007
by Routledge
2 Park Square, Milton Park, Abingdon, Oxon OX14 4RN

Simultaneously published in the USA and Canada
by Routledge
270 Madison Ave, New York, NY 10016

*Routledge is an imprint of the Taylor & Francis Group,
an informa business*

Typeset in Times New Roman by
Prepress Projects

Printed and bound in Great Britain by
MPG Books Ltd, Bodmin, Cornwall

British Library Cataloguing in Publication Data
A catalogue record for this book is available from the British Library

Library of Congress Cataloging in Publication Data
Banik, Dan, 1969–
Starvation and India's democracy/Dan Banik.
p. cm. – (Routledge advances in South Asian studies series)
Includes bibliographical references and index.
1. Famines – India – Prevention. 2. Food supply – Government policy
– India. 3. Famines – India – Kalahandi (District) 4. Poverty – India
– Kalahandi (District) 5. Famines – India – West Bengal. 6. Poverty
– India – West Bengal. 7. Democracy – India. I. Title.

HC439.B27 2007

363.8′5610954 – dc22

ISBN10: 0-415-40729-X (hbk)
ISBN10: 0-203-96288-5 (ebk)

ISBN13: 978-0-415-40729-8 (hbk)
ISBN13: 978-0-203-96288-6 (ebk)

CONTENTS

ILLUSTRATIONS

Figures

Tables

Boxes

ACKNOWLEDGEMENTS

This book is the product of an interest in starvation and famine that started almost a decade ago and I have greatly benefited from discussions, suggestions and criticisms made by those who have taken an interest in my work. I owe an enormous debt to James C. Scott, Barbara Harriss-White and Subrata K. Mitra, who have not only taught me much but also provided useful comments, advice, encouragement and friendship. To Amartya Sen, who has been a major source of inspiration and with whom I had instructive discussions, I acknowledge a special debt.

For detailed and immensely helpful comments on earlier drafts, I am extremely grateful to Marc Cohen, Bob Currie, Stephen Devereux, Milton J. Esman, Walter P. Falcon, James Garrett, Anne Gjerdåker, Carl H. Gotsch, Bernt Hagtvet, Ron Herring, Hugh LaFollette, Charles Lindblom, Desmond McNeill, Ben White and two anonymous referees.

For very useful counsel and suggestions I wish to thank Tony Atkinson, Wenche Barth-Eide, Luka Deng Biong, Tom Christensen, Edward Clay, Giovanni Andrea Cornia, Meghnad Desai, Tim Dyson, Asbjørn Eide, Thomas Hylland Eriksen, Peter Evans, Edward Friedman, Des Gasper, Stuart Gillespie, Wolfgang Hoeschele, Jon Hovi, Paul Howe, Randhir B. Jain, George Kent, Francesco Kjellberg, Atul Kohli, Uwe Kracht, William Lafferty, Stig Toft Madsen, Raino Malnes, Philip McMichael, Barbara D. Miller, Karl Ove Moene, John D. Montgomery, Mick Moore, Per Pinstrup-Andersen, Pamela Price, Sanjay Reddy, Fred Riggs, Susan Rose-Ackerman, Arild Engelsen Ruud, Palagummi Sainath, Arjun Sengupta, Tor Skålnes, Olav Stokke, M. S. Swaminathan, Olle Törnquist, Stein Tønnesson, Rene Veron, Robert Hunter Wade, Jon Wetlesen and Øyvind Østerud.

In India, I received assistance from a large number of individuals and organisations. My thanks to Swapan Banerjee, Subhra Banerjeee, Biman Bose, Atri Bhattacharya, Susant Bhol, Kanchan Chakrabarty, Indrani and Saurabh Chaudhuri, Bhakta Charan Das, Feroze, Moloy Goswami, Pradeep Jena, Sanjib Joshi, Kailash, Uma Shankar Kar, Amareswar Mishra, Surja Kanta Mishra, Ashok Mitra, N. Murali, Janardan Pati, Jagdish Pradhan, G. K. Prasad, N. Ram, N. Ravi, Jawhar Sarkar, Tathagata Satpathy, Hemant Sharma and the staff of Purulia Circuit House.

ACKNOWLEDGEMENTS

The book is based on the main findings of two research projects – 'Public Action in Combating Famine: The Case of India' and 'The Silent Emergency: Child Malnutrition in India' – both generously funded by the Research Council of Norway, which not only allowed me to spend several months at a stretch in India between 1998 and 2005 but also gave me the freedom to attend numerous seminars and conferences in Europe and the United States. An additional Research Council grant made it possible to spend three months at the International Food Policy Research Institute (IFPRI) in Washington, DC, in the summer of 2006 and I wish to thank Marie Ruel and her colleagues at the Food Consumption and Nutrition Division for providing me with such an excellent work environment. The Centre for Development and the Environment (SUM) at the University of Oslo has been my 'home' since mid-1996 and I have received generous support from friends and colleagues. In particular, I wish to thank Bente Herstad, Desmond McNeill, Kristi Anne Stølen and Alida Boye for their support and encouragement over the years. Sigve Bøe Skattum very kindly, and at very short notice, drew the maps used in this book. Dorothea Schaefter and Tom Bates at Routledge have been most helpful and I am grateful for their infinite patience. I also wish to thank Andrew R. Davidson at Prepress Projects for insightful comments and excellent work on the manuscript.

Ava and Devdas Banik have fuelled my interest in poverty research and have been a source of unconditional support. Two wonderful years of being married to Vibeke has opened a whole new world to me, one of new knowledge, particularly on European history, and exciting Saturday morning discussions on world politics at the breakfast table. I dedicate this book to her and our joint product – little Alexander.

ABBREVIATIONS

ACC	The United Nations Administrative Committee on Coordination
ADM	Additional District Magistrate
ADMO	Additional District Medical Officer
AGP	Asom Gana Parishad
AIMIM	All India Majlis-E-Ittehadul Muslimmen
APL	above poverty line
BDO	Block Development Officer
BJD	Biju Janata Dal
BJP	Bharatiya Janata Party
BMI	body mass index
BPL	below poverty line
CAG	Comptroller and Auditor General
CBI	Central Bureau of Investigation
CDMO	Chief District Medical Officer
CDPO	Child Development Project Officer
CED	chronic energy deficiency
CMR	crude mortality rate
CDR	crude death rate
CPI	Communist Party of India
CPI(M)	Communist Party of India (Marxist)
CPI(M-L)	Communist Party of India (Marxist-Leninist)
CRF	Calamity Relief Fund
DCFS	District Controller of Food and Supplies
DCSO	District Civil Supplies Officer
DM	District Magistrate (same as Collector)
DPAP	Drought Prone Areas Programme
DRDA	District Rural Development Agency
DSP	Deputy Superintendent of Police
DSWO	District Social Welfare Officer
DSWD	District Social Welfare Department
DWCD	Department of Women and Child Development

EAS	Employment Assurance Scheme
EM	excess mortality
FAD	food availability decline
FAO	Food and Agricultural Organization of the United Nations
FBL	All India Forward Block
FCI	Food Corporation of India
FEWS Net	Famine Early Warning System Network
FPS	Fair Price Shop
GOI	Government of India (Central government)
GP	Gram Panchayat
GR	Gratuitous Relief
ha	hectares
IAS	Indian Administrative Service
IAY	Indira Awas Yojana
ICDS	Integrated Child Development Services
ICS	Indian Civil Service (pre-independence period)
IMR	infant mortality rate
INC	Indian National Congress ('Congress')
IPS	Indian Police Service
IRDP	Integrated Rural Development Programme
ITDA	Integrated Tribal Development Agency
ITDP	Integrated Tribal Development Programme
JD	Janata Dal
JE	Junior Engineer
JGSY	Jawahar Gram Samridhi Yojana
JRY	Jawahar Rozgar Yojana
KBK	Kalahandi, Bolangir and Koraput districts in Western Orissa
LIP	Lift Irrigation Projects
LPG	liquefied petroleum gas
LTAP	Long Term Action Plan (for the KBK districts)
MFP	minor forest products
MIP	minor irrigation projects
MLA	Member of the State Legislative Assembly
MMR	maternal mortality rate
MP	Member of Parliament
MWS	Million Wells Scheme
NABARD	National Bank for Agriculture and Rural Development
NAC	Notified Area Council
NCCM	National Centre for Calamity Management
NCHS	National Centre for Health Statistics
NDA	National Democratic Alliance
NFCR	National Fund for Calamity Relief
NFBS	National Family Benefit Scheme
NFHS	National Family Health Survey

NGO	non-governmental organisation
NHRC	National Human Rights Commission
NIC	National Informatics Centre
NMBS	National Maternity Benefit Scheme
NNMB	National Nutrition Monitoring Bureau
NMMP	National Mid-day Meals Programme
NOAP	National Old Age Pension
NRS	National Readership Survey
NSS	National Sample Survey
OAP	Old Age Pension
OAS	Orissa Administrative Service
PDS	Public Distribution System
PEM	protein energy malnutrition
PHC	Public Health Centre
PIL	public interest litigation
PMO	Prime Minister's Office
PS	Panchayat Samity
PUCL	People's Union of Civil Liberties
PWD	Public Works Department
PWPI	Peasant and Workers Party of India
RDA	recommended daily allowance (food intake)
RDC	Revenue Division Commissioner
RJD	Rashtriya Janata Dal
RMC	Regulated Market Committee
Rs	rupees
RSP	Revolutionary Socialist Party
SC	Scheduled Caste
SCN	United Nations Sub-Committee on Nutrition
SDO	sub-divisional officer
SGSY	Swarna Jayanti Gram Swarozgar Yojana
SJPR	Samajwadi Janata Party – Rashtriya
SMR	Standardised Mortality Rate
SNP	Special Nutrition Programme
SP	Superintendent of Police
SRC	Special Relief Commissioner (Board of Revenue)
SRS	Sample Registration System
SS	Shiv Sena
ST	Scheduled Tribe
TDP	Telegu Desam Party
TPDS	Targeted Public Distribution System
UF	United Front
UIP	Upper Indravati Project
UN	United Nations
UNICEF	United Nations Children Fund

URTI	Upper Respiratory Tract Infection
VLW	village level worker
WFP	World Food Programme
WHO	World Health Organisation
WA	weight for age
WP	widow pension
ZP	*Zilla Parishad*

INDIA

Jammu & Kashmir

Himachal
Pradesh

Punjab

Uttaranchal

Haryana

New Delhi

Arunachal Pradesh

Rajasthan

Uttar Pradesh

Sikkim

Assam

Nagaland

Bihar

Meghalaya

Manipur

Gujarat

Madhya Pradesh

Jharkhand

Tripura

Mizoram

Chhattisgarh

West Bengal

Kolkata

Orissa

Maharashtra

Bhubaneswar

Goa

Andhra Pradesh

Karnataka

Pondicherry

Lakshadweep

Tamil Nadu

Andaman & Nicobar

Kerala

ORISSA

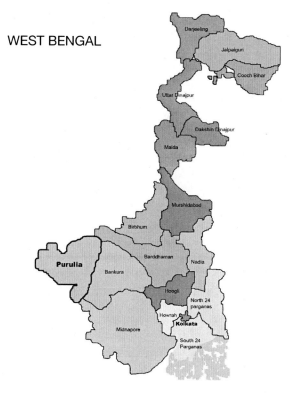

WEST BENGAL

1

INTRODUCTION

The Nobel laureate Amartya Sen has famously claimed that no famine has ever occurred in a democratic country. In contrast to China, which experienced the worst famine in recorded history in 1958–61, India has successfully prevented famine since independence in 1947. This success, Sen argues, is primarily due to India's democratic political structure, which allows for a free press, opposition parties and the freedom for civil society to organise and advocate. Indeed, India's achievement is all the more impressive when one considers that famines were prevented despite large-scale poverty, undernutrition and the production of less food per capita than the famine-hit countries of Africa in the 1970s and 1980s. And together with impressive economic growth, the country has also made substantial progress in promoting human development in the past five decades – life expectancy has doubled, child mortality has fallen by more than 50 per cent, and fertility has declined by more than two-fifths. However, the success in preventing famine has not been replicated in the field of chronic hunger, which remains a major concern and affects large groups in the population.

This book builds on Sen's claim that no famine has ever occurred in a democratic country, but goes further and examines the ability of democratic institutions to tackle starvation which lacks the sensational characteristics of a famine. It examines the characteristics of the Indian political system and the nature of the problem of starvation in order to understand why some issues are effectively dealt with and not others. Despite unprecedented technological progress in the twentieth century, the *threat* of famine continues to loom over many countries, including India. The topic warrants increased attention as new definitions and understandings of famine are resulting in situations where events that were not previously counted as famines are increasingly viewed as famines. Similarly, depending on how one understands and defines 'democracy', one could claim that famines also take place in certain democratic societies. In this context India provides an instructive example, where over 200 million men, women and children suffer from a combination of chronic malnutrition and severe undernutrition, and more than 2.5 million children die every year before reaching the age of five. This is clearly a major problem that needs to be seen in parallel with Sen's claim that democratic

1

India has successfully avoided famine. In doing so, the book highlights the 'silent emergency' of high levels of undernutrition and starvation in democratic India, which ironically persists in spite of large surpluses of foodgrains produced in the country each year. Thus, the features of democracy – including a vibrant press and active political parties, which appear to help prevent famine in India – are notably ineffective in preventing starvation deaths. This book tries to explain why this is so by focusing on empirical material drawn from two states on India's east coast – Orissa and West Bengal. There is, in particular, a focus on reported instances of 'starvation deaths' – which can be placed in a continuum between chronic (daily) hunger and sensational famines – in the tribal-dominated and drought-prone Kalahandi district in western Orissa, which over the past few decades has achieved notoriety as India's 'starvation capital'. Despite regular press coverage and expressed political concern over severe drought-induced distress, Kalahandi has remained highly vulnerable to starvation. The book provides an explanation for this by studying levels of poverty and inequality, impact of drought, state action in improving nutritional standards, and how democratic institutions and public action work towards reducing vulnerability to starvation. The case of Kalahandi is then compared with the tribal-dominated and drought-prone Purulia district in the neighbouring West Bengal state, where no starvation-related deaths have been reported despite recurrent drought and food shortages.

Although the book draws its empirical reference from India, its goal is to engage in a theoretical and cross-cultural analysis of the interaction of political institutions, media, civil servants, voluntary organisations and citizens groups in the prevention of famine and starvation deaths. In addition to India, the relationship between governance and the reduction of extreme poverty and vulnerability has become increasingly important in countries where chronic undernutrition, starvation and the threat of famine are a regular feature of daily life for large groups of people. Indeed, in recent years, famines or the threat of famine has loomed large over countries in Asia (e.g. Bangladesh and North Korea), sub-Saharan Africa (e.g. Ethiopia, Sudan, Niger, Malawi, Mali, Zimbabwe) and Latin America (e.g. Bolivia, Colombia, Brazil). Hence it is not only important to revisit the democracy and famine prevention argument but also to examine why millions of people around the world – irrespective of regime category – continue to suffer from severe undernutrition and starvation.

The extent of hunger and government interventions

When India gained independence in 1947, the country faced two main nutritional challenges. The first was the threat of famine due to low agricultural production together with the lack of a proper food distribution system. The second was chronic and acute undernutrition due to poor access to safe drinking water, sanitation and health care, which were further aggravated by the widespread prevalence of infections and disease (Planning Commission 2000: 2). In the past five decades, the threat of famine has been dramatically reduced. Similarly, there has been considerable reduction in the incidence of certain nutritional-deficiency diseases like kwashiorkor, marasmus, pellagra and beriberi although undernutrition levels among children remain high. General improvements in nutritional status have been attributed to rapid foodgrain productivity growth and improvements in dietary intake and health care.[1] Successive Indian governments have intervened in private food markets in order to control and stabilise prices and supplies and to prevent food shortages. As Pacey and Payne (1985) note, state intervention in food markets in India has largely been undertaken in three ways. First, in times of bad harvests with short supplies and high prices, the government has responded in a variety of ways – rationing of food stocks, imposition of movement restrictions on agricultural produce, import from other countries, and the control of market prices through the public distribution system. Second, in good harvest years when market prices are low and supplies abundant, the government has intervened by relaxing the rationing system, reducing procurement from farmers and relaxing the inter-state movement restrictions for foodgrains. Third, in times of exceptionally good harvest and subsequent very low market prices, the government has granted various forms of price support to producers, and encouraged export. Currently India also has several active programmes that have the potential to make a substantial contribution to the reduction of undernutrition. These include the provision of subsidised food through the Public Distribution System (PDS), targeted food supplementation through the Integrated Child Development Services (ICDS), the National Mid-Day Meals Programme (NMMP) and emergency feeding programmes for the poorest of the poor. In addition, the government has initiated micronutrient programmes for the distribution of iron-folate, vitamin A and salt iodisation together with food-/cash-for-work programmes that boost food availability and accessibility through schemes like the Employment Assurance Scheme (EAS) and Jawahar Rozgar Yojana (JRY).

However, and despite a large food surplus since the mid-1990s, the above-mentioned safety-net-oriented schemes have had only moderate success. As a result, the food and nutritional security of a large portion of the population, especially in rural and inaccessible areas, remains precarious. Even though the national food supply position has steadily improved over the years – staple food production peaked at 209 million tonnes in 2000 – and foodgrain stocks accumulated, a large majority of Indian households have failed to improve their per capita foodgrain consumption. Data from successive National Sample Surveys show high levels of vulnerability both in terms of the ability to purchase food available in the market and with regard to price increases, unemployment and temporary loss or reduction of income. Chronic energy deficiency (CED) and micronutrient deficiencies are widespread among both children and adults in India. For example, while mortality rates were halved between 1947 and 2000, the corresponding reduction in undernutrition was only 20 per cent (Planning Commission 2000: 5). The major cause of CED continues to be inadequate food intake, infections and poor child caring practices resulting from low dietary intake, poor sanitation facilities and inadequate health care and poor infant feeding practices. In the public imagination, the home of malnourished adults and children is sub-Saharan Africa, although all available data clearly show that the worst affected region is South Asia. The enormity of the problem is borne out by the fact that India accounts for 40 per cent of the world's malnourished children while containing less than 20 per cent of the global child population. According to one study more than half of the Indian children under four years of age are moderately or severely malnourished, 30 per cent of newborns are significantly underweight, and 60 per cent of Indian women are anaemic (Measham and Chatterjee 1999). Despite considerable government interventions, success at improving nutritional status has varied across regions, states, gender, age and social groups. Although undernutrition is especially high among children less than two years of age, rural women and certain caste and tribal groups, nutritional status varies enormously from region to region (ibid.: 10). For example, in spite of the prevalence of low dietary intake, the infant mortality rate and the percentage of the population facing severe undernutrition in Kerala are far lower than other states primarily thanks to 'more equitable distribution of food between income groups and within families and better access to and utilisation of health care' (Planning Commission 2000: 5). Indeed, despite higher average dietary intake than Kerala, three states – Orissa, Uttar Pradesh and Madhya Pradesh – have more than 25 per cent of the population facing severe undernutrition (ibid.: 8). Similarly, nutrition spending, as a percentage of state domestic product, varies considerably among states, with Tamil Nadu (0.58 per cent), Orissa (0.36 per cent) and Gujarat (0.29 per cent) spending far more on nutritional programmes in 1994–95 than West Bengal (0.08 per cent), Andhra Pradesh (0.1 per cent) and Rajasthan (0.13 per cent).[2]

Although experts now agree that addressing the needs of women is a crucial aspect of combating child malnutrition, this aspect has been largely ignored in India (Swaminathan Foundation 2000). Malnutrition among women is common and severe during pregnancy, and one-third of all babies in India are born with low birth weight. In comparison, approximately 16 per cent of babies in poor countries are born malnourished, i.e. with birth weight of 2.5 kilograms or less (Martorell 1999). Low birth weight is a good indication that 'the infant was malnourished in the womb and/or that the mother was malnourished during her own infancy, childhood, adolescence, and pregnancy' (Ramalingaswami et al. 1996). Further, approximately 60 per cent of Indian women suffer from iron deficiency anaemia, a proportion that rises to a staggering 83 per cent during pregnancy (ibid.).

An important determinant of whether a child grows well relates to the 'quality of childcare', a topic largely neglected in academic research as it is considered to be a private activity and consequently difficult to quantify. One-third of India's labour force consists of adult women who are mostly engaged in heavy manual tasks that place additional caloric demands on them. The heavy burden of bearing children and poor eating habits compounds the problem further. According to Measham and Chatterjee (1999: 12), 'a vicious intergenerational cycle commences when a malnourished or ill mother gives birth to a low birth weight female child: she remains small in stature and pelvic size due to further malnourishment, and produces malnourished children in the next generation'. Moreover, the low status of women in many parts of India results in women and female children getting less than their fair share of household food and health care. And it is generally assumed that the situation is usually worse in tribal areas, where female literacy rates are often below 10 per cent. Large groups of Indian women have limited opportunities and freedoms and, for certain caste and tribal groups, local customs and traditions, together with poor economic status, contribute to the neglect of proper child care. Such customs also restrict interaction with other women and exposure to knowledge and information on education and health matters.

Berg (1987: 1) claims that, in large parts of the developing world, 'malnutrition is everybody's business but nobody's main responsibility'. This is particularly true in the Indian case where nutritional interventions are typically characterised by an uncoordinated response (Measham and Chatterjee 1999). Government officials do not have a specific ministry or department of nutrition to turn to, since numerous ministries at central and state levels implement these programmes.[3] There is, in general, a lack of overall coordination of nutritional interventions, and implementing agencies tend to work in splendid isolation with little or no contact with policy-making organs (Banik 2001).

Starvation and Kalahandi's notoriety

The most glaring example of widespread food and nutritional insecurity in recent years is Kalahandi district, located in the state of Orissa. Kalahandi has become synonymous with drought and starvation. In the past couple of centuries, it has played host to drought, periodic food shortages and famine on numerous occasions. For example, after the colonial administration declared a famine in 1887 – following three successive years of crop failure – widespread mortality was reported. Famine struck the region again in 1899 – locally referred to as 'Chappan Salar Durbhikshya' (The Famine of the Century) – after the failure of rains in successive years severely affected foodgrain production.[4] There were occasional food shortages during the first two decades of the twentieth century although no major famine occurred until 1919, when the price of foodgrain rapidly increased resulting in profiteering and unauthorised export to neighbouring regions by grain merchants. The government's relief efforts – which included the provision of loans and supply of foodgrains from buffer stocks – had little impact in preventing mass starvation and loss of lives and the situation worsened when a cholera epidemic arrived together with influenza. Leading up to Indian independence in 1947, Kalahandi continued to experience regular periods of food shortage, which were drought-related in 1920–21, 1922–23 and 1925–26 and flood-related in 1927 (Kalahandi Gazetteer 1980: 141).

Even after 1947, the district faced food shortages on a regular basis although there are no detailed estimates of the number of victims who may have died from starvation. In terms of its severity and impact, the drought in 1965–66 remains one of the worst recorded in Kalahandi's history. The district recorded its lowest annual average rainfall in history (669.2 mm) and over 75 per cent of the harvest was lost (Mahapatra 1994: 107; Currie 2000: 81–83). The severity of the drought also led the Prime Minister, Indira Gandhi, to visit the district in 1966 and announce that the central government would substantially increase its financial allocation for development programmes in the region. This gesture by the Prime Minister, notes Currie (2000: 84), 'was to win Indira Gandhi and the Congress party lasting support among poorer sections within the region'. Besides droughts causing widespread crop loss in the 1970s, the district also suffered from a major flood in 1977 which caused severe damage to roads, bridges and telecommunications.

Much of Kalahandi's current notoriety, however, can be traced back to the mid-1980s when a string of press reports on child sale and starvation deaths – and subsequent criticism of the government in Parliament – influenced the Prime Minister, Rajiv Gandhi, to visit the district in 1985. This was also when the rest of India began hearing of Kalahandi on a daily basis as media interest, especially in the national press, increased manifold. With severe droughts in 1986–87, the situation in the district was grim and a few concerned individuals and organisations petitioned the judiciary alleging starvation deaths and the general neglect of the district by the Orissa government. Subsequent inquiries conducted by court-appointed officials concluded that starvation deaths had indeed taken place, and a couple of high-ranking civil servants in Orissa were indicted for failing to take preventive action. These petitions and the subsequent court rulings further increased media interest in the Kalahandi story in the 1990s.

The district was back in the national limelight in 1993 when newspaper reports indicated thousands of people in the district who were severely affected by a severe drought and almost 500 people were reported to have starved to death. And when large parts of India were reeling under drought in 1996–97, Kalahandi was once again one of the worst affected areas. In a span of a few months, over 600 people were reported to have been taken severely ill from diarrhoea, gastroenteritis and tuberculosis, and 94 lives were lost according to official statistics. Unofficial reports put the figure at over 300. There were almost daily reports in the English-language and Oriya press on starvation deaths, epidemics, distress sale of assets and large-scale out-migration from the district. These reports, and pressure from a group of opposition-party politicians and legislators in Orissa, prompted the central government in December 1996 to ask the National Human Rights Commission (NHRC) to investigate 21 specific cases of alleged starvation deaths in Kalahandi and other districts of Orissa on an urgent basis. The ensuing NHRC report concluded that starvation deaths had taken place in 18 of the 21 cases and the investigating team warned that, unless immediate measures were taken, the situation would worsen. The Orissa government, however, dismissed these findings and vehemently denied even the likelihood of starvation deaths taking place in the state. Instead, it blamed the central government for neglecting Orissa and for failing to provide adequate calamity relief funds to successfully tackle drought. Kalahandi faced major droughts again in 1998 and 2000, and a similar pattern was observed with the press regularly highlighting starvation deaths in the district and Orissa government consistently refusing to admit such deaths. And in the absence of independent investigations – further complicated by widely disparate understandings of starvation and its causes among civil servants and health officials – whether deaths have indeed resulted from starvation is not resolved factually. Thus, the topic of starvation deaths is a contested arena; although everyone seems to agree that such deaths are bad, two types of tactics are used by the government – denial and blame-shifting.

The Kalahandi case is particularly interesting since in addition, to widespread media publicity, the issue of starvation deaths in the district has figured regularly and prominently in parliamentary debates with successive opposition parties criticising the central and state governments for their failure to provide relief to the drought-affected population. This suggests a failure of public action. Indeed, in the period 1996–2000 – the focus of this book – vulnerability to starvation in Kalahandi was one of the highest in India, with hundreds perishing each year from food-related causes and thousands being forced to migrate to neighbouring states in search of work. Starvation deaths, however, do not just take place in Kalahandi, and there are several districts spread across other states where large groups face acute distress on a regular basis that may culminate in death from starvation. In a 1996 survey, the central government identified 41 districts in 12 states that were 'prone to starvation deaths'. And in addition to Kalahandi, three districts from Orissa – Nuapada, Koraput and Bolangir – figured on the list.[5] The Kalahandi case is, however, especially interesting given the sustained media publicity, VIP visits (almost all Prime Ministers of India have visited Kalahandi) and judicial interventions which have focused attention on drought and deprivation in the district. These actions also gradually resulted in the projection of Kalahandi as India's starvation capital and there was national consensus that the district symbolised poverty and suffering like no other area of the country. Yet starvation deaths continue to occur every year.

The argument

With the experience of Kalahandi in mind, this book critically examines the relationship between democracy, starvation and famine prevention, taking as a starting point Amartya Sen's claim that no famine has ever occurred in a democratic country. Although Sen admits that democratic India has succeeded in preventing famine, he repeatedly highlights the fact that the country has failed miserably to address the problem of chronic undernutrition. However, he does not provide an explanation for this failure. This book empirically applies Sen's hypotheses on the relationship between democracy and public action on the one hand and the prevention of famine and starvation deaths (resulting from severe undernutrition) on the other. In doing so, it links India's success in famine prevention with its failure to reduce high levels of undernutrition and subsequent starvation deaths among vulnerable and highly food-insecure groups.

The argument is twofold. First, I revisit Sen's original argument on democracy's role in preventing famine and argue that, despite recent criticism, it can be refined and further strengthened by focusing on operational definitions of 'famine' and a more nuanced understanding of 'democracy'. This is particularly relevant for the Indian case as there is still some confusion whether the country has actually avoided a famine since independence. Second, I use Sen's democracy–famine argument to examine whether and how democracy is able to prevent starvation deaths as well. In doing so I argue that, in addition to opposition parties and the press, there is a need to understand the role and capacity of, and interaction among, a wide range of institutions including the bureaucracy, judicial and legislative branches of government, civil society organisations and citizens' action in preventing starvation deaths.

To return to the first argument, I propose two sets of ways in which the relationship between democracy and famine prevention can be refined and further strengthened. I argue that it is imperative to clearly distinguish the term 'famine' from related terms like 'malnutrition', 'undernutrition' and 'starvation deaths', as these terms are frequently used interchangeably, causing much confusion among academics, policymakers and practitioners. A clarification on such conceptual issues is of urgent importance for the purposes of early warning, diagnosis and timely response to food crises. In this quest, I present a fivefold typology of operational definitions comprising 'undernutrition', 'severe undernutrition', 'famine threat', 'famine' and 'great famine'. In the light of recent criticism directed at Sen, I demonstrate that his argument applies only to cases of large-scale loss of life as symbolised by the categories 'famine' and 'great famine', and not to cases that fall under 'undernutrition', 'severe undernutrition' or 'famine threat'. Consequently, I demonstrate that Sen is right in that democratic India has successfully prevented famine. In order to understand the relationship between democracy and famine prevention, I argue that it is important to identify certain key features of democracies that enable them to tackle famine better than 'non-democracies'. In this task, I re-examine Sen's argument with the use of the concepts of 'democracy' and 'freedom' and argue that Sen's statements are best understood when loosely or broadly interpreted in contrast to a narrow and rigorous interpretation. Although elections are important, they do not guarantee adequate public deliberation on socio-economic rights, and in this sense a democracy provides necessary but not sufficient conditions for famine prevention. Thus, while democratic institutions have the potential to increase political concern and responsiveness towards preventing major crises like famine, there are no guarantees that all democracies will successfully manage to avert a famine. In terms of the Indian case, the country has in the past witnessed, and will continue to experience in the future, numerous situations that can best be described as 'famine threats'. Thus far, India has managed to prevent such 'famine threats' from escalating into 'famines' and there is reason to believe that India will continue to enjoy success on this issue. In this respect, Sen is correct: democracy and public action do work well towards preventing famine in India.

The second argument is related to examining how a democracy addresses the issue of starvation deaths. In other words, what helps to prevent starvation deaths? Taking as a starting point the notion of open and accountable government in a democracy, I focus on the instrumental role and capacity of democratic institutions to fight starvation. There is a need to specify and understand how anti-starvation policies are actually implemented, and the conditions under which democratic political rights and resulting public action succeed in respecting, protecting and fulfilling important social and economic rights and freedoms.[6] A broad aim of this empirical section of the book is to focus on the interaction between specific institutions in nutrition policy and the existing 'rules of the game' that characterise this interaction. This is primarily undertaken by adopting a bottom-up (or process-oriented) perspective on the role, functioning and effectiveness of state and non-state institutions in reducing vulnerability to undernutrition and starvation. An extended understanding of 'public action' is analysed with a focus on certain key actors including the press, NGOs, judiciary, bureaucracy, opposition political parties, Panchayats[7] and parliament. The overall aim is to examine the interaction between the executive, legislative and judicial branches of government in addition to the influence of civil society organisations both in making information on starvation deaths publicly available and in holding relevant authorities accountable for apparent failures to prevent such deaths.

In order to test some of the conclusions from the Kalahandi case, the book also briefly reviews the experience of Purulia district in neighbouring West Bengal. The purpose is not to undertake a detailed discussion of the Purulia case but to examine the impact of the drought-induced food crisis in Purulia in 1998, and subsequent public action that prevented starvation deaths. What are the lessons to be learnt from the two cases? Interestingly, Purulia shares many of the characteristics of Kalahandi. It has high levels of poverty, low levels of literacy and a high percentage of Scheduled Caste (SC) and Scheduled Tribes (ST) in the population.[8] Most importantly, the entire district is drought-prone and, apart from the district capital, Purulia town, most of the villages suffer from food shortages and water scarcity during years when the monsoon rains are erratic and unevenly distributed. However, despite recurrent drought episodes, high population density, undeveloped agricultural potential, stagnation in industry, and high levels of undernutrition, no starvation deaths have ever been reported in Purulia. What explains Purulia's success in preventing starvation deaths in comparison to Kalahandi? What lessons can be learnt from the two cases? Most importantly, is it possible to identify certain conditions under which democracy and public action work better to prevent starvation deaths?

Research design

The study is based on both quantitative and qualitative data collected at national, state and local levels in India. A major secondary source of information was the large amount of newspaper reports on food shortage, drought relief and starvation published in major English-language, Bengali and Oriya dailies in the period 1996–2000. In addition, a rich variety of empirical material was gathered from policy documents, reports (inquiry reports, departmental reports and NGO annual reports), proceedings of court cases, parliamentary debates and questions, pamphlets, memoranda, administrative budgets, department instructions and regulations, and official correspondence between bureaucrats, politicians and journalists. The collection of statistical information was combined with in-depth field visits to the case study areas. Fieldwork was undertaken in four phases totalling over a year in the periods November 1998–March 1999, December 2000–March 2001, September 2003–January 2004 and December 2004–January 2005. It was organised at four levels: state capital (Bhubaneswar and Calcutta), district (Bhawanipatna and Purulia town), block (Thuamul Rampur, Lanjigarh and Bhawanipatna blocks in Kalahandi and Purulia, Balarampur and Manbazar blocks in Purulia) and village. The choice of blocks and villages within the two districts was based on information on severity of drought, extreme poverty, food insecurity and destitution gathered from published press reports and in consultation with local journalists, politicians, NGO workers and district officials.

A considerable amount of empirical data was collected through over 300 semi-structured interviews and informal discussions with different categories of informants during the three phases of fieldwork. The working languages used were English, Hindi and Bengali. In Bhubaneswar and Calcutta, the primary interviewees included high-ranking politicians, civil servants, MPs and MLAs, editors, journalists and correspondents of national and regional newspapers, major NGOs, and academics. In Bhawanipatna and Purulia town, interviewees included district officials, clerks, doctors, political leaders and party workers, community leaders, NGO staff, journalists, shop owners, traders, school and college teachers and visiting officials from Bhubaneswar and Calcutta. Valuable information was also gained from discussions with caretakers of government guesthouses, drivers, cooks, servants and gardeners. At the block and village levels, interviews were conducted with members of the poorest and most vulnerable households, BDOs and their staff, revenue inspectors, extension officers, Panchayat representatives, school teachers, traders, shop owners, farmers, moneylenders, and visiting government officials and medical teams. Special emphasis was placed on 'network mapping' and observation of the major aspects of socio-economic and political life in the selected villages.

Outline of the book

In Chapter 2, I propose two sets of ways in which Sen's argument on the relationship between democracy and famine prevention can be further strengthened. These are related to the manner in which the concepts of 'famine' and democracy are understood and operationalised. The discussion provides the foundation for an examination of the role and capacity of a democracy in preventing starvation deaths. Chapter 3 provides an overview of poverty and undernutrition in Kalahandi, the official social security provisions in operation and the common local coping strategies adopted by villagers in response to drought. It also establishes the district's high vulnerability to severe undernutrition and the likelihood of starvation deaths. Administrative guidelines for responding to drought in Orissa are critically examined in Chapter 4 followed by an analysis of government response to drought in the period 1996–2000, particularly in terms of agricultural production and the provision of employment. There is also a specific focus on implementation structures and the subsequent modest impact of nutritional interventions including the PDS, ICDS, NMMP and Gratuitous Relief programmes. The focus in Chapter 5 is on legal and quasi-legal interventions on starvation deaths and the right to food which have attracted considerable attention within India and abroad. This is followed by an analysis of the impact of such interventions particularly in terms of changes in administrative response to drought and the views of civil servants on undernutrition and allegations of starvation deaths in Kalahandi. In Chapter 6, I discuss the role and capacity of the national, regional and local newspapers in providing early warning information of drought and impending food crises with predictive significance. Do such news reports actually trigger the authorities into action? If not, why? And what characterises reports of starvation deaths and how do journalists understand the phenomenon? The first part of Chapter 7 focuses on politics in Orissa and the extent to which political leaders and their parties criticise official policy and influence government response to drought and starvation. The Panchayat system, although relatively new in Orissa, is also examined particularly in relation to the implementation of development programmes and the ability of its representatives to influence the district administration's response to drought and destitution. Against the background of recurrent centre–state feuds over calamity relief funds, the chapter also discusses the extent to which federalism in India prevents a more timely and effective response to drought and starvation. Parliamentary discourse on Kalahandi's problems is the focus of Chapter 8, and the content and context of debates and questions on drought and starvation during two Lok Sabha (the lower house of the Indian Parliament) periods are examined. There is a particular focus on the activity and influence of MPs from Orissa, especially two successive MPs from Kalahandi. In order to test some of the major conclusions from the Kalahandi case, Chapter 9 briefly reviews the West Bengal government's response to the drought in Purulia district in 1998, where no starvation deaths occurred despite severe food and water shortages. The analysis particularly focuses on the role of the CPI(M) party, the bureaucracy and the Panchayat system. Finally, Chapter 10 summarises the major conclusions of the study and identifies certain 'lessons' or conditions under which democracy and public action are not successful – or are insufficient – in preventing starvation deaths.

2

DEMOCRACY AND STARVATION

In his influential book *Poverty and Famines* (1981), Amartya Sen radically changed ideas on the causation of starvation and famines. Conventional wisdom until then had suggested that famines were variously caused when food availability declined on account of dramatic shifts in climatic conditions, mismanagement of natural resources and overpopulation. Placing such approaches under the category of 'Food Availability Decline' (FAD), Sen launched a forceful refutation of the FAD thesis, observing that starvation and famines occur even when there is an abundance of food available in a country or a region. Based on a study of famines in Africa and South Asia, he argued that the main causation of famine was not food supply failure, but rather demand failure or 'entitlement collapse'. In terms of the Kalahandi case, it is particularly important to examine whether starvation deaths are the result of insufficient food production or lack of individual freedoms; hence this chapter starts with a brief overview of Sen's entitlement and capability approaches which provide the foundation for a focus on the role of democracy and public action in combating starvation and famine.

Sen argues that overall production or availability of food is often an inaccurate indicator of what the vulnerable groups in a community actually require, and the entitlement approach therefore focuses 'on the ability of people to command food through the legal means available in society, including the use of production possibilities, trade opportunities, entitlements *vis-à-vis* the state, and other methods of acquiring food' (Sen 1981: 45). In a much-cited passage, he writes:

> Starvation is the characteristic of some people not *having* enough food to eat. It is not the characteristic of there *being* not enough to eat. While the latter can be a cause of the former, it is but one of many *possible* causes. Whether and how starvation relates to food supply is a matter for factual investigation. Food supply statements say things about a commodity (or a group of commodities) considered on its own. Starvation statements are about the *relationship* of persons to the commodity (or that commodity group).
>
> (ibid.: 1)

Accordingly, starvation and famine take place when economic change – in the form of a fall in 'endowment' (e.g. alienation of land, or loss of labour power due to ill health) – or an unfavourable shift in the conditions of 'exchange' (e.g. loss of employment, rise in food prices, reduction of social security provisions, etc.) make it no longer possible for a person to acquire any commodity bundle with enough food. For the prevention of famine, 'entitlement protection' is important, i.e. the processes whereby lost entitlements of groups vulnerable to famine are recreated. These include several types of public policy interventions like the promotion of participative economic growth, the protection of the environment, the abolition of armed conflicts, and the development of social security systems (Sen 1990a: 3–4). The intrinsic importance of the entitlement approach – which is primarily concerned with individual and household command over 'commodities' – must, argues Sen, be seen in relation to the concept of 'capability' which refers to the basic capacity that enables people to function, i.e. it 'represents the various combinations of functionings (beings and doings) that the person can achieve' (Sen 1992: 40). Understood in this sense, capability is a 'set of vectors of functionings' that reflect 'the person's freedom to lead one type of life or another' (ibid.). For Sen, poverty is the result of a failure of basic capabilities to function, i.e. poverty is capability deprivation, which includes the capability of being adequately nourished, leading a long and healthy life, being literate, etc. And 'larger entitlements contribute to wider capabilities' (Drèze and Sen 1989: 13n21). The example provided is that of a pregnant woman having far greater nutritional and medical needs than a non-pregnant woman. If both women have the 'same command over food and health care as another', it may not give the pregnant woman 'the same capability to be well nourished and healthy' (ibid.: 13). Similarly, take the case of two persons, A and B, suffering from starvation: Person A is, for instance, starving because of lack of access to food while Person B is starving on purpose on account of religious or political beliefs. If one were to employ traditional welfare economics, concerned primarily with *outcomes*, to evaluate the two cases, it would not capture the essential difference. However, using the capability approach one would be able to recognise that Person B, who is starving on purpose, could have, in essence, made a different choice – one not to starve (Atkinson 1998: 9). Such an analysis will then have profound implication for policy recommendations.

Public action

The brief overview on entitlements and capabilities provides the basis for understanding the importance of the concept of public action, which requires 'causal investigations of capabilities and of variations in the relation between entitlements and capabilities' (Drèze and Sen 1989: 13n21). Having argued for a capability-centred approach to assessing the standard of living, Sen (1990b, 1991) introduces the concept of public action and defines it as including 'not only what is done *for* the public by the state, but also what is done *by* the public for itself'.

Thus, public action entails concern for – and the motivation to do something to improve – the lives of others. It involves not only government policies but also the range of actions undertaken by individuals and groups to extract government accountability and to seek remedial action. The importance of public action thus lies in its potential for enhancing 'the capability of people to undertake valuable and valued "doings and beings"' ranging from 'such elementary capabilities as the ability to avoid undernourishment and related morbidity and mortality, to more sophisticated social capabilities such as taking part in the life of the community and achieving self-respect' (Drèze and Sen 1989: 12). And without recognising 'this basic human motivation' to get involved in the lives of others, 'it would be impossible to understand the part that political parties, social leaders, journalists, relief agencies and grass-root activists can play in encountering famines and chronic deprivation' (ibid.: 13).

A focus on the notions of 'capability' and 'public action' helps not only to assess the nutritional needs of the vulnerable but also to acknowledge the importance of access to complementary services like health care, clean drinking water, sanitation, etc. In order to see how public action works in achieving capabilities, Sen further recommends a focus on legislation in a country.

> The relevant legislation includes not only the protection of certain basic provisions of public support and social security, but also – at a deeper level – the guaranteeing of democratic rights of free elections, uncensored news reporting and unfettered public criticism. Even though these political features may, on a superficial view, look rather remote from the elementary economic problem of hunger and starvation, they are, in fact, closely connected. They promote the political incentive for governments to be responsive, caring and prompt.
>
> (Sen 1990b)

The idea of public action is thus closely linked with the idea of social security and involves the application of social means to both prevent and combat vulnerability to poverty and deprivation. Drèze and Sen (1989: 16) distinguish between two distinct types of social security. First, social security as *protection* is associated with 'preventing a decline in living standards as might occur in, say, an economic recession or – more drastically – in a famine'. Second, social security as *promotion* is concerned with 'the enhancement of general living standards and to the expansion of basic capabilities of the population' and is understood mainly as a long-term challenge. The provision of social security thus conceived can entail direct support in the form of free food and health services, cash support, employment insurance and basic education. It can also include indirect support in the sense that, if economic growth is followed by 'widespread participation of the population', then social security can make 'a substantial – and lasting – contribution to eliminating deprivation' (ibid.). However, the 'public', to whom social security is provided, is 'not a homogenous entity, and there are divisions related to class, ownership, occupation, and also gender, community and culture' (ibid.: 17). On the basis of this diversity, it is natural that, although public action ought to be beneficial for all groups in society, there will be considerable pressures from different groups seeking a larger share of benefits than others. Therefore, any form of public action needs take into account various cooperative conflicts (ibid.: 17–18).

Thus, public action involves public delivery of goods and services by both state and non-state (e.g. market) actors. However, this is only part of the picture and it is crucial that the public – heterogeneous as it usually is – participates in the process of social change in both 'collaborative' and 'adversarial' ways. For example, the public needs to be collaborative in aspects of government policy – literacy drives, health campaigns, land reforms, famine relief measures – that require such cooperation for successful implementation. The public also needs to influence government initiatives and demand proper government response by performing an adversarial and critical role. This is achieved by political activism, critical news reports and informed public criticism.

> The distinction between the 'collaborative' and 'adversarial' roles of the public has some relevance to this dichotomy between the advantages of public commitment *vis-à-vis* those of political pluralism. While a leadership committed to radical social change can often inspire more public collaboration, having a committed leadership is not adequate for – and may even be hostile to – the exercise of the adversarial role of the public. Since both the roles have value in combating deprivation, it is natural to look for the possibility of combining the advantages of committed leadership with those of pluralist tolerance.
>
> (Drèze and Sen 1989: 278)

Drèze and Sen (1989) go on to argue that both collaborative and adversarial features of public participation are required for successfully combating famines, undernutrition and endemic deprivation. The ideal combinations of both these features may be challenging and difficult to implement given social, political and economic constraints in many poor countries. Nonetheless, this does not detract anything from the main argument that both features are necessary for preventing famines and endemic deprivation. Drèze and Sen (ibid.: 279) further argue that it is 'essential to see the public not merely as "the patient" whose well-being commands attention, but also as "the agent" whose actions can transform society'.

India's success in preventing famine

Basing his analysis on an initial comparison between India and China, Amartya Sen argued, in his now famous Coromandel lecture (1981, published as Sen 1984), that independent India has successfully prevented famines thanks to its democratic political structure. Indeed, in spite of near-famine conditions in 1965–67,

1970–73, and during the more recent droughts in the 1980s and the 1990s, the last major famine in India took place in Bengal in 1943–44 under undemocratic and colonial rule.[1] In contrast, and as a direct consequence of the disastrous policies of the 'Great Leap Forward', China experienced a famine in 1958–61, which resulted in the deaths of around 30 million people (Ashton *et al.* 1984; Drèze and Sen 1989). Sen claims that the primary reason for China's failure to prevent this catastrophe was the absence of democracy in the country:

> This particular aspect of the Chinese famine – its linkage with the lack of democracy in China – fits into a more general pattern of association between democracy and successful prevention of famines, or – seen the other way – between the absence of democracy and the lack of any guarantee that serious attempts to avert famines will be undertaken.
>
> (Sen 1984)

Sen (1983a, 1984) goes on to argue that India's success is not primarily the result of raising food output per head, as it is often thought to be. Famines have been prevented despite lower food production than in many countries in the Sahel, and a lower rate of economic growth than China.

> India has not had a famine since independence, and given the nature of Indian politics and society, it is not likely that India can have a famine even in years of great food problems. The government cannot afford to fail to take prompt action when large-scale starvation threatens. Newspapers play an important part in this, in making the facts known and forcing the challenge to be faced. So does the pressure of the opposition parties. In the absence of these pressures and free newspapers famines can develop even in countries that normally perform better than India.
>
> (Sen 1984: 84)

Sen's ideas are therefore based on two key assumptions: (1) the informational aspect – the prowess of an independent and crusading media that can provide early warning of impending food crises and the imminent risk of starvation – and (2) the political incentive – a pluralist, multiparty political system that can criticise government inaction or failures to tackle a crisis (e.g. the failure to initiate timely relief and rehabilitation measures). Thus, a political system in which one is free to criticise government policies can 'spread the penalties of famine from the destitute to those in authority' (Sen 1990b). The Chinese political system exhibited neither of the two above features during the famine of 1958–61, and subsequent research by others largely substantiates Sen's claim. For instance, from the time when people began to starve in large numbers, it would take two years before the Communist Party was able to come to grips with this disaster. Without a democratic system of checks and balances, Chairman Mao's policy decisions on development and famine relief were never really questioned.[2] Interestingly,

16

the political repression of the Great Leap Forward followed a largely tolerant but brief Hundred Flowers period during which the government allowed considerable dissent. However, as Becker (1996) writes, already early on in the Great Leap Forward, Mao warned that dissent would not be tolerated. Political and other dissenters were systematically imprisoned and tortured. In addition to the millions who perished, large numbers of people either were arrested and sent to death camps or fled their homes. Then, four years after the famine, repression intensified with the launch of the Cultural Revolution.

In contrast to China, Drèze and Sen (1989) propose that famine prevention in India has been a direct result of extensive 'entitlement protection' efforts that have primarily relied on the operation of two complementary forces. First, the administrative system aims at recreating lost entitlements caused by floods, droughts, economic slumps, etc. Second, the political system is instrumental in getting the administrative system to work as and when required. Administrative action, however, may be non-operational and ineffective in the absence of a 'political trigger'. Hence, the role of democracy is crucial. In his latest book on the subject, Sen (2000) revisits the democracy–famine prevention relationship, but interestingly qualifies his earlier statements by using the term 'substantial famine', although he does not clarify what he means by 'substantial'.

Indeed, no substantial famine has ever occurred in a democratic country – no matter how poor. This is because famines are extremely easy to prevent if the government tries to prevent them, and a government in a multiparty democracy with elections and free media has strong political incentives to undertake famine prevention. This would indicate that political freedom in the form of democratic arrangements helps to safeguard economic freedom (especially freedom from extreme starvation) and the freedom to survive (against famine mortality).

(Sen 2000: 51–52)

Sen also notes that democracies have the potential to respond to large crises far better than non-democracies and that this factor may not be much noticed in non-crisis times.

The security provided by democracy may not be much missed when a country is lucky enough to be facing no serious calamity, when everything is running along smoothly. But the danger of insecurity, arising from changes in the economic or other circumstances or from uncorrected mistakes of policy, can lurk behind what looks like a healthy state.

(Sen 2000: 52–53)

By influencing government policy via public action in the form of political activism, criticism and opposition, many actors in Indian society contribute towards triggering government response towards the prevention of famine. And analysis

17

of Sen's writings on public action provides three main categories under which his various statements can be placed. These include the role of the news media, state action for social security and famine relief, and democracy and the role of the opposition.

The role of the news media

Since widespread starvation does not occur simultaneously in all regions of a country, the news media can provide a sensitive system for early warning and prediction of famines (Sen 1987: 14). An active and vigorous newspaper system can usefully supplement the work of economic analysis and formal early warning techniques (that focus on nutritional, agricultural and health indicators) 'by re-porting early signs of distress with predictive significance' (ibid.). Thus, freedom of speech and expression in society can result in the provision of quick and cred-ible information and feedback to the authorities, and Sen notes:

> A free press and the practice of democracy contribute greatly to bringing out information that can have an enormous impact on policies for famine preven-tion (for example, information about the early effects of droughts and floods and about the nature and impact of unemployment). The most elementary source of basic information from distant areas about a threatening famine are enterprising news media, especially when there are incentives – provided by a democratic system – for bringing out facts that may be embarrassing to the government (facts that an authoritarian government would tend to censor out). Indeed, I would argue that a free press and an active political opposition constitute the best early-warning system a country threatened by famines can have.
>
> (Sen 2000: 180–181)

Hence, as long as the press is free, Sen believes it will perform this task of pro-viding information and early warning. This will in turn make it difficult for the authorities not to react with a sense of urgency and therefore such informal early warning can prove to be far more effective than formal early warning indicators of famine.

State action for social security and famine relief

Public action and its success depend considerably on the 'feasibilities of different courses of action' which involve taking into consideration causal factors that may cause deprivation and hunger, in addition to the power and types of interventions undertaken by various agencies in the field (Drèze and Sen 1989: 17).

In particular, the character of the state, and the nature of the government undertaking state actions, can be crucial. The questions raised include not merely the administrative capabilities of governments, but also the political commitments and loyalties as well as the power bases of the holders of political power.

(ibid.)

On the question of the agency best equipped to anticipate and tackle famine threats and ameliorate deprivation, Sen (1987: 14) naturally enough argues that the responsibility should fall on national governments. Consequently, the state must also take into account various 'complementarities and tradeoffs between different avenues of action' in the process of 'developing an overall effective public programme for eliminating hunger in all its forms' (Drèze and Sen 1989: 18). Besides state action, market incentives that offer profits are also important. Drèze and Sen emphasise the incentives that 'motivate governments to implement well-planned public policies, induce families to reject intra-household discrimination, encourage political parties and the news media to make reasoned demands, and inspire the public at large to cooperate, criticize and coordinate'. Thus, even though there may be conflict between state action and market incentives, they argue that these must not be seen to be in constant competition with each other:

The need to consider a plurality of levers and heterogeneity of mechanisms is hard to escape in the strategy of public action for social security. The internal diversities involved in an effective public action programme can be quite extensive. For example, several countries have achieved some success in preventing famines by combining cash transfers to vulnerable groups in the form of wages for public employment with reliance on the private sector for moving food to affected regions, along with public participation in food distribution to prevent the emergence of collusive manipulation by private traders. These combined strategies illustrate the fruitfulness of taking an integrated and pluralist view of public action.

(ibid.)

In addition to market mechanisms, the role of various non-state actors – national and international voluntary agencies, the extended family, the community – may usefully supplement state action. Therefore, although the state should be active in providing social security, state action cannot and should not replace the traditional importance of non-state groups and institutions (ibid.: 19).

Democracy and the role of the opposition

The promotion and strengthening of a democracy, argues Sen (2000: 157–158), is crucial for the process of development on three grounds. First, democracy has *intrinsic importance* in that it is a value in itself and has a direct relevance in the promotion of basic capabilities, which include social and political participation. Second, democracy makes possible various *instrumental contributions* in

19

ensuring that people are able to express and support their claims of economic needs and receive political attention. Third, democracy has a *constructive* role in the very understanding and identification of what constitutes 'needs' in a social context. Civil and political rights enable participation in public debates and discussions, and allow criticism which is important for the understanding and conceptualisation of economic needs, and the eventual response to meet them. Sen argues that each of these three features needs to be considered while evaluating a democratic system.

In terms of preventing famine, although newspapers may provide information and early warning, state action needs to be accountable if it is to serve its real purpose. This is where a democratic political culture is important, although Sen cautions that rules, procedures and practices must not be seen as 'mechanical devices for development' since their 'use is conditioned by our values and priorities, and by the use we make of the available opportunities of articulation and participation' (ibid.: 158). For instance, the public needs to understand and be aware of issues and participate actively in shaping the course of state action. How citizens of a country make use of various opportunities available to them in order to voice their demands and claim remedial action – 'public enlightenment' – is vital in addition to democratic rules and procedures (ibid.: 154).

Democracy also allows citizens to make use of a range of opportunities available, but to what extent these are used, argues Sen, will depend on the functioning of multiparty politics and the nature of dominant values in society (ibid.: 154–155). The role of political parties and organised opposition groups is particularly important as they can exert political pressure to prevent famine.[3] Thus, the nature of domestic politics will determine the level of responsiveness showed by the political authorities.

> How soon, how urgently and how actively the government will act will also depend on the nature of politics of the country, and the forces that operate on the government to act without delay. Depending on the nature of the political structure, it is often possible for an inactive and uncaring government to get away with implicit manslaughter, if not murder. Many governments have been extraordinarily sluggish and insensitive to information coming in about threatening famines. Here again the extent of public knowledge of and involvement in social issues can be crucial. Effective famine anticipation and counteracting policies are not merely matters of economic analysis, they are also significantly dependent on the nature of political agitprop and active journalism, which operate on the government, influencing its concerns and forcing its hand.
>
> (Sen 1987: 14–15)

After independence from British rule, the newly elected rulers of India gave clear priority to preventing famine and the idea matured with political activism. In contrast to highly visible forms of suffering like famine, political actors in India have done little to put the silent and less visible forms of suffering on the political agenda. Sen is therefore very critical of the 'docility of the opposition' which has allowed the Indian government to 'get away with unconscionable neglect of these vital matters of public policy' (Sen 2000: 155).

A critique

Sen's numerous contributions to the debate revolutionised famine studies by shifting the focus from food supply to food distribution, access and demand in the form of entitlement. Although the entitlement approach was largely well received, several studies challenged Sen's attack on FAD approaches (Bowbrick 1986, 1987; Nolan 1993),[4] and others have worked to further improve the entitlement argument (Osmani 1995; Ravallion 1996). As Devereux (2000: 20) correctly observes, 'Sen's insistence on contesting the existence or magnitude of food supply shocks during famines provoked critics into challenging his calculations or believing (incorrectly) that Sen was asserting that food availability decline was never a feature in any famine'. In addition, the entitlement approach has been criticised for not focusing adequately on famine causation. When Sen writes on how people starve in famines, he limits his explanation to the people–market relationship under stress and thereby 'perpetuates a technocratic view of famine that excludes politics and intent as causal factors, and *political* action (rather than "*public*" action) as an appropriate – even necessary – solution' (ibid.: 20–21). Similarly, Edkins (2000: xx–xxi) argues that Sen's critique of approaches advocating the FAD thesis is based on a 'purely technical concept' of entitlements, and that Sen does not emphasise the importance of social relations for the rise and maintenance of entitlements applying the force of law. By not focusing on the legal and social systems, Sen 'allows his work to provide techniques for dealing with famine as an economic breakdown within a system but does not permit him to question the system itself' (ibid.). Similarly, Bhatia (1993: 37) criticises the approach for not having 'roots in history' and for providing an explanation of famine as 'more of an accident than a culmination of historical forces at work'.

The entitlement approach is also accused of not having a 'place for violence' (de Waal 1990; Edkins 2000) and for downplaying the role of war and complex political emergencies (Nolan 1993). Others accuse it of suffering from an inherent Indian bias in that Africa is studied with the use of Indian (Asian) categories (de Gaay Fortman 1990, cited in Rubin 2001: 36). Whereas Fine (1997) wants to focus more on both state and 'socially determined' power, Gore (1993) claims that Sen ignores how legal rules operate and neglects gender biases.

Several authors have further criticised Sen for identifying famine with an extraordinary 'event' of starvation instead of a lengthy drawn-out 'process' through which death results from several other factors including gradually destitution and the impact of disease. According to Rangasami (1985: 1798), one of Sen's earliest critics, the entitlement approach views famine in 'biological' terms, as an event inevitably leading to starvation and excess mortality. Rather, she argues, famine should be understood as a 'politico-socio-economic process'. For instance, during British rule in India, particularly in the period 1880–1905, relief administrators were aware of the effects of unemployment, decline in real wages and food shortage. Hence Rangasami's point is that famine progresses from dearth, famishment, and morbidity and that 'the culmination of the process comes well before the slide into disease death' (ibid.: 1748). An understanding of famine as an extraordinary event becomes further problematic as Sen focuses mainly on the final end result and not the process. Thus, Rangasami argues that Sen ignores the fact that, when government intervention is finally undertaken, lives may be saved without assets being recreated (ibid.: 1750).

Returning to the democracy–famine prevention relationship, Sen sees the opposition's desire to undercut and discredit the ruling party as leading to demands for anti-famine action. However, he romanticises the role of the free press when he assumes that it will necessarily be constructive in its pursuit to promote the interests of the poor and those vulnerable to famine. In doing so, he ignores factors like political ownership and control of the media, lack of adequate training and remuneration to journalists, and the incentives that the press has in covering certain sensational crises while ignoring others. Bhagwati (1995) argues that Sen's argument is not very persuasive since information about a major famine will spread even under authoritarian conditions. And even if such information – 'horizontally from province to province or vertically from ruled to rulers' – is inadequate or absent, the 'reality of the famine is known in the locales where it occurs' (ibid.: 59). Thus, for Bhagwati the critical question is whether democracy provides better conditions for allowing affected groups to press for improvements, and he concludes by arguing that 'a free press is important, but it is best to have a press that also reflects broader interests than those of the elite' (ibid.: 60).

Keen (1994: 5) criticises Sen for overlooking the fact that states and politically powerful groups may actively promote famine by obstructing relief for rational purposes of their own. For example by withholding famine relief the price of grain increases; during the Irish famine (1845–50), lobbying by grain merchants had a great impact on the British decision to not import food. Similarly grain merchants in Malawi lobbied against famine relief in 1949, and blockades against food supplies and other forms of relief have often functioned as weapons of war in both domestic and international conflicts. For example, during the Nigerian civil war of 1967–70, the blockade of Biafra caused hunger within rebel camps, and starvation-induced submission constituted a major aspect of government policy. Further, by withholding relief, famine can be contained at certain locations, making it difficult for the affected population to migrate in search of food. Another reason for withholding relief can be to minimise the side-effects of famine like, for instance, 'the perceived threat to the health and security of local people posed by famine migrants' (ibid.). Rangasami (1985: 1748) similarly argues that Sen's famine approach focuses exclusively on victims of starvation whereas famine 'is a process in which benefits accrue to one section of the community while losses flow to the other'.

Despite the merits of the above criticisms, Sen's approach to famine is neither limited to the entitlement approach nor solely in his most famous book, *Poverty and Famines*. In order to get a complete picture of Sen's views on famine prevention, the concept of 'entitlement' must be seen in tandem with the notions of 'capability' and 'public action'. For example, while Sen in *Poverty and Famines* does not speak of the importance of democracy, power and public action in preventing famines, he does so with increasing frequency in subsequent works. In essence, Sen justifies the promotion of a society with ample democracy as a solution to famine, although there is some ambiguity regarding how far he intends to do so. Because of the nature of the political structure, it is often possible for an inactive or uncaring government to escape accountability when it fails to mobilise an adequate response during a crisis. At the core, Sen proposes that democratic traditions enable a government to be responsive and accountable to human needs; consequently, inappropriate policies and inadequate actions can come under criticism by the political opposition, interest groups, voluntary organisations and the media, and this triggers the government into action. However, Sen largely repeats the argument without much elaboration of exactly how such democratic processes work in promoting a person's entitlement to food and why some issues (e.g. famine) energise the government and others do not. Neither does he elaborate on or develop the concept of democracy. Hence in the remaining sections of this chapter I argue that Sen's argument can be made more persuasive if one focused on an improved understanding of certain key concepts. In this quest, I propose two sets of ways in which Sen's argument can be refined and further strengthened to respond to some of the above-mentioned criticisms. The first is related to the manner in which 'famine' is understood and operationalised; the second concentrates on the relationship between democracy and public action on the one hand and the prevention of famine and chronic hunger on the other.

How should famine be understood?

The term 'famine' came into English from the Latin *fames*, meaning hunger, and most dictionary definitions of famine range from extreme/severe/broad/acute scarcity or shortage of food leading to violent hunger to acute shortage of anything. In general, conventional definitions see famine in terms of 'mass starvation', 'excess mortality' and 'community crisis' (Blix *et al.* 1971; Currey 1978; Cox 1981). For example, Rivers *et al.* explicitly state, 'Starvation is a semantic prerequisite for the definition of famine' (1976: 355, quoted in Devereux 1993: 12). Aykroyd (1974: 2) argues that ' "mass starvation" and "famine" mean much the same thing' and Alamgir (1980: 7) observes that 'famine implies hunger, starvation, malnutrition, and something more – excess death'. Currey and Hugo (1984: 1) define famine as a community crisis, 'a syndrome with webs of causation through which communities lose their ability to support marginal members who consequently either migrate in families because of lack of access to food, or die to starvation or starvation related disease'. And according to Keys *et al.* (1950) 'famine denotes the semi-starvation of many people – a substantial proportion of the population of some sizeable area'.

Thus, conventional definitions of famine tend to emphasise the physiological condition of famine victims, and famine deaths are understood to take place on account of inadequate or total absence of food intake. Sen himself has largely influenced the development of such conventional wisdom by clearly underlining the relationship between starvation and famine in the following way:

> Famines imply starvation, but not vice-versa . . . Starvation is a normal feature in many parts of the world, but this phenomenon of 'regular' starvation has to be distinguished from violent outbursts of famines.
>
> (Sen 1981: 40–41)

Two issues are crucial here. First, although starvation can lead to famine, it need not always be so as the process of starvation may be stopped before death occurs. Second, even if a handful of individuals die of starvation it does not qualify as a 'famine'. As Woldemariam (1984: 4) observes, 'Ordinary hunger is not famine; undernourishment is not famine; malnutrition is not famine; even though all these terms are used interchangeably as if they are synonymous' (cited in Devereux 1993: 12).

Such conventional views of the relationship between starvation and famine have, in recent years, been challenged by de Waal (1989) on three accounts. First, based on studies of famines in Africa, he argues that people may voluntarily choose to starve when faced with a choice between not eating and selling assets. Second, he claims that mortality in recent African famines like the Darfur famine in Sudan in the 1980s was more a result of disease than of starvation. He writes:

> the concept of famine in Darfur is primarily one of destitution, and not mortality and starvation . . . Europeans believe that famine implies death by starvation, Africans who are exposed to famines do not.
>
> (de Waal 1989: 257)

Third, de Waal detaches the excess mortality component from famine. Describing how famine victims in Sudan differentiated between famines 'that kill' and those that do not, he writes that local perceptions of famine in Darfur were threefold, including minor famines that cause hunger, severe famines resulting in destitution, and catastrophic famines that caused mass deaths. Moreover, when people died during 'famines that kill', mortality was primarily related to hardship, disorder, disease and epidemics resulting from unhygienic conditions in overcrowded refugee camps. De Waal thus disputes the conventional wisdom of associating famine deaths exclusively with starvation or food component and argues for a 'health crisis' model of famine mortality as opposed to a 'food crisis' model.

On the first point de Waal is correct in observing that people may on occasion choose to starve rather than sell their assets. This type of strategy may particularly be chosen when victims of starvation understand their suffering to be of a temporary nature, i.e. they may hold out hope for a change in their dietary intakes in the not-too-distant future. Thus, the process of starvation may be partly self-inflicted in that individuals possessing assets have the choice of selling these and thereby avoiding the effects of starvation for a definite period of time. However, I would argue that, when the pangs of hunger continue for a while (and children start falling ill) and there is little hope for accessing food, it is not unreasonable to assume that starving households will start a distress-induced sale of their assets. Hence, although de Waal is correct in that people may choose to starve, it seems plausible that this may be true only for a short period of time. With prolonged starvation and imminent death, voluntary starvation is less likely to occur.

The second point, de Waal's argument that famine deaths are caused more by disease than starvation, is an important one but requires qualification since undernutrition and disease often combine to cause deaths and it is difficult to ascertain the major cause of mortality. In cases of prolonged starvation and re-sulting destitution, body organs begin to lose weight at a fast pace, then start to malfunction and finally stop functioning one after the other. The immune system is weakened, increasing the likelihood of infections, which in turn increase the likelihood of death due to disease. In addition, those subsequently exposed to communicable diseases (e.g. in refugee camps) may have been forced to migrate from their villages once their food entitlements disappeared (Ravallion 1996; Devereux 2000). And Scrimshaw *et al.* (1968) observe that undernutrition in a community can lower the resistance to infection, and in turn infections worsen the existing situation. Hence, there is good reason to argue that undernutrition and infection are 'inextricably interwoven, with resultant increased mortality' (Jelliffe and Jelliffe 1971: 57). Although undernutrition and starvation act as catalysts, death is almost invariably the result of infection and disease. Diet and disease interact in a complex and mutually reinforcing manner such that it is often impossible to identify which is the primary cause of 'stress'. Payne (1994) highlights this difficulty when he notes:

> An infection can result in loss of appetite and hence initiate undernutrition; it can also result in the depletion of body stores of specific nutrients and hence malnutrition. Dietary deficiencies, on the other hand, can reduce the effectiveness of response of the body's immune system, making infection more likely and increasing its severity. In these ways, either diet or disease can act as initial causes of stress and both can interact in a mutually reinforcing way.
>
> (Payne 1994: 83–84)

The effects of starvation and disease are worsened in famine conditions with various forms of social disorganisation like overcrowding, inadequate sanitation facilities and an increase in disease carriers such as rats, lice and mosquitoes. An inability to bury or burn dead bodies further leads to a worsening of hygiene (e.g.

in refugee camps). Thus, starvation, in combination with unhygienic conditions and uncontrolled population movements as a result of social disruption, increases the likelihood of disease transmission and the severity of disease attacks on under-nourished individuals (Foege 1971; Cox 1981). Epidemics and infectious diseases like typhus, relapsing fever, dysentery, diarrhoea, gastrointestinal infections, ty-phoid, tuberculosis, measles, whooping cough, etc. are common in famine areas and cause mortality. Mortality rates are usually higher for vulnerable groups like children, the infirm, pregnant and lactating women and the aged, who are weak and require more energy (Jelliffe and Jelliffe 1971: 57; Cox 1981: 13). The point here is that diet and disease interact together to produce illness and death and it is difficult, if not impossible, to establish which of the two is the primary cause of mortality in areas of famine.

De Waal's third point relates to the distinction between 'famines that kill' and those that 'do not kill'. The idea that famines do not imply starvation deaths on a large scale is difficult to accept mainly because famine has traditionally been as-sociated with widespread mortality. In a sense, without the notion of 'mass starva-tion', famine loses its distinctive feature as compared with terms like 'epidemics', 'undernutrition' and occasional 'starvation deaths'. Although an understanding of famine as both a gradual process leading to starvation and a dramatic event needs to be recognised, it is far-fetched to associate famines with a zero mor-tality scenario. Famine implies death. And the attempt by de Waal to translate and interpret local expressions in Darfur to mean famine is not a good enough reason to abandon using the term in its original sense. Indeed, rather than using the term famine broadly to describe a wider range of nutritional conditions, there is actually a greater need in the academic and policy debate to operationalise famine narrowly and distinguish it from related phenomena like undernutrition and starvation. Instead of widening the concept, I am arguing for delimitation. Thus, the disagreements over famine definitions really boil down to the issue of how flexible the term famine should be. On the one hand, a narrow defini-tion of famine focusing exclusively on mass starvation and excess mortality has the advantage of being distinct from 'undernutrition' and small-scale starvation deaths. This prevents confusion in the usage of these terms and is the only way we can understand the causes of famine and appropriate responses. On the other hand, a wide definition of famine has the advantage of giving importance to local perceptions of famine in certain regions of the world which need not equate it with excess mortality. Depending on the context in which the term is used, famine will signify different things to different people. However, an all-inclusive and broad definition of famine in its current usage is difficult to operationalise and can cause difficulties in terms of early warning and detection (and declaration) and the ensuing response.

The need for such an operationalisation is borne out from de Waal's own writ-ings. For example, he first observes that in 1966–67 'democratic or liberal institu-tions . . . failed to prevent famine' in the Indian state of Bihar (de Waal 2000: 11). A couple of paragraphs later, and referring to the same case, he writes: 'severe famine was prevented, but undernutrition and poverty were not' (ibid.). Thus, what should be considered a famine and what should not is intrinsically related to how one defines the term. It is also important to ask how large the number of deaths need be in order for the situation to be branded as a famine. Should famines be seen as an exceptional 'event' with a given time-frame, or should it be seen as a continuous 'process' of undernutrition resulting in mass starvation, disease and finally full-blown famine? These questions are relevant precisely because, if one applies a definition of famine that requires a large number of deaths or equates famines with extraordinary catastrophes of the kind witnessed in Ethiopia (1970s and 1980s), then Sen is right in his observation that India has never had a famine since independence. If, on the other hand, one operates with a famine definition that allows for a lesser number of casualties within an extended time period, then Sen's observation of India's success in preventing famine may appear more problematic given the frequency with which starvation deaths are reported in the Indian press.

Indeed, Sen (1981: 1) is inattentive to famine definitions although he writes: 'Famines imply starvation, but not vice-versa. And starvation implies poverty, but not vice-versa.' In recent years, Sen (2000) has also used the word 'substantial' together with 'famine', perhaps in an effort to qualify his earlier assertions, although it is unclear what he means by 'substantial'. And within Sen's framework, it is particularly difficult to place the phenomenon of 'starvation deaths' – where people die from starvation but the situation cannot be described as one of 'mass starvation' that characterises a 'famine'. Sen operates with a dualistic distinction between chronic hunger on the one hand and famine on the other. In reality, numerous levels or phases between these two extremes must be recognised, and it is surprising that Sen has in subsequent work remained silent on definitions that emphasise the socio-economic and the political aspects of starvation and famine.

Why operationalise famine?[5]

A good operational definition of famine does not currently exist despite the enormous academic literature on famines. Given that the wide variety of famine definitions currently available has not been of much help to practitioners, a necessary first step is to at least arrive at a consensus on what famine *does not* mean, i.e. identify a set of conditions/factors that should definitely not be a part of a famine definition. In order to do so it is important to understand famine both as a *process* (as different phases that are precursors to an actual manifestation) and an extraordinary *event* (sensational episode of mass deaths and excess mortality). A clearly formulated definition of famine analytically distinguished from related terms can be beneficial on at least two interrelated counts – *early warning information* of an imminent crisis and the *declaration of famine and the process of holding political and administrative authorities accountable* for failing to prevent large-scale loss of life.

Early warning of impending food crises followed by rapid state and non-state intervention is crucial when households begin to feel the impact of food shortage, infections and disease. A good early warning system is one which recognises the start of such a period of suffering. This in turn depends on threshold levels applied by governmental agencies and others for the provision and launching of relief assistance. When this threshold is specific and low, households can be assisted at an early stage. However, and all too often, thresholds are applied at a very late stage of already reached severity such that it may be too late to mobilise assistance. It is important not just to intervene early but also to intervene with the right forms of assistance (e.g. not just provide food aid but also non-food items). Government officials, aid agency personnel and journalists often do not have ready-made criteria and/or may not be adequately trained to provide early warning information of an impending crisis. For instance, during recent food crises in Ethiopia in 1999–2000 and in Niger and Mali in 2004–05, the governments of these countries and international agencies either described the situation as famine or used various terms like food crisis, complex emergency, etc. In general, 'there is often a reluctance to use the "F" word'.[6] It is therefore important to arrive at a consensus on a range of operational signals that can be applied for classifying a crisis and its level of severity. And although there are already some attempts by the World Food Programme and the Famine Early Warning System Network (FEWS Net) to track vulnerability to food shortages, they do not always emphasise the operational link between various stages of undernutrition and starvation leading to famine. For example, the three levels of 'alert' used by FEWS Net – 'watch', 'warning' and 'emergency' – simply use general and ambiguous phrases like 'food security crisis'.[7] Moreover, such attempts are not universally accepted, being largely practised individually by the agency concerned. A good operational definition of famine can therefore supplement such individual efforts and help to establish the foundations of a methodology that all agencies working in this field can incorporate as part of their routines. Thus, such an exercise is not just an academic/semantic matter.

Currently, national governments, voluntary organisations and international aid agencies use a variety of terms to describe and define an imminent or on-going food-related crisis affecting large groups of people. These include 'hunger', 'severe food insecurity' and 'food emergency', which are often used to describe 'famine'. This leads to confusion and disagreement among actors in charge of the provision and distribution of relief. The timing of a declaration of 'famine' by a government is important. An early declaration can provide useful information of an imminent crisis and can propel national and international agencies to focus on a specific group or region in the process of mounting an emergency response. For example, it was only when a famine was declared in Sudan in the mid-1980s that famine relief became a focus of government policy. At other times, a late declaration of famine serves to focus attention on mass deaths already taking place.

A major shortcoming of conventional theories of famine has been their failure 'to assign *culpability* for famine to anyone other than the victims themselves and the banal mechanics of market forces' (Devereux 2000: 21). The very act of declaration can also be a subject of misuse. For instance, governments are tempted to easily declare a famine, even when a situation does not resemble one, for purposes of receiving international assistance or for diverting attention from policy failures elsewhere. Unrestricted usage of the term, however, can backfire when it is later proved that the observed phenomenon, although a crisis, was not a famine. In other instances, governments (e.g. the Ethiopian regime in 1983–85) are reluctant to declare a famine for fear of embarrassment and national and international criticism of their failure to prevent such suffering. Thus, the credibility of the term famine is at stake. Whereas frequent usage may lead to a 'cry wolf' syndrome in which famine loses its ability to shock and convey a sense of urgency, there may also be a general reluctance among certain regimes or organisations to admit to a crisis even when they are convinced that the situation truly warrants such a declaration. The problem is that current definitions and theories are tied to a framework that sees famine as a failure to be remedied by scientific or technical solutions. Edkins (2002) argues that such approaches, using 'theoretical considerations of cause as a starting point, leads to technologised responses that are not only incapable of responding adequately to the politics of mass starvations but are themselves implicated in that politics'. There is therefore a pressing need to question how famine and resulting mass starvation is allowed to occur and who is responsible for it. This is important for locating responsibility or culpability for causing large-scale loss of lives which could otherwise have been prevented.

Operational criteria[8]

Despite the frequent use of the term 'hunger', the term is without a proper scientific definition. It can refer to a broad range of phenomena of varying levels of severity and there is no agreement on applicable methods of measuring it. At the most general level, hunger is a 'symptom or a sensation which is expressed as a craving for food' (Robson 1972: 2). However, this sensation or craving may result from a wide variety of causes, some voluntary and others involuntary. As Payne (1994: 86) puts it, sometimes hunger is 'a signal of desperation' while at other times it may simply be 'an expression of keen healthy appetite'. In contrast, there is large-scale agreement that 'undernutrition' (often used interchangeably with 'malnutrition'), in the strictest sense, is caused by a lack of appropriate nutrients in the food consumed by an individual and may result not only from the *quantity* of food consumed (excessive or inadequate) but also the *quality* of food intake (e.g. lack of vitamins, protein and micronutrients).

It is further important to distinguish undernutrition from related terms like 'starvation' and 'famine'. Figure 2.1 is an attempt to distinguish these terms by showing the causal linkages between them. A deterioration of the physiological condition can occur because of poor health and inadequate food intake. Undernutrition can result not only from inadequate intake of food but also from poor health and sanitation conditions and inadequate care. In comparison, 'starvation' is usually the direct result of inadequate food and over a period of time can lead

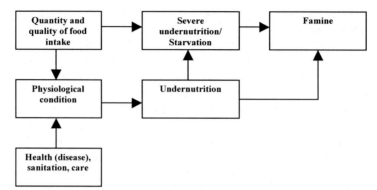

Figure 2.1 The linkages between undernutrition, starvation and famine.[9]

to mass death in a society leading to famine. A combination of inadequate food intake and poor health can also lead to a general undernutrition which if sustained over a long period of time can result in famine.

Undernutrition is characterised by the body receiving insufficient energy from the food consumed so that it has difficulty maintaining normal physical and chemical functions. In addition, there is little energy supply for demanding physical work in adults and for growth in children. In contrast, 'starvation' is a process resulting from a period of sustained undernutrition. During this period, the level of energy intake is below the level of energy expenditure such that there is a continuous loss of body weight which may ultimately lead to death. There are varying degrees of starvation. For example, 'short-term starvation' may last a few days or perhaps a week, and may not lead to death. It can also be 'seasonal' in nature, occurring at regular times each year (for example, in months following a severe drought and destitution) and can last on and off for several weeks. Short-term and seasonal starvation result in increased morbidity and mortality among nutritionally vulnerable groups like children and the elderly (Dirks 1993). Deaths may, however, go unreported, especially when they occur in areas normally outside the reach of the media and often not covered by government-run nutritional programmes. 'Starvation deaths' may result from a prolonged period of sustained undernutrition and the total absence of any forms of food for x days, where x depends on various factors including the general physical condition and nutritional status of an individual before the start of the starvation process, the rate of body weight loss, body size, metabolic changes, adverse climatic conditions and the level of physical activity undertaken during the period of starvation.

There is no watertight definition of 'famine'. However, the use of the term invariably implies a quantum leap in the magnitude of suffering not associated with undernutrition and individual cases of starvation. As Stephen Devereux writes:

> Chronic malnutrition describes nothing more than a poorly balanced diet, lacking in essential nutrients, while 'undernutrition' is the physical syndrome associated with prolonged food deprivation. Neither constitutes sufficient

evidence for famine, which is a wide-ranging crisis, not simply a biological syndrome.

(Devereux 1993: 13)

Thus, at the outset, 'famine' can be defined as a community crisis resulting from a general state of mass starvation caused by a decline in the food intake per capita over a prolonged period. The end result of a famine is excess deaths caused, directly or indirectly,[10] by the inability of vulnerable groups to acquire sufficient food to sustain life. Table 2.1 provides a classification of five possible categories or phases of undernutrition and famine-related stress on individuals and households.[11] It shows how chronic undernutrition can progress into a famine if adequate interventions are not undertaken quickly. A general description of each category is provided below.

- *Undernutrition*
  This is the consumption of incorrect types of food (quality) and/or inadequate intake of food (quantity). An improvement in the nutritional status of the population is dependent on public action – including food subsidy programmes, direct food supplementation programmes, pensions and labour-intensive programmes – and local coping strategies like seasonal migration, loans from moneylenders, distress sale of assets, etc.
- *Severe undernutrition*
  This phase is characterised by a decline in the level of food consumption and high food insecurity among sections of the population. This may be caused by a shortfall in foodgrain production, sharp increase in prices, sudden unemployment or loss of income. Inadequate intake of food provides insufficient energy or micronutrients for the maintenance of normal physical and chemical functions. Sustained undernutrition leads to starvation, and the continuous loss of body weight can ultimately lead to death among certain individuals and groups more vulnerable than the rest of the population (e.g. children, pregnant women, nursing mothers, the elderly, sick adults). Local coping strategies may include reliance on alternative sources (e.g. forests) for food items, borrowing from moneylenders, distress sale of assets and an increase in seasonal and forced migration.
- *Famine threat*
  A condition of severe undernutrition and starvation worsens and starts affecting larger groups in the population who increasingly face destitution. This may result from a combination of *initial causes* (e.g. successive drought/flood-induced crop failures, war, destruction of roads and communication) and *aggravating factors* (e.g. degree and duration of food insecurity, high market prices of food items, lack of safe drinking water, animal/human epidemics, loss of shelter, extremely cold/hot climatic conditions). There may also be an increase in the incidence of people affected with severe dehydration, dysentery, diarrhoea and upper respiratory tract infections. With prolonged

31

Table 2.1 A typology of famine and related terms

Type of stress	Brief description	Possible indicators	Examples
Undernutrition	Chronic undernutrition (poor quality and quantity of food consumed)	High IMR and MMR Low BMI Food consumption well below national mean High levels of 'mild' and 'moderate' malnutrition among children: stunting <20%, underweight <10%, wasting <5% Diarrhoea, dysentery, tuberculosis, respiratory disorders, anaemia, sparse hair, etc.	Large parts of the developing world
Severe undernutrition	Decline in the level of food consumption and high food insecurity among sections of the population	Increase in IMR and MMR Food consumption below average local consumption levels; eating of newer types of food collected from alternative sources stunting 20–29%, underweight 10–19%, wasting 5–9% Very low BMI among adults Increased mortality: CMR <0.5/10,000/day	Specific regions in almost all developing countries at regular times during a year. India (Kalahandi) Sudan (Darfur)
Famine threat	A condition of severe undernutrition and starvation worsens and starts affecting larger groups in the population who face destitution	Critically low BMI Stunting 30–39%, Underweight 20–29%, Wasting 10–15% Increase in CDR due to starvation and infectious disease Increase in mortality rates (CMR ≥1 but <2/10,000/day) Higher mortality rate for males	India (Bihar 1965–66, Maharashtra 1971–72) Ethiopia (1999–2000) Mali (2004) Niger (2005)
Famine	Community crisis, destitution for large groups and widespread mortality from mass starvation and epidemics	Stunting >40%, underweight >30%, wasting >15% CMR >2 but <15/10,000/day Total excess mortality ≤300,000	West Africa (Sahel, 1969–74) Somalia (1974–75) Mozambique (1982–85) Sudan (Darfur and Kardofan, 1984–85) Sudan (Bahr el Ghazal, 1998)
Great famine	Catastrophic magnitude, extremely high CMR and excess mortality	CMR >15/10,000/day Total excess mortality ≥300,000	India (Bengal, 1943–44) China (1959–62) Nigeria (Biafra, 1968–70) Ethiopia (1983–85) North Korea (1995–99)

Note: IMR, infant mortality rate; MMR, maternal mortality rate; BMI, body mass index; CMR, crude mortality rate.

stress, there is the possibility of an increase in 'starvation deaths', the extent of which will depend on the prior nutritional status of the community, the nature of family/kinship relations and assistance and the nature of government response depending on the existing type of political system.

In certain cases, there may be a substantial number of starvation deaths in particularly remote areas and within a specified time period. If the situation does not improve dramatically a full-blown famine is highly likely. Whether this takes place or not will depend on the availability – and speedy and timely distribution – of national/regional food reserves, the amount and type of international aid sanctioned, existing transport facilities, migration patterns, the morale of victims of starvation, etc.

- *Famine*

This is a community crisis (destitution for large groups) and results in widespread mortality from starvation and epidemics. Physical activity is primarily limited to food-procuring activities and all potentially edible items may be consumed including seeds, wild roots, poisonous plants, tree bark, insects, manure, etc. There may be an increase in thefts, riots, prostitution and child selling, and a decline in fertility. The elderly may be left behind by younger family members who migrate in search of food and work. While kinship groups and friends may initially be able to provide some assistance, this will usually be reduced as famine progresses and norms of social behaviour stop being practised as these groups can no longer assist themselves. In the end there are no viable coping strategies and the result is complete destitution. It becomes a situation of survival for the fittest. Famines with excess mortality (EM) below 300,000 are included in this category. Example of such famines are West Africa (Sahel, 1969–74, EM = 101,000), Somalia (1974–75, EM = 20,000), Mozambique (1982–85, EM = 100,000), Sudan (Darfur and Kardofan, 1984–85, EM = 250,000) and Sudan (Bahr el Ghazal, 1998, EM = 70,000) (based on mortality estimates provided in Devereux 2000: 6).

- *Great famine*

These famines are characterised by a very high level of excess mortality (more than 300,000) and the post-famine impact on the population is greater than the previous 'famine' category as there may not be many able-bodied persons capable of restructuring local society. Famines that can be placed in this category include the following (based on Devereux 2000: 6): India (Bengal, 1943–44, EM = 2,100,000–3,000,000), China (1959–62, EM = 30,000,000), Nigeria (Biafra, 1968–70, EM = 1,000,000), Ethiopia (1983–85, EM = 590,000–1,000,000) and North Korea (1995–99, EM = 2,800,000–3,500,000). However, the severity and impact of 'famine' and 'great famine' must also be seen in relation to the total number of inhabitants in an area or the total population of a country. For example, if 300,000 people perished in a small country with a population of a few million people, its impact would be more severe than if the same number of people died in a country like India or China.

The main purpose of the attempt to operationalise famine is to propose some way of clearly distinguishing famine from related phenomena which allows for more accurate diagnoses and quicker and more efficient responses. It also shows how famines can be the end result of a long process starting with chronic undernutrition and gradually assuming more acute dimensions. Hence, it is possible for national and international agencies to react as early as possible and prevent further escalation of the problem. Famines and famine threats can be avoided if authorities are made aware of the seriousness of chronic and severe undernutrition and the urgency with which these problems need to be addressed. And they can be held accountable for their failure to react at an earlier stage if a stage of famine is reached. The task of operationalising famine is, however, fraught with numerous difficulties. For example, the proposed cut-off points will invariably be contentious and, although the exact composition of various indicators should be arrived at through consensus and dialogue involving all affected parties (including nutritionists, medical practitioners, relief workers, residents of famine-prone areas, etc.), it may be immensely difficult to organise such meetings in practice. Reaching a consensus on the use of anthropometrical measures in specific regions may also prove elusive. Indeed, numerous indicators can be used – sometimes requiring methodological and regional modifications – depending on the availability and reliability of data. Here, I have proposed the following sets of indicators: infant mortality rates (the probability of dying between birth and exactly one year of age, expressed per 1,000 live births), maternal mortality rates (the annual number of deaths of women from pregnancy-related causes per 100,000 live births), body mass index (a measure of body weight relative to height), WHO measures of undernutrition (prevalence of severe undernutrition among children under five years of age measured in terms of height for age (stunting), weight for age (underweight) and weight for height (wasting)), crude mortality rates (the mortality rate from all causes of death for a population) and total excess mortality (when the Standardised Mortality Rate, SMR, for a particular region is higher than the provincial SMR). In practice, however, some of these indicators may be replaced by even more accurate measures.

Another challenge could be that policymakers, aid agencies and national governments may not be too keen to reach a consensus that can be universally applied to all situations. In addition, there may be concerns that the definition of famine is so narrow that it may be difficult to assign culpability in non-famine situations. Further, even in famine situations, national governments may avoid taking responsibility and blame it on initial causes, aggravating factors and previous regimes. And given the severe weaknesses (and usual delays) of crisis response among donors and international development agencies, such operational definitions of famine may simply not be enough. However, this should not detract us from pursuing such an exercise, and the goal ought to be to move away from a situation where the urgency to provide assistance during 'famines' prevents us from responding to cases of 'severe undernutrition' and 'famine threats' with an equal sense of urgency and commitment.

Are famine-hit countries democratic?

A controversial aspect of the relationship between democracy and famine prevention relates to whether certain countries like Bangladesh (1974) and Sudan (1985–86) should be considered democracies during recent famines. Conversely, there are several cases like Nigeria (1974), Kenya (1984) and Zimbabwe (1982–84) where largely non-democratic regimes have successfully prevented the escalation of major food crises into famine. De Waal (1997: 7–8) suggests that India's success in averting famine since independence is due to the 'vigilance of its political achievement'. He goes on to argue that that it is important to locate human rights within political processes, and identifies 'a specific "political contract" that has ensured an enforceable freedom from famine in India'.[12] This political contract is apparently 'the result of a popular movement successfully articulating a right, and forcing a reluctant government to comply with its claims' (ibid.: 11). In contrast to India, most of Africa has not implemented a similar political contract between the state and its citizens and this, according to de Waal, explains Africa's poor record at famine prevention:

> there has been little or no opportunity for famine prevention to emerge as a right in Africa. The only exceptions may be among certain urban populations, where the right to relatively cheap food has become deeply entrenched. The central reason for this is that famine never became the politicised issue in the same way that it was in India.
>
> (de Waal 1996: 28)

De Waal accepts there have been a handful of exceptions and 'partial exceptions' to this argument, for instance, when the Wollo famine in Ethiopia (1973) was used by revolutionaries to remove Emperor Haile Selassie. While combating famine was a major priority of the revolution, it was 'quickly hijacked by a military dictatorship which in due course went on to inflict an even more severe famine on the Ethiopian people' (ibid.: 28). Similarly, during the height of the civil war in Ethiopia in the 1980s, the Tigrayan People's Liberation Front (TPLF) expressed a clear anti-famine commitment and was able to gain considerable popular support among the people in the Tigray region. However, and ironically, after the TPLF came to power in 1991, its anti-famine contract weakened considerably, and there have been several 'minor famines' in Ethiopia since the early 1990s. De Waal also writes that the 1984–85 famine in Sudan weakened the Nimeiri government considerably and the opposition allied to remove the government by citing its failure to prevent famine. However, once they removed Nimeiri, these so-called 'democratic forces' abandoned the famine issue. Thus de Waal asserts that an anti-famine contract has never really materialised properly in Africa, and that this explains recurrent famines in the continent.

Although de Waal makes a useful contribution to the debate, he overstates the existence of a 'political contract' in preventing famine in India. And one wonders who would 'contract' for freedom from famine but accept the continuation of high levels of undernutrition? Do tribal and other vulnerable groups 'contract' for poverty and disempowerment? Thus, de Waal's suggestion appears to imply a Faustian bargain in which there is explicit consent to chronic food insecurity in exchange for freedom from famine. Certain states in India – where there are political demands for protective social security – have indeed managed to provide some form of basic social security to large portions of its populations. For example, Kerala and West Bengal are characterised by generally high levels of political awareness among the rural population and this has meant that local issues, including those relating to food security, are highly politicised. It is therefore possible that, in these states, signals of imminent food crises and starvation will be quickly communicated to the authorities by local party workers, thus preventing major loss of life. However, and in terms of India's general success at preventing famine, there is little evidence of a 'political contract'. Instead, the key issue appears to be whether local authorities and the state government are willing to acknowledge and declare a 'crisis' and what drives such a process of acknowledgement and declaration. Indian public administration usually manages to respond to crises in an impressive manner and Drèze and Sen (1989, 1995) are correct to observe that politicians trigger bureaucratic response. However, in order to activate this trigger, politicians must first publicly declare a crisis and risk being criticised for failing to prevent it in the first place. Being very visible and involving large-scale suffering, famines can be prevented since no politician can afford to give the impression of doing nothing to tackle the crisis. In contrast, the quiet persistence of chronic undernutrition and recurrent episodes of small-scale starvation-related deaths in isolated areas are less visible and do not receive the kind of attention they deserve. These silent forms of suffering require that political authorities admit, acknowledge and declare a 'chronic crisis' and then take appropriate steps to combat it, which may involve very different public responses from those adopted to prevent high-profile famines.

Rubin (2001: 78) provides an interesting viewpoint when he argues that Sen's claim can be divided into two distinct interpretations – 'strict' and 'weak'. According to a strict interpretation, 'a famine would never be able to occur in a democratic society with a free press', while a weak interpretation entails merely 'hypothesising that democracy and free press increase the government's responsiveness thus not excluding the possibility of a famine in a democratic society altogether'. This view largely conforms to my argument that Sen's claim works best when broadly interpreted, whereby democracy, a free press and resulting public action increase the likelihood that the government will be actively involved in preventing famine. Such an interpretation leaves open the possibility that famines may take place in weak and unstable electoral democracies. For example, transitional democracies, where electoral procedures have recently been introduced, can witness famines simply because democratic institutions are underdeveloped and a 'collaborative' and 'adversarial' political culture has not taken root properly.

Returning to the example of the famine in Sudan in the 1980s, the experiment with parliamentarianism in 1986–89, while important from the electoral point of view, was not able to guarantee and safeguard basic freedoms to the Sudanese. Indeed, it imposed shariah as national law. Similarly, the Bangladesh famine in 1974 took place despite the presence of an elected government in Dhaka. The country had recently become independent from Pakistan, and the government, elected in 1973, was not able to put in place an effective system of governance to tackle natural disasters and resulting food shortages. Thus, famines in so-called democratic Sudan and Bangladesh can be explained by broadly interpreting Sen. Although democracy increases government responsiveness to crises, the ability to prevent famine ultimately depends on the how local institutions function and their capacity and the government's commitment to protect, fulfil and promote basic human rights and freedoms. And democratically elected governments may end up being highly corrupt. The international dimension – excluded by Sen – is also crucial. For example, some governments may be urged to implement a particular policy which may increase food insecurity in subsequent years (e.g. International Monetary Fund advice to Malawi which influenced the government to sell its entire maize stock in 2001).

Interestingly, non-democracies may also enjoy considerable success in preventing famine as long as certain freedoms (although not extensively political in nature) are guaranteed – including freedom of speech and expression together with the freedom to organise – even though regular free and fair elections are not held. The military regime's success in preventing famine in Nigeria during drought-induced food shortages in 1972–73 is a case in point. In particular, the Nigerian press played a crucial role in providing early warning information to the authorities and galvanised national support for relief operations. The result was an impressive state response to prevent famine (Reddy 1988). Similarly, Drèze and Sen (1989) have highlighted the success of Zimbabwe, Kenya and Cape Verde in preventing famine in the 1980s despite the fact that none of these were multiparty democracies.

Freedom is more than democracy. Democracy presupposes freedom, not vice versa. Thus, democracy may or may not be the best guarantor for freedom in a given situation, historically or geographically defined. There is currently a general consensus of an intimate relationship between democracy and freedom, and several definitions of democracy, except narrow minimalist versions, explicitly contain references to various individual freedoms. It is also largely assumed that democracy possesses the capacity to foster basic human freedoms, i.e. certain minimum freedoms relating to those of association, speech, expression and opposition are essential in order for elections to be meaningful. The argument is that checks and balances inherent in democratic systems prevent excessive abuse of power and arbitrary oppression while guaranteeing rights and entitlements to citizens and correcting policy errors. Hence, the association between democratic governance and its ability to promote human rights and freedoms provides a strong justification of the general preference of democracy over other forms of government. However, the democracy–freedom association is not as simple as it is often taken to be and at the outset it is necessary to view them as distinct concepts. Minimalist conceptions of democracy, termed 'electoral democracy' by Diamond (1996: 21), highlight the importance of 'minimal levels of freedom in order for competition and participation to be meaningful'. In other words, and following Schumpeter's (1947: 269) definition, democracy is a system 'for arriving at political decisions in which individuals acquire the power to decide by means of a competitive struggle for the people's vote'. At the other end of the spectrum lies the broad concept of 'liberal democracy' which includes periodic, free and fair electoral contestation together with universal adult suffrage. This category includes a wide range of features including a system of checks and balances, the availability of alternative and multiple channels for expression and representation of views, and the right of being politically equal under the rule of law (Diamond 1996: 23–24). Between 'minimalist' and 'liberal' democracies, however, there are several intermediary conceptions of democracy which 'explicitly incorporate basic civil freedoms of expression and association, yet still allow for considerable restriction of citizenship rights' (ibid.: 25). These intermediary views are distinct depending on 'whether political and civil freedoms are seen as relevant mainly to the extent that they ensure meaningful *electoral* competition and participation, or are instead viewed as necessary to ensure a wider range of democratic functions' (ibid.).[13]

Thus, minimalist democracy involves 'the selection of rulers or policies' and 'freedom' relates to the ability to 'engage in certain behaviors or to hold and express views without governmental interference' (Bova 1997: 112–113). The issue at hand is the capacity of democracies, in comparison to non-democracies, to extend freedoms from those initially granted into more substantial ones. In consolidated and stable democracies with a well-developed political culture, 'the range of rights and liberties available to citizens . . . goes well beyond what is strictly required for the existence of democracy itself' (Dahl 1992: 236). While this may often be the case, democracy and freedom do not enjoy a directly proportional relationship and maximising both is a challenge for many societies. As Przeworski *et al.* (2000: 34) aptly argue, 'Whereas democracy is a system of political rights – these are definitional – it is not a system that necessarily furnishes the conditions for effective exercise of these rights.'

The point here is that a focus on certain basic freedoms is relevant and important to capture the complex web of processes by which victims of, and those vulnerable to, starvation and famine articulate their problems – directly or indirectly through prominent citizens and organisations – and seek redress from the ruling authority. By comparison, many definitions of 'democracy' attach considerable if not exclusive attention to the role of elections. Sen himself has observed that democracy has two related features: the voting aspect and the open public deliberation aspect. He cites the example of Pakistan under General Musharraf and, while agreeing that free and fair elections need to be held as soon as possible, simultaneously argues that it is important to remember that public deliberation in Pakistan under Musharraf has been much more open than other previous democratically elected governments.[14] Although Sen is correct in observing that free public deliberation in a democracy provides a better foundation for combating economic need, there is a need to qualify this since he assumes that democratic institutions by themselves will guarantee public deliberation and an effective response against poverty and deprivation. This need not really be the case, particularly in countries like India where democracy remains an unfinished project and where civil and political rights do not result in the active promotion of socio-economic rights and freedoms, particularly in relation to politically marginalised groups in the population. Instead of merely being concerned with the ideal role of democracy, it is important to address a second-order question which relates to the nature and extent to which civil and political rights and freedoms *actually* play an instrumental role.[15]

Thus, although elections are important, they do not guarantee successful public deliberation in preventing starvation and famine. In this sense, a democratic system provides necessary but not sufficient conditions for famine prevention and the promotion of socio-economic rights and freedoms. Although democracies guarantee certain basic freedoms, there is no guarantee that citizens are actually in a position to utilise these freedoms properly. As Beetham (1999: 91–92) observes, understanding democracy exclusively with regard to a set of political institutions implies that institutions alone are all-important for democracy. This ignores the intrinsic role that human rights and freedoms play in the notion of democracy. Thus, how effective institutions are, i.e. how democratic they are, will depend on the guarantee and exercise of civil and political freedoms in society. And it is important to emphasise both the extent of freedoms guaranteed in a democracy and the 'enabling conditions, institutional as well as social' (Przeworski *et al.* 2000: 34) that allow individuals to act freely in the political sphere – even though they may vary considerably from situation to situation. By studying such enabling conditions with regard to both individuals and institutions, it may be possible to better explain state capacity to combat acute and endemic deprivation even when the formal mechanisms of an electoral democracy are in place.

Understanding the ability of democracies to prevent starvation deaths

If we interpret Sen's claim broadly and agree that democracy and a free press increase government responsiveness, the next question to ask is why the same democratic freedoms are less able to combat less sensational forms of suffering, like chronic undernutrition, that often result in starvation and death. Sen admits that India has generally failed to address the problem of chronic hunger, although he does not take the argument further to explain why this is so. He writes:

> Democracy has been especially successful in preventing those disasters that are easy to understand and where sympathy can take a particularly immediate form. Many other problems are not quite so accessible . . . While the plight of famine victims is easy to politicize, these other deprivations call for deeper

analysis and more effective use of communication and political participation – in short, a fuller practice of democracy.

(Sen 2000: 154)

How does democracy work in practice? More importantly, what challenges do democracies face in terms to tackling the problems of starvation? There is a need to investigate the intricacies of the democratic processes at work in promoting basic human rights and a person's entitlement to food. Currie (2000: 24) offers a good start, observing that it is important to recognise the 'relation between government and interest groups within civil society, and specifically to the degree of "partiality" of the state within a modern political democracy'. Consequently, the state is never a 'neutral arbiter', which impartially controls 'conflicts between competing groups within the polity'. Ruling parties invariably 'share common interests with dominant groups in order to sustain themselves economically and to preserve stable political governance'. This is a claim supported by Rangasami (1985: 1797) who, writing on the Indian experience, notes that 'the state intervenes only to halt the starvation process but will not consider intervention in the economic process' that would make chronic undernutrition and starvation difficult in the first place. This further accentuates vulnerability to famine. Similarly, Alamgir (1978) observes that authorities in Bangladesh tend to react only when vulnerable groups fall below the 'famine line'. Politically, the government can tolerate large sections of the population under the 'poverty line' as chronic poverty is not understood as being an urgent problem requiring a prioritised response.

The above discussion leads us to question who exactly constitutes the 'public' and in what way the public highlights the issues related to chronic undernutrition and starvation in democracies. The 'public' is not a homogeneous entity and in most developing countries there are divisions related to class, caste, ownership, occupation, gender, community and culture. Institutions like opposition parties, interest groups, non-governmental organisations, bureaucrats, academics, farmers groups and trade union movements have the potential to work towards creating a public sphere, generating political pressure, in which the issue of starvation results in not private but public acts. By exercising political pressure, these actors play a major part in determining actions undertaken by governments, and even authoritarian political leaders have, largely, accepted the discipline of public criticism and social opposition. Public action in this sense serves to enlighten the public and draws attention to problems that may otherwise be neglected. This in turn may lead to the precipitation of remedial action on the part of governments faced with critical pressure. However, there has been debate within South Asian studies about the nature of the 'public' in highly segmented societies, and many scholars have worked towards finding definitions of the 'public' and 'public sphere' by borrowing from, in particular, the work of Habermas (1989). However, some scholars also tend to adapt Eurocentric definitions to developing country contexts. In non-European societies a public sphere can be thought of as the discourse that takes place across the boundaries of caste and clan segments, creating notions of common welfare and shared fates. It is perhaps easy for persons in highly segmented societies like India to objectify those outside their extended kin group as 'others' about whom one need not bother. Therefore, and from a methodological angle, the task of identifying 'public action' as the explanatory variable for political pressure on government remains a complex one.

There is a further need to identify the sets of conditions under which public action can be successful or unsuccessful in promoting government commitment to tackle undernutrition and starvation. This requires a closer look at the 'range of political actions adopted by citizens to put pressure on government, and the range of responses adopted by office-holders' (Currie 2000: 24). In addition to formal articulation of interests in democracies, an analysis of public action should also take into account interest articulation through 'alternative channels' which are adopted whenever 'the democratic political process fails to meet the needs and expectations of citizens'. For example, politicians and bureaucrats may offer preferential treatment to particular groups in the community, award project contracts on the basis of bribes, deny the existence of a problem despite clear evidence to the contrary, etc. On their part, citizens can also bypass democratic procedures and adopt alternative strategies like refusing to pay back government loans, resorting to violent protests and disrupting social services. Similarly, Törnquist (2002: 31) suggests that in many developing countries citizens often prefer to bypass democratic means to further their ends. They may find it more attractive to pursue their agendas by choosing 'non-democratic and even anti-democratic avenues (e.g. violent protests, paying or bargaining for protection and influential positions and contacts within the administration, government and elite circles)'.

Most importantly, democracies in the developing world, including India, appear to excel at crisis-induced responses. A formal political declaration of a crisis is almost always required for the administrative machinery to start relief operations. For such a declaration to be made, however, the crisis must be clearly visible and acknowledged as an 'emergency' by political and administrative elites. I believe this factor explains the success that democracies have enjoyed in preventing famines. As discussed in previous sections, famines imply mass starvation deaths and most democratically elected governments may find it difficult to refuse to declare a crisis when faced with an impending famine. By comparison, politicians treat chronic undernutrition as part and parcel of the situation, where large numbers of people live below the poverty line. This is because those in authority do not expect to be held accountable for persistently high levels of undernutrition, and are confident that such issues are accepted by society as a natural feature of a poor country with a large population.

Interestingly, however, there may be occasional willingness of opposition parties to politicise extreme deprivation among certain sections of the population. As the evidence from the ensuing case studies will show, the main incentive to do so is to malign the ruling party in the period immediately preceding elections. In order to counter this, ruling party leaders may feel the need to descend on a poor and remote village in an attempt to downplay the accusation of extreme

41

destitution. Thus, politicians from all parties, more so those with considerable power and influence, prefer to play the 'role of the saviour'. The general argument here is that politicians in democracies appear to have an incentive in ensuring that a large section of the population remains poor. They have little incentive to actively promote and be committed to long-term measures aimed at removing extreme poverty and vulnerability to starvation if the possibility of playing the role of a saviour outweighs the cost of being held responsible for the crisis. A core feature of democracy involves periodic elections, and the presence of large groups of people living in extreme poverty creates opportunities and incentives for politicians (particularly those who wish to seek re-election) to intervene when deprivation becomes particularly acute (Banik and Brekke 2004). By reacting to the sensational and visible impacts of natural disasters or by taking action on the basis of newspaper reports alleging starvation and child sale, politicians may try to convey the message that the poor need to be saved from sliding into destitution and death. Short-term and ad hoc relief operations may be launched amidst much fanfare and with a strong media presence. Clothes and food may be distributed personally by high-profile leaders and, in general, promises are made that such deprivation will not be allowed to happen again. In doing so, politicians try to win political support from the poor and those who sympathise with the poor. If election is not on the cards, the desire to play the role of the saviour is greatly diminished. The crucial point here is that political interest is related not only to whether deprivation occurs but also to its context.

While politicians from all parties are in a position to play this game, those who can blame previous governments for the current plight of the local poor are in a better position to don the garb of the saviour. When ruling party politicians blame previous governments for current ills, opposition party leaders may direct their ire at the current government. However, the incentive and motivation to play the role of the saviour may be further influenced when, in the period between elections, ministers and senior civil servants are expected to make high-profile visits to disaster sites. As the discussion on calamity relief in Chapter 7 will show, the failure to send a minister to inspect and oversee ad hoc relief operations may be perceived as being tantamount to callous disregard on the part of the government, even though such visits often do more harm than good. Indeed, VIP visits to crisis areas usually divert attention from the victims of a crisis. Security concerns and the media entourage that follows VIPs make local authorities spend more time and resources looking after distinguished visitors than those in need of relief.

Thus, any attempt to explain the failure of democracies like India to successfully address the problem of chronic hunger needs to focus on the interaction between specific institutions, and the existing 'rules of the game' that characterise this interaction. In this task, there is a need to emphasise a bottom-up perspective on the role, effectiveness and capacity of formal democratic institutions, as articulated by the local population including those vulnerable to starvation. For example, the role of political parties and the press must be examined in terms of their capacity to provide credible information (early warning and follow-up) to, and extract accountability from, the government on issues of drought and star-vation deaths. Also, how do politicians and media persons distinguish between famine and chronic hunger and what is the nature of government intervention in improving the general nutritional and health status of those vulnerable to starva-tion? Moreover, long-term measures and short-term government interventions may favour certain groups depending on their level of political consciousness. It is also crucial to understand the traditional coping strategies adopted by the local population to tackle food shortages and a sudden fall in purchasing power. Large groups in the population often fall outside the gambit of government pro-grammes. How do they survive and what methods do they employ to combat recurrent drought conditions and food shortages?

Finally, implementation of anti-hunger policy and the role of the bureaucracy are not highlighted by Sen, and have further not received much attention in recent famine studies. This is surprising given that an accurate assessment of the situa-tion at the field level is crucial for the initiation of preventive measures to combat food crises. Examining the role that street-level bureaucrats play in providing early warning information is crucial in addition to understanding the nature of the 'political trigger' that pushes the administrative machinery into action once a crisis is officially declared. Similarly, the role and activity levels of civil society organisations in criticising government policy and seeking judicial redress for the lack of human rights protection is also important. Besides, as judicial interven-tions in protecting and promoting the right to food in India have of late increased following petitions to the courts from NGOs and interest groups, it is particularly interesting to examine the extent to which such measures have influenced po-litical and administrative action. Before addressing these issues specifically, it is necessary to examine the characteristics of Kalahandi's poverty and the vulner-ability of large sections of its population to starvation. This is the focus of the next chapter.

3

KALAHANDI'S POVERTY

The political history of Kalahandi (meaning 'black pot')[1] is synonymous with the Naga dynasty, which ruled Kalahandi from the early eleventh century to 1948. The Naga administration revolved around feudal lords (*Zamindar*) and the village headman (*Gountia*), who collected revenue on behalf of the King. Communications and trade within the region were poor and there were no regular and organised bazaars to trade goods (Kalahandi Gazetteer 1980). After the introduction of direct British rule in 1853, successive Naga princes were allowed to retain their privileges on condition that they surrendered a large portion of their annual revenue to the government. The administrative structure of the Kalahandi princely state was reorganised by separating an area directly under the control of the prince (*Khalsa*) from that of the *Zamindari* (an area divided into five sections, each under the control of a Zamindar). The Zamindars, in turn, relied on the village Gountia to provide a fixed amount of revenue, while in certain special (*khas*) villages, revenue was directly collected. In return for his services, the Gountia received a large plot of fertile and rent-free land (*bhogra*), which could not be sold, transferred or mortgaged (Currie 2000: 69). Over time, a strategy of high levels of revenue extraction by Zamindars combined with an elite group of Gountias controlling the most fertile strips of land gradually impoverished large sections of Kalahandi's population. The British did, however, usher in general economic development in the area by building new roads and improving access to drinking water by digging wells. Gradually a market system with a cash-economy base developed, ending Kalahandi's relative isolation from other areas of Orissa.

After Indian independence, the Kalahandi princely state merged with the state of Orissa in January 1948, and the Zamindari and Gountia systems were abolished in 1951–52 and 1956, respectively. With the enactment of the Orissa Land Reforms Act in 1960, which provided fixed ceilings on surplus landholdings, traditional forms of forced labour (known as *bethi* and *begari*) were abolished (ibid.: 77–78). Several important pieces of legislation followed, empowering the district administration to return to tribal groups land that had earlier been illegally confiscated from them by non-tribal and exploitative moneylenders (ibid.).

Kalahandi today

Located in south-western Orissa and extending over an area of over 8,000 square kilometres, the district today is the product of a series of political decisions designed to facilitate effective administration.[2] The district administration is located in Bhawanipatna and headed by the Collector – an officer of the Indian Administrative Service (IAS).[3] The district is further divided into two sub-divisions (Bhawanipatna and Dharamgarh) each under a sub-divisional officer (SDO), and 13 blocks, each headed by a block development officer (BDO). For purposes of revenue collection, Kalahandi has seven *Tehsils* – each under a *Tehsildar*, who is in turn assisted by a team of revenue inspectors – and the task of managing law and order is managed by the Superintendent of Police (SP) and his staff at the district police department. A three-tier system of local self-government, variously termed *Panchayats* and *Panchayati Raj*, provides advice to the district administration on development-related activities and monitors programme implementation. Despite early attempts to institutionalise the Panchayati Raj system in Orissa in the early 1960s, the system only became fully operational in 1997. As a result, Panchayats enjoy very little power and influence in comparison to other states like West Bengal and Kerala.

The majority of the district's 1.3 million inhabitants live in the plains; the hilly tracts are scarcely populated. Almost 17 per cent of Kalahandi's population belong to the Scheduled Caste category (mainly *Dom, Ganda, Chamar, Ghasi, Dhoba, Mehra, Beldar* and *Panika*) and Scheduled Tribes constitute 29 per cent of the population, with the major tribal groups being *Kandhas, Banjara, Bhatada, Bhunjia, Binjhal, Dal, Gondh, Mirdha, Munda, Paroja, Saora* and *Sabar*. The district's literacy rate is abysmally low – 31.08 per cent in comparison to the official Orissa and national averages of 49.09 and 52.1 per cent, respectively. The literacy rate for women is a meagre 15.28 per cent; it is assumed that the corresponding figures for tribal groups are even lower. The majority of the population are either cultivators (43 per cent) or landless agricultural labourers (41 per cent) (Kalahandi District Statistical Handbook 1997). The urban areas of Kalahandi are inhabited by mainly lower middle-class households comprising primarily local traders and salaried employment in public services. The district is rich in natural resources (including bauxite, graphite, manganese ores, iron and quartz), albeit with little industrial development owing to lack of energy sources and inadequate infrastructure. Although 31 per cent of the district is covered by forests, there are growing concerns over a gradual depletion of the forest cover due to excessive cattle grazing and the unrestricted felling of trees.

Kalahandi's economy, like most other areas in rural India, is primarily dependent on agriculture, which employs more than 80 per cent of the labour force. There are four main types of land available for cultivation – *bahal, berana, mal* and *att. Bahal* and *berana* are fertile lowlands – primarily in the possession of wealthier and non-tribal groups – and provide higher yields than *mal* and *att* categories. *Mal* is terraced and sloped land, able to receive surface drainage water from the less fertile *att* uplands. Both *mal* and *att* lands are best suited for crops that do not require much soil moisture (Kalahandi Gazetteer 1980: 127). The agricultural season is divided into *kharif* (April–September) and *rabi* (October–March) seasons. The traditional *kharif* crops are paddy, maize, millets (*ragi, jower*), jute, vegetables, chilli and groundnut. In the *rabi* season, wheat, winter paddy, oilseeds, potato, tobacco, onion, garlic, coriander and some pulses are grown. In the hilly tracts of the district, small groups of tribal farmers engage in permanent cultivation, with the help of water from streams and canals. Most tribal farmers, however, practice 'slash and burn' shifting cultivation (variously called *podu chas, dongar chas, kudki chas* and *kudu chas*) with paddy, maize and minor millets being the major crops.

The characteristics of poverty

In addition to high levels of illiteracy and excessive dependence on agriculture, a majority of Kalahandi's inhabitants lack proper housing, health and sanitation facilities. Most rural houses are constructed out of grass leaves, reeds and bamboos which do not provide adequate shelter against oppressive heat and heavy rainfall, and half of all villages are not electrified (Government of Orissa 2000). Poverty is widespread among all classes and castes of society, but it is particularly prevalent among SC (largely landless labourers) and ST groups who practice shifting cultivation on infertile land and depend on forest resources and products to supplement their diets and incomes.

Inequality in agricultural landholdings

Given that Kalahandi's economy is predominantly rural and agrarian, land is the most important asset. In recent decades there has been a large increase in the number of marginal farmers owning less than one hectare of land and around 40 per cent of Kalahandi's cultivators are currently classified in this category. Despite their large numbers, however, marginal farmers only account for 11.7 per cent of the total cultivated area (Kalahandi District Statistical Handbook 1997). The average size of operational landholdings in Kalahandi is 1.94 hectares, far higher than the Orissa average of 1.34 hectares. Since the landholdings of only SC groups in Kalahandi are smaller than the Orissa average, the explanation of Kalahandi's poverty relative to other districts in Orissa appears to lie elsewhere. For example, the long-term trend of land transfer and fragmentation of cultivable plots has resulted in an explosion in the number of marginal farmers in recent decades. Although the average size of operational landholding in Kalahandi is well above the state average, cultivable land in the district varies enormously in terms of fertility, amount of rainfall received and the availability of irrigation facilities – all of which combine to have a bearing on agricultural productivity. The most fertile and low-lying lands (which both receive more rainfall and have better access to irrigation) are almost invariably owned by large farmers. Moreover, despite legislation on land reform, land ceilings and tenancy rights, the Orissa government has a poor enforcement record. Most marginal farmers and landless labourers remain under the control of local landlords who charge exorbitant rents and seldom share the costs of production. As Buch and Baboo (1997: 17–18) note, 'Since the tenants are uneducated and unaware of the law, the landlords always devise means to get away with any fresh legislation that might hamper their interests.' And such 'insecurity in the tenurial status means that the tenants do not take interest in the improvement of the land' which in turn adversely affects crop production (ibid.: 18).

Below Poverty Line (BPL) households

Every five years, the District Rural Development Agency (DRDA) carries out household surveys in order to identify beneficiaries of rural development programmes. Households with an annual income of less than Rs 11,000 (estimated to be equivalent to ownership of 5 acres of land) are classified as BPL and ranked into the following four sub-groups according to annual income: Rs 0–4,000, Rs 4,001–6,000, Rs 6,001–8,500, Rs 8,501–11,000. The results of a survey conducted in 1997 were widely criticised on methodological grounds and the Orissa government ordered a review of the conclusions. Although the data from the revised survey were unavailable, corresponding data from 1992 bear out three main features of poverty in Kalahandi. First, the district has the third highest percentage of BPL households in the state, and over 70 per cent of these households earn less than Rs 6,000 a year. Second, the district average of BPL households is astonishingly high at 86.77 per cent of the total population. Third, the poorest occupational groups are landless agricultural labourers and marginal farmers, comprising 66 per cent of the total BPL households. These two groups are also most vulnerable to drought.

Even in the year 2000, the BPL list compiled in 1992 formed the basis for selecting beneficiaries for all social security programmes in Kalahandi. The district administration, however, initiated several attempts to update the lists by organising an annual general meeting (*palli sabha*) of all villagers within a Gram Panchayat area. During such assemblies, a tentative list of recipients of food subsidies, pensions and other benefits was circulated and approved by the attendees. In general, however, the *palli sabhas* were not properly announced and often thinly attended. In addition, villagers complained of irregularities in the compilation of such lists, particularly since Panchayat representatives tended to favour their friends and relatives and in the process excluded those in genuine need.

Social security and anti-poverty programmes

In the period 1998–2000, six major pension and benefit schemes were in operation in Kalahandi. Among these was the National Old Age Pension scheme whereby the central and state governments provided Rs 75 and Rs 25 per month, respectively, to each pensioner above 65 years of age. In addition, eligible persons received Rs 100 under the Old Age Pension and the Widow Pension programmes. The National Maternity Benefit Scheme provided pregnant women from BPL households with Rs 300 for the first two live births. And upon the death of the main bread earner of a family, the nearest relative received Rs 5,000 (in case of natural death) and Rs 10,000 (accidental death) from the National Family Benefit Scheme. Through the Balika Samrudhi Yojana programme, the central government provided cash incentives to couples in order to encourage the birth and well-being of girl children.

Four major programmes, jointly financed by central and state governments, aimed specifically to reduce poverty in Kalahandi. Indira Awas Yojana provided financial assistance for the construction of houses (including smokeless ovens and lavatory facilities) for certain SC and ST groups. The Million Well Scheme assisted small and marginal farmers in the construction of nearby wells for the provision of limited, yet crucial, irrigation water. The Swarna Jayanti Gram Swarozgar Yojana programme encouraged groups of villagers (a minimum of 10 members) to form self-help groups and save a part of their income. After six months, the group qualified for various amounts of cash support from Panchayat institutions and government banks. Finally, the Integrated Tribal Development Programme was in operation in Lanjigarh and Thuamul Rampur blocks, where more than half of the population belonged to tribal groups. The programme supported a large number of activities, including dairy development, fisheries, soil conservation, schools, stipends to tribal students, etc.

Despite good intentions, most above-mentioned social security and anti-poverty programmes in the district suffered from problems related to targeting. In other words, the outdated and unreliable BPL lists excluded many poor and vulnerable households. District officials also complained that although they submitted so-called 'utilisation certificates'[4] – documenting that previously allotted funds had been used up and that a new installation of funds was urgently required – central and state governments were slow to respond with fresh allocations. Without adequate funds officials argued that it was of little use to update the BPL lists since, even though new members could be included in a revised list, they would not necessarily receive any benefits.

Nutrition, health and the likelihood of starvation deaths

Rice is the staple food, consumed regardless of social position and source of income. It is common practice in rural areas to consume boiled rice soaked in water overnight together with chillies, onions and a simple curry made of leafy vegetables. Members of poor households eat rice once a day and on occasion the diet is supplemented with coarse grain, small millets and herbs. Pulses, wheat, fish and meat are primarily consumed by economically well-off classes. The nutritional pattern of tribal groups differs from the rest of the population as the limited production of paddy on small plots of infertile highlands is often sold immediately after the harvest in order to repay debts. Hence, many groups have traditionally relied on the collection of edible items from the forest (roots, plants, fruits and flowers) in order to meet the nutritional needs for a period of four to six months each year. In certain villages, there was also evidence of regular (often daily) consumption of liquor fermented from the *mahua* flower. A local NGO – Antodaya – claimed that a large number of tribal males have in recent years become addicted to locally brewed liquor available at *bhattis* (temporary liquor shops) and that several families were forced to mortgage assets in order to repay *bhatti*-related debts.

Pregnant and nursing women, children below five years and the elderly are among those most vulnerable to disease in Kalahandi. Despite a reduction in the incidence of mass mortality in the district in recent years, Table 3.1 shows that the infant and maternal mortality rates remain alarmingly high. The reliability of such statistics, however, varies greatly. For example, whereas the chief medical officer claimed that the IMR for Kalahandi was 55 in 1999, the social welfare officer put the figure at 68. According to an Orissa government survey, Kalahandi's IMR was 140 against the state average of 97.[5] Notwithstanding such statistical irregularity, several doctors claimed that basic nutritional and health indicators for Kalahandi were far worse than the figures compiled by the district health and social welfare departments.

The alarmingly high IMR indicated widespread malnutrition and low immunological defence to disease. Most children in the study villages showed visible symptoms of nutritional deficiencies resulting from protein-calorie malnutrition and lack of vitamins in the diet, including large and protruding bellies, thin arms and legs, watery eyes, discoloured hair, etc. According to local doctors, adults and children in many areas of the district suffered from vitamin B deficiencies and every fourth adult showed clinical symptoms indicating malnutrition over a prolonged period, and hence risked being affected by splenomegaly (enlargement of the spleen) and hepatomegaly (enlargement of the liver). One of the best available methods for measuring overall nutritional status of children under six years of age is to measure the mean annual weight for age (WA), which provides a composite indicator of long-term and current growth retardation. Data on child malnutrition – based on ICDS surveys in Kalahandi – were made available by

Table 3.1 Basic health indicators of Kalahandi, 1993–99

Year	IMR	MMR	Birth rate	Death rate
1993	91	2	20	9
1994	75	2	16	5
1995	81	2	20	7
1996	69	2	21	8
1997	63	1	23	8
1998	69	2	20	8
1999	55	1	24	8

Source: Office of the Chief District Medical Officer, Kalahandi.

the district social welfare officer. These surveys classified malnutrition into the following four grades using annual WA data: Grade I (90–100 per cent of WA, 'mild'), Grade II (75–90 per cent of WA, 'moderate'), Grade III (60–75 per cent of WA 'moderate/severe') and Grade IV (less than 60 per cent of WA, 'severe'). As Table 3.2 indicates, around 30 per cent of Kalahandi's children enjoy normal health and dietary patterns whereas the rest suffer from various degrees of malnutrition. The data also confirmed the social welfare department's claim that impressive progress had been made in combating the severest forms of malnutrition since 1998. However, evidence from the study villages painted a different picture and the problem appeared to be just as serious in 2001 as it was during my first visit in 1999. Although the official figures for 'moderate' and 'severe' malnutrition were far lower than what was observed in the study villages, they nonetheless pointed to the high probability of finding large numbers of malnourished children in Kalahandi's villages. Moreover, monthly ICDS survey data for the period July–December 2000 further showed that the two tribal-dominated blocks that formed a major focus of this study – Lanjigarh and Thuamul Rampur – figured prominently among those with the highest incidence of moderate and severe forms of malnutrition. Thus, while the district average was 0.2 per cent, the incidence of severe (Grade IV) malnutrition in these areas was 0.27 per cent and 0.50 per cent, respectively.

Malnutrition surveys in India have generally been limited to children and there are few surveys available on adult malnutrition. This also applies to Kalahandi except for a nutrition survey conducted by the Orissa government in three blocks of the district in 1997.[6] The survey used the mean annual WA composite indicator of long-term and current growth retardation to classify malnutrition among children into three categories – mild, moderate and severe.[7] Other indicators used to determine the nutritional status of children and adults were vitamin A and B deficiency, anaemia, upper respiratory tract infection, tooth caries and sparse hair. The survey concluded that between 6.25 and 9.3 per cent of the children in three blocks of Kalahandi were severely malnourished and the incidence of anaemia among children ranged between 35 and 37 per cent. Not surprisingly, the incidence of child malnutrition was highly correlated with the nutritional status of women and all three blocks showed a high incidence of anaemia (between 40 and 60 per cent) and vitamin B deficiency (between 17 and 30 per cent). Although the

Table 3.2 Malnutrition among children under 5 years, Kalahandi, 1998–2000

	Nutritional status of children 0–6 years					
Year	*No. of children surveyed*	*Normal (%)*	*Grade I (%)*	*Grade II (%)*	*Grade III (%)*	*Grade IV (%)*
1998	130,857	31.10	36.40	29.35	2.68	0.45
1999	130,383	30.66	37.72	29.05	2.25	0.31
2000	144,950	32.15	37.44	28.41	1.80	0.20

Source: Adapted from data collected from Kalahandi's social welfare office.

survey data are limited to only one village in each of the three blocks, field visits
in the focus villages of this study and interviews with local doctors confirmed the
poor overall nutritional status of adults and children in rural Kalahandi.

Traditionally, malaria, diarrhoea and tuberculosis have been predominant in
Kalahandi in addition to cholera, typhoid, dysentery, respiratory disorders, gastroenteritis, filarial infections and whooping cough. Disease-related deaths tend to
increase during severe drought years and the consumption of contaminated water
in recent years has resulted in an increase in waterborne diseases. Table 3.3 lists
the death toll from various diseases in the period 1993–2000. The large number
of deaths from diarrhoea, in particular, corresponds to the drought years of 1993,
1996 and 1998.

Towards the end of 2000, Kalahandi had 13 mobile health units (one for each
block), which were used to check epidemics. Public Health Centres (PHCs) located at the block level were required to conduct regular disease surveillance. In
this task they were assisted by primary health workers who regularly monitored
the incidence of diarrhoea, gastroenteritis, acute respiratory disorders, jaundice,
etc. Each PHC was also required to send a weekly report of the situation to the
district health authorities.

The discussion so far bears out the fact that a large number of adults and children in Kalahandi suffer from various forms of malnutrition, undernutrition and
disease which are related to poverty and poor dietary practices. With reference to
the definitions of starvation discussed in Chapter 2, the possibility of 'starvation
deaths' – from the total lack of any food for several consecutive days – appears
likely in Kalahandi although such deaths are not widespread. Reports of alleged
starvation deaths in the district, however, must be understood in a wider context,
taking into account mortality from a combination of malnutrition, undernutrition
and disease. As the discussion in Chapter 5 will demonstrate, the actual process
of identifying a starvation death is immensely difficult and challenging both for
medical doctors and district officials. Given that there is no 'starvation death' category in official reports and statistics, officials (including doctors) tend to focus
exclusively on the final result (immediate cause of death from a specific disease)

Table 3.3 Deaths from major diseases in Kalahandi, 1993–2000

Year	Malaria	Diarrhoea	Tuberculosis
1993	10	167	34
1994	–	29	17
1995	3	24	17
1996	20	188	20
1997	28	40	22
1998	54	203	19
1999	67	13	20
2000	47	12	16

Source: Office of the Chief District Medical Officer, Kalahandi.

and not the actual process (underlying process of progressive and sustained malnutrition and undernutrition) which brought about the outcome.

Drought and coping strategies

Rainfall from the south-west monsoon is the primary factor that determines agricultural production in India since only approximately 38 per cent of the net area
sown in the country has access to irrigation. The actual impact of drought often
depends on its severity gauged in terms of the length of the episode, the total
amount of area affected and the socio-economic characteristics of the population
residing in drought-hit areas. Thus drought has the potential of adversely affecting
people in numerous spheres of life – environmental, economic and social (Mooley
1994: 606). It also usually affects everyone although those with large assets, in the
form of land, farm animals and food stocks, do not normally face the same level
of distress as vulnerable groups with 'hand to mouth existence and with very little
margin or staying power' (Dubashi 1992: A30). Nonetheless, people residing in
drought-prone areas acquire, over time, an ability to deal with food shortages and
loss of income, and the complex methods for tackling hardship and 'preserving
assets which are needed to sustain a living in the future' usually fall under the
broad category of 'coping strategies' (Young and Jaspars 1995: 6–7). The nature
of such strategies employed varies depending on types of livelihood, land use
patterns, the system of trade, marketing, credit, etc. and local populations 'learn
through experience of drought and famine which specific strategies are best in
their situation' (ibid.: 7).

In most villages of rural Kalahandi, agriculture provides the primary source
of food in the period August–January, as harvesting of the first (and sometimes
second) crop takes place. Starting in the month of November, a large portion of
the income generated from the sale of agricultural produce is also used to repay
foodgrain and cash loans taken up earlier in the year. From mid-January and until
May–June, the forests provide a secondary source of food, and various forms of
fruits, roots, and flowers are collected for consumption. *Sal* seeds and *kendu* and
palas leaves are also collected from forests since they fetch good prices in the
open market. Firewood and bamboo collection is especially popular in certain
areas as it provides raw materials for paper mills and the construction of small
houses. Other coping strategies to combat food insecurity involve the consumption of less preferred food, limiting the portion size of food, borrowing food or
money, 'maternal buffering' (practice of a mother deliberately eating less to ensure children have enough to eat) and the skipping of meals for whole days.[8] The
use of tobacco and the consumption of locally-brewed liquor (from *mahua* flower
and date palm juice) also serve as important coping strategies against hunger.

Starting in March–April, loans from moneylenders assume importance and
food is purchased with the help of loans until August. Indeed, private moneylenders (*sahukars*) exert considerable influence among the rural poor with their
grassroots presence, providing easy access to those in need of a quick loan. In

contrast to banks and cooperative societies, borrowers do not need to go through a lengthy application process and even the landless can receive loans despite not possessing landed security or other collateral. Most moneylenders in the study villages were 'outsiders', non-Oriyas (often belonging to the well-off Marwari community) who had settled in Kalahandi from neighbouring Andhra Pradesh and Madhya Pradesh. Such loans were used to meet household consumption needs, including expenses related to food, clothing and social ceremonies like the annual *Nuakhai* festival in August/September to celebrate the first harvest of the agricultural season. Some small and marginal farmers also use these loans to purchase seeds, fertilisers and agricultural equipment before the start of the agricultural season in June. Despite the enactment of the Orissa Money Lenders Act of 1939 and its subsequent amendments, most moneylenders engage in illegal practices related to the mortgage of land and charge exorbitant interest rates (often as high as 50 per cent per month).

Assistance from immediate family members residing in the vicinity is also an important coping strategy. If such assistance is unavailable, other relatives, friends, neighbours, patrons, large farmers and charitable organisations are approached. These networks function as 'shock absorbers' in times of crisis, and are well captured in a local folksong: *Judh bele pithir bhai, akal bele duhagai* (A brother in battle is just as important as a yielding cow during a drought).[9] The extent and regularity of help from fellow villagers is, however, dependent on how the drought affects the 'givers' and the 'receivers'. For example, drought in a particular village could affect the majority of the villagers equally (when most are marginal farmers) and sometimes unequally (in villages with some medium and large farmers). In general, assistance from those outside the immediate family is highly uncertain and therefore not always a reliable coping strategy.

An alternative strategy – and an important contribution of some NGOs in Kalahandi – is to form local 'self-help groups', where villagers contribute a fixed amount of money and/or foodgrains every month so that local 'cash banks' and 'grain banks' can be created. In times of acute need, any member of the group can withdraw a sum of money or grain from the common fund. Antodaya, an NGO working in Thuamul Rampur block, appears particularly successful in organising tribal women to form such self-help groups, and within a span of three years the organisation claimed to have organised over 900 women in both small (5–6) and large (10–15) groups. The idea of such self-help groups also appears to appeal especially to women since many are victims of marital and alcohol-related violence. Self-help groups, claim NGOs, also provide the most effective weapon against the stranglehold of moneylenders. There was, however, little evidence to indicate that such schemes had actually been successfully implemented all over Kalahandi, since there was a general absence of effective and well-functioning NGOs in many areas.

Another common coping strategy is distress sale or mortgage of assets – draught animals, cows, goats, poultry, cheap ornaments, kitchen utensils, etc. – during severe drought years. With little water and fodder available, there was an increase in the distress sale of cattle during the 1996 drought. Middlemen from neighbouring states visited several areas of the district for the purchase of cattle at low prices either from the villages directly or from weekly markets held at select locations between villages. The cattle was then herded to neighbouring districts like Rayagada and sold to principal traders who in turn sent the cattle to Hyderabad in neighbouring Andhra Pradesh. A traditional folksong from Kalahandi describes the practice of distress sale in the following manner: *Lipila kuna ke lipa, Amar sagake padichhe dukha, Kanar phasia bika* (Brush the wall again and again, my companion is in trouble. Sell the earring) (quoted in Mishra 1989: 43).

One of the most important coping strategies during both drought and non-drought years is migration. Seasonal migration in normal agricultural years has a long tradition in Kalahandi, mainly influenced by factors such as guaranteed employment, higher wages and sometimes even a sense of adventure and the desire to visit far-off places. Once the harvesting operations of the *kharif* crop are completed, small and marginal farmers together with landless labourers have no employment opportunities in the lean season. Instead of sitting idle, they prefer working in agriculture, construction and transport sectors in major cities of the country, leaving in November–February and returning towards the end of May or early June with the onset of the monsoon rains. This form of migration is more likely from the plains of the district that are well connected with the rest of Orissa by rail and road. These are also areas where private agents and their assistants responsible for recruiting migrants operate on a regular basis, promising higher wages and attractive working facilities in neighbouring Madhya Pradesh (e.g. cities like Raipur, Bilaspur and Jabalpur) and Andhra Pradesh (e.g. Hyderabad). A typical migrant is usually an SC or ST (male) landless agricultural labourer or marginal farmer, above 18 years of age. In some cases entire families including women and children migrate, although it is common to leave elderly parents behind.

In contrast to seasonal migration, distress-induced migration is primarily the result of factors which include drought, land alienation, debts and high levels of food insecurity. This form of migration, which had increased in Kalahandi in the 1990s, is a final resort when other coping strategies fail. Such migration usually starts as early as September–October, when there is little possibility of harvesting a crop, and long before a formal declaration of drought by the district administration. The acute distress affecting poor households also serves to further the interests of recruiting agents and their assistants, who take the opportunity to recruit even cheaper labour than they can normally expect with regard to seasonal migrants. Several NGOs in Kalahandi argued that distress-induced migration had of late become 'seasonal' in character and an integral part of the regular coping strategies adopted by vulnerable households given three successive droughts in 1996–2000.

Wages earned by migrant labourers are crucial for the survival of poor households. Labourers often receive an advance amount of Rs 400–500 per individual for work in brick kilns, mines and chemical industries, and lesser amounts (in the range of Rs 200–350) for agriculture-related work which is considered to be less hazardous. These advances together with the money saved from daily wages are used to feed the household, repay loans, repair houses, purchase seeds and fertilisers and to bear expenses related to social events like religious ceremonies and weddings. Being largely illiterate and ignorant of local laws in foreign cities, migrant labourers from Kalahandi are largely exploited, often not receiving the correct wage rate and compensation in the event of work-related accidents. Given poor working conditions in major Indian cities, a news report in early September 2000 reported that a group of 'harassed and disillusioned' migrants had returned from Mumbai, Nagpur, Raipur and Bilaspur 'preferring to face the hardships of life in the rural settings rather than stomach the exploitation and harassment of the concrete jungles'.[10] The routine exploitation of migrants by agents has also become a part of Kalahandi folklore, and a popular song from the district echoes the frustration of both seasonal and distress-induced migrants: *Dakinela thikadara, Ghara duara chadi bidese ghara, Petakaje harabara* (The contractors took us, Bereft we the native, now habiting on antique land, Hankering for the belly).[11]

4

DROUGHT AND STATE ACTION

Drought and famine are not new to India. Indeed, in *Arthasastra* – a classic trea-
tise on government written in India over 2,000 years ago – Kautilya writes that
when famine is imminent a good king should 'institute the building of forts or
waterworks with the grant of food, or share [his] provisions [with the people], or
entrust the country [to another king]' (quoted in Drèze 1990: 19). Over centuries,
numerous interventions were undertaken, including free kitchens, free distribution of foodgrains, remission of taxes and other forms of revenue, monetary advances and the construction of canals, roads and embankments in order to provide employment (Srivastava 1968: 28; Walker 1989: 101). However, there are
no records of a comprehensive famine relief policy in the country until the arrival
of the British.

Before the arrival of the British East India Company in 1765, famine was a
relatively localised and infrequent affair. Although famines became more severe
and widespread during the tenure of the East India Company (1765–1858), it
showed little interest in providing organised famine relief (Walker 1989; Drèze
1990). Anti-famine policies, however, were given high priority when the British government took over the country's administration in 1858. Although several
major famines occurred – most notably in Orissa (1865) and in Bihar and Bengal
(1873) – many lives were saved when the government undertook a very expensive but effective policy of procurement and distribution of grain (Brennan 1984:
94–95). Existing famine relief policies were nevertheless found to be inadequate
and a Famine Commission (established in 1880) formulated the Famine Codes of
1883 based on the principle that it was the government's responsibility to ensure
that there would be no loss of lives during food shortages. The Codes were essentially administrative guidelines to help the local administration anticipate and
declare famines and thereafter provide quick and efficient relief (Brennan 1984;
Hubbard 1988; Walker 1989). There were also institutionalised career incentives
for district officers to resolve and manage food crises successfully (Harriss 1988:
161).

With the help of these Codes, the government was able to prevent crop failures
from developing into famines in the period 1880–96. Following major famines in

several parts of the country in 1896–97 and 1899–1900, a new Famine Commission revised the Famine Codes in 1901 and subsequently several provinces took steps to frame new, or revise their old, famine codes. For example, the Bihar and Orissa Famine Code was first formulated in 1913 and later revised in 1930. Upon independence, India continued to use the Famine Codes although separate relief manuals or relief codes were drafted for each state in order to address droughts, floods, earthquakes and other disasters. In the ensuing sections of this chapter, specific provisions of the Orissa Relief Code relating to drought are first discussed followed by the actual government response undertaken in 1996–2000, including interventions in agriculture, irrigation, employment generation and nutrition.

Relief code guidelines for response to drought and famine

The Orissa Relief Code (hereafter Code) was drafted in 1975 with the aim of providing an administrative 'approach to relief' that was 'both preventive and curative' (Orissa Relief Code 1996: Introduction). Drought is defined as the 'failure of the rains' which 'either defers commencement of agricultural operations or affects growth of crop' (para. 22). The Code further notes that 'the intensity of drought depends upon whether the concerned areas have been visited by droughts successively for a number of years' (ibid.). There are also several provisions for 'early warning' including the importance of collecting 'rainfall statistics' to enable 'timely warning of climatic dangers, prevents surprise and provides information for a plan of campaign' (ibid.). The Code further provides that, after the end of the annual rainy season, rain gauges in the district must be checked by district officials (para. 23a,b) and that periodic assessments of crop loss must be undertaken by field staff every year through two types of experiments – an eye-estimation of crop loss followed in specific cases with crop-cutting experiments in villages where crop loss appears to be more than 50 per cent (para. 28a,b; Appendix V: iii). Revenue field staff members are required to compile and send reports to the district revenue department, quantifying crop loss under two categories – number of villages with crop loss between 50 and 74 per cent and those with 75 per cent and above (Appendix V: iv).

The Code instructs the Collector to submit fortnightly reports on weather and crop conditions throughout the year to his superiors in Bhubaneswar. There is a particular focus on an 'analytical report' by 10 July every year containing information on the following indicators: rainfall patterns, the district administration's plans for the agricultural season, the state of irrigation facilities, current market prices of essential commodities, stock of foodgrains available, the health situation, the functioning of the social security network and safety-net-oriented programmes, etc. (para. 24a,b). The reports from each district must then be verified by senior state-level officials (who may undertake field visits) and then submitted to the Orissa government within a week (para. 25d).

Based on available early warning and other information from the districts – including monthly situation reports and other relevant documents submitted by the Collector – the Orissa government has the primary responsibility for formally declaring a drought in the state (para. 29a). The declaration of drought in a block and/or classifying an entire district as drought-hit is important because 'without formally declaring any area/pocket as drought-affected, no relief operation should ordinarily be launched' (para. 29c). Hence, only in exceptional cases of extreme distress can the state government instruct field officers to start relief operations in the form of labour-intensive works for employment generation without a formal declaration of drought. Once drought has been formally declared, the state government is required to submit a report to the central government's Ministry of Agriculture and Cooperation (para. 30). It must also formulate a 'master plan' for the declared drought-hit areas for the implementation of 'durable, remunerative, productive and asset-creating schemes and projects.' Moreover, the government has the responsibility of preparing long-term contingency plans so that 'as soon as drought situation develops, or the situation worsens, these projects may be switched on without loss of time' (ibid.). Highlighting that 'Speed is the essence of relief operations,' the Code specifies the implementation of a wide range of measures which include the following (para. 7): labour-intensive works; emergency assistance to the destitute ('gratuitous relief'); nutritional and supplementary feeding programmes; coordination of relief measures by NGOs; care of orphans and the destitute; strengthening the PDS; improving health and veterinary services; credit to farmers; special relief to weavers and artisans; stocking foodgrains in strategic places; provision of drinking water; suspending the collection of land revenue; enquiry into starvation cases and prompt action taken on such reports.

The Code clearly states 'Unlike in the past, the responsibility for relief now squarely rests on the State and extends not only to mere prevention of drought or flood but also maintenance of a certain standard of economic health of the people' (Introduction). In addition to government relief efforts, paragraph 6 of the Code encourages state officials to enlist the 'assistance of NGOs and voluntary organisations to augment the Government effort in carrying out relief measures'.

Since there are numerous government departments involved in relief operations, the task of coordinating relief activity is both crucial and challenging.[1] At the district level, the Collector coordinates all relief operations, assisted by his or her deputies, revenue officers and BDOs. If the required number of officers in a drought-hit district is inadequate, the Relief Code provides that additional officers can be transferred from other districts (para. 17). While there is an emphasis on the involvement of Panchayats in the administration of relief (para. 19.2), the Code provides for a District Level Committee on Natural Calamities to assist the Collector. This committee – which is composed of district officials, representatives of registered voluntary organisations and Panchayats, and all elected political leaders from the district – must meet 'as often as required' in order to offer advise on precautionary measures, the nature of relief operations and the location of the relief works (Appendix III, IIIa and IIIb). At the state level, the Special Relief Commissioner based in Bhubaneswar is responsible for relief operations in drought-affected areas. In addition, the administrative heads of various government departments are delegated financial powers which specifically relate to drought relief (para. 12). The State Level Committee on Natural Calamities – chaired by the Chief Minister and comprising of ministers, leader of the opposition, ministers in the central government from Orissa, elected MLAs and MPs and other senior administrative personnel – functions similar to its district counterpart (Appendix II). It meets 'whenever necessary' and advises the state government on the nature and extent of relief measures required to tackle a crisis. The Code further provides that in case of 'extensive and acute distress . . . the State Government may appoint separately a Special Relief Commissioner for expeditious and effective relief measures' (para. 12, section 6).

Nutritional interventions

As soon as a drought is declared, the Collector is responsible for ensuring the availability of adequate amounts of food and for taking steps to 'supply essential food articles to the people through the public distribution system and otherwise' (para. 33.1). The Code recognises that poor and vulnerable groups may not have the required purchasing power to acquire foodgrains available in the market. Therefore, it recommends that the district administration must strengthen existing social security schemes and intensify efforts to provide food through the PDS and the ICDS programmes. The Code further prescribes two main nutrition-related interventions targeted at vulnerable groups, one indirect in the form of generating employment through labour-intensive works and the other direct in the form of 'gratuitous relief' (para. 33.2). The district administration is urged to generate extra employment opportunities (or 'mandays') through various programmes funded by the state and central governments. These include the EAS, JRY, JGSY and MWS. The state government may also authorise the district administration to implement Food for Work (with free food supplied by international organisations) and Grain for Work (with free wheat supplied by the central government) programmes. Employment can also be provided through the 'development of water resources, irrigation potential, etc.' (para. 150a) and district officials are advised to submit a list of 'suitable relief works' which may help agricultural production and boost household income (para. 151a) to the District Level Committee on Natural Calamities for approval (para. 151e).

Gratuitous Relief, as envisioned by the Code, requires the district administration to feed those 'who have been incapacitated temporarily due to the impact of such a calamity or illness or otherwise and cannot earn their living' (para. 163). These include the handicapped, the infirm and those unable to carry out physical work in the labour-intensive schemes. The Code provides for three types of gratuitous relief: 'emergent relief', 'ad hoc gratuitous relief' and 'gratuitous relief on cards'. Emergent relief relates primarily to distress caused by floods and cyclone, and the district administration is required to provide dry and/or cooked food, clothing, shelter and other basic necessities like kerosene oil, salt and match boxes (para. 165). The remaining two forms of gratuitous relief are most relevant for the Kalahandi case.

Ad hoc gratuitous relief is a short-term intervention targeted at 'people affected by a natural calamity to avoid starvation, extreme hardship, etc.' In particular, there is a focus on persons who cannot participate in government-sponsored employment generation programmes, including 'persons whose attendance on the sick or infant children is absolutely necessary' and 'able-bodied persons but temporarily rendered weak due to want of food or malnutrition or as a result of illness' (para. 167a). Assistance in the form of rice, wheat, *ragi*, maize, etc. (depending on local availability) can be sanctioned by the Collector to 'deserving cases' up to a fortnight in order to 'enable the recipients to come back to their normal avocation' (para. 167b). There is no provision for cash payments although in cases of extreme distress items of clothing (e.g. saris, dhotis and blankets) may be distributed (para. 167c).

Through gratuitous relief cards (GR cards), vulnerable groups are entitled to food rations once every fortnight. Such cards are sanctioned by the district administration for an extended duration, depending on the nature of the natural calamity and the resulting distress experienced by vulnerable groups (para. 168a). In a drought year, the block-level officials are encouraged to compile a list of potential beneficiaries in consultation with Panchayat representatives (para. 170) and the following groups are eligible: the aged and physically infirm who do not receive any pensions or other social security benefits; children below 12 years of age who are not covered by supplementary or emergency feeding programmes; individuals who cannot work due to malnutrition and disease. The Code also provides for the inclusion of 'idiots', 'lunatics' and 'blind persons' in this programme (para. 169).

Administrative response to drought in Kalahandi, 1996–2000

From 1996 to 2000, Kalahandi faced a drought every second year. As Table 4.1 shows, the drought in 1996 was one of the worst in the district's history and 11 of its 13 blocks were severely affected. 1998 proved to be another difficult year with

Table 4.1 Drought and crop loss in Kalahandi, 1996–2000

Year	Annual average rainfall (mm)	No. of blocks affected	No. of Gram Panchayats affected	No. of villages affected with crop loss above 50 per cent
1996	1,037.60	11	123	1,005
1997	1,612.30	2	10	22
1998	1,125.07	11	89	511
1999	1,210.00	1	1	1
2000	1,164.20	8	97	599

Source: District Collector's report to a central government visiting team, 23 November 2000.

widespread crop loss in over 500 villages. A severe drought hit Kalahandi once again in 2000, severely affecting paddy cultivation in eight blocks. The district usually receives more than 80 per cent of its total annual rainfall between June and September, and on average there are 54 rainy days every year. Since the start of meteorological data collection and recording, the average annual rainfall in Kalahandi has been 1378.3 mm. The annual average rainfall data for the years 1993–2000 are given in Table 4.2.

While it is clear that Kalahandi received less than average rainfall in 1996, 1998, 1999 and 2000, the district's annual average is normally far higher than most other districts in Orissa. Hence, the two key features of drought in Kalahandi are the *timing* and the *distribution* of rainfall during the monsoon months. First, rainfall water for agricultural purposes is most needed in the month of June. Erratic rainfall in the June–September period can be disastrous for agricultural production (e.g. *kharif* crops like paddy, *ragi* and maize) as germination of seeds starts in July with the crop expected to mature in August and September. Even if the rains return later, the timing may not be appropriate. Second, the distribution of rainfall is equally important; in the period 1996–2000, the hilly tracts of Kalahandi (e.g. Thuamul Rampur) with little agricultural activity received far more rain water than the fertile plains (e.g. Dharamgarh) during the crucial months of June and July. In other words, more than adequate rainfall in the uplands of Kalahandi is generally of little use as the soil in these areas has very little water retention capacity.

The principal rivers of Kalahandi are rain-fed and go dry during the summer months starting in April. If the rains fail to arrive on time (in May–June) and/or are unevenly distributed, agricultural activities suffer and farmers become highly dependent on irrigation facilities. As a senior district official observed, even in the best of times only 35 per cent of the cultivable area is irrigated and, although the district administration takes 'preventive steps', the magnitude of a drought episode 'can be quite overwhelming'. Efforts to expand irrigation facilities in the district have been rendered difficult on account of the difficult geographical

Table 4.2 Annual rainfall in Kalahandi, 1993–2000

Year	Annual average (mm)	Percentage deviation from historical average of 1,378.2 mm
1993	1,553.8	12.69
1994	2,045,3	48.40
1995	1,580.4	14.65
1996	1,037.6	−24.74
1997	1,612.3	16.98
1998	1,125.0	−18.35
1999	1,210.0	−12.19
2000	1,164.2	−15.52

Source: Compiled from District Statistical Handbook (1993–97) and information from the Collector's Office.

terrain and lack of funds. The undulating terrain of Kalahandi provides few suitable areas for the storage of rain water, and ground water levels are often minimal in most areas given the presence of hard rocks 9 to 12 metres below the surface. This makes it difficult to bore tube wells and implement lift irrigation. District officials claimed that despite numerous surveys of potential areas and sources for irrigation over the years, the lack of adequate funds have been a major problem. For example, Kalahandi received only Rs 2.5 million for 'protective irrigation'[2] and repair of lift irrigation points (LIPs) in 2000 – an amount which proved to be grossly inadequate given the severity of the drought.[3] The Chairman of Kalahandi, Zilla Parishad, echoed the sentiments of many when he blamed the funds crunch on the 'inability of our MP and MLAs to secure grants from central and state governments'.[4]

In the past farmers relied extensively on traditional irrigation structures like tanks (local water catchments) and wells that were constructed in accordance with the topography and climate of the region. However, the capacity of these traditional sources of irrigation to supply water is gradually decreasing as they are seldom repaired – and are generally neglected – by the district administration. The few attempts to renovate a select few tanks and wells were fraught with numerous difficulties. For example, the structures required constant monitoring and renovation which in turn required additional irrigation department staff, and the large number of renovation works required additional funds which were unavailable. Moreover, several ponds and tanks were privately owned and large groups of marginal farmers did not have access to ponds in times of water scarcity (Pradhan 1993, cited in Mahapatra 1994: 138). Reflecting on the problems of maintenance of tanks and wells, a senior district official observed that undertaking repairs caused difficulties since social conflicts arise as soon as some are denied water while others have access to it.[5]

Despite being perennially drought-prone, existing irrigation facilities in Kalahandi were extremely poor. The *Upper Indravati Project* – started in 1978 for the provision of hydro-electric power and irrigation to Kalahandi and adjoining districts – was yet to be completed[6] and local irrigation systems relied mainly on water from canals constructed by placing embankments on rivers and small tributaries. Unfortunately, these were only to be found in the plains, especially in the agriculturally prosperous blocks of Junagarh, Dharamgarh and Jaipatna. Although LIPs were prioritised by the district administration, they required abundant water supply from rivers. Therefore, when the administration provided around 250 drought-affected farmers with subsidised diesel pumps within a span of two weeks during the drought in 1998, it had little effect as the rivers were dry. Senior district officials in Kalahandi argued that new and effective strategies of watershed management – the storage of water for the agricultural season and human consumption – was one of the most important strategies to combat drought. A survey conducted in 1997 by an NGO, however, revealed that most water harvesting structures in Kalahandi were ineffective because of faulty project implementation, technical flaws, the improper selection of sites and poor workmanship. The survey also found that the agencies involved consistently flouted construction norms and did not consult villagers in the implementation process.[7]

Agricultural production

Crop yields and cropping intensity have increased since the late 1980s. Agricultural production is diverse and includes foodgrains, pulses, oilseeds, and sugarcane. This has been partly facilitated by improved road and railway communications between Kalahandi and other parts of Orissa, and partly by the increased production of remunerative cash crops like cotton. However, agriculture remains subsistence-oriented rather than a commercial venture. From Tables 4.3 and 4.4, three general trends can be observed in terms of agricultural production in the period 1996–2000. First, paddy is the most important crop and there was a substantial increase in the area under cultivation in the *rabi* season although the drought years of 1996 and 1998 resulted in a sharp decline in production. After 1998, however, paddy production once again passed 300,000 tonnes and surprisingly the drought in 2000 did not substantially reduce production. This is explained by the increased use of high yielding varieties of seeds, fertilisers and surplus production in the two traditionally prosperous blocks of Dharamgarh and Junagarh which received increased irrigation water from the Indravati dam project. Second, although there was a gradual increase in the production of cereals and pulses in both *kharif* and *rabi* seasons, overall production decreased in drought years. Cotton production was the major success story in the district, having increased tenfold since 1996. Third, there was an overall improvement in the performance of the *rabi* crop partly thanks to government efforts to promote multiple cropping patterns and the provision of high yielding varieties of seeds, and partly thanks to the availability of irrigation water in a select few regions of the district. However, farmers in the study villages claimed that production would have been even higher had the agriculture department supplied larger amounts (and better quality) of seeds and fertilisers at cheaper rates.

Although agricultural production has been under severe threat in drought years, it would be misleading simply to view the production figures for individual drought years without considering long-term trends. Thus, there was a steady increase in total foodgrain production in Kalahandi in the 1996–2000 period and per capita foodgrain production in the district – even in drought years – remained above Orissa and national averages. In fact, Kalahandi was one of the largest producers of rice in Orissa and, as Table 4.5 shows, the Food Corporation of India (FCI) consistently procured large amounts of rice from the district in both drought and non-drought years. And yet large sections of Kalahandi's population were reported to have suffered from food shortage and starvation – a phenomenon best captured by Sen's concept of entitlement failure. The Kalahandi case provides support to Sen's critique of the FAD approach (discussed in Chapter 2) in that people starve not merely because of a fall in food production but through a process in which they gradually lose their basic entitlements and purchasing power. Even

Table 4.3 Agricultural production, Kharif season (April to September), 1996–2000

	1996		1997		1998		1999		2000	
Crop	Area (ha.)	Production (tonnes)	Area (ha.)	Production (tonnes)	Area (ha.)	Production (tonnes)	Area (ha.)	Production (tonnes)	Area (ha.)	Production (tonnes)
Paddy	183,460	161,955	192,248	338,740	178,519	206,725	182,400	311,904	175,821	314,895
Cereals	18,647	9,947	17,509	14,717	16,639	12,171	19,944	15,494	17,546	13,651
Ragi	8,683	3,531	7,842	7,371	7,035	5,206	10,130	7,294	10,033	6,521
Pulses	108,230	34,414	97,951	51,809	82,695	23,107	104,735	41,890	95,839	43,127
Oilseeds	47,147	16,586	39,813	25,066	29,600	12,667	33,031	17,065	26,621	11,979
Cotton	2,077	1,501	3,107	2,640	5,603	4,262	8,978	8,224	15,510	11,632
Fibres	1,324	746	987	712	1,185	569	1,197	1,009	1,381	691

Table 4.4 Agricultural production, Rabi season (October to March), 1996–2000

	1996–97		1997–98		1998–99		1999–2000		2000–2001	
Crop	Area (ha.)	Production (tonnes)	Area (ha.)	Production (tonnes)	Area (ha.)	Production (tonnes)	Area (ha.)	Production (tonnes)	Area (ha.)	Production (tonnes)
Paddy	1,034	1,518	3,410	6,584	2,480	3,945	19,148	39,100	17,700	53,100
Wheat	713	759	956	946	800	720	936	867	1,600	2,800
Maize	163	224	198	220	216	229	629	998	600	950
Pulses	103,873	29,154	131,052	62,446	127,258	39,409	131,207	60,955	124,000	58,470
Oilseeds	24,352	13,450	33,004	22,159	33,075	17,713	32,862	20,074	32,800	28,758
Sugarcane	1,221	7,033	3,193	16,398	2,367	18,095	2,670	20,932	6,000	51,000

Source: Office of Deputy Director of Agriculture: Kalahandi Range, Bhawanipatna.

Table 4.5 Levy rice procurement from Kalahandi by Food Corporation of India,
1996–2000

Year	Target (tonnes)	Achievement (tonnes)	No. of rice mills
1996–97	40,000	41,290	22
1997–98	100,000	67,117	26
1998–99	80,000	48,280	31
1999–2000	100,000	80,176	38

Source: Office of Deputy Director for Agriculture, Kalahandi district.

during the so-called 'worst drought of the century' in 1996, there was always food available in Kalahandi's markets, but vulnerable groups facing unemployment and little alternative sources of income could not purchase such food. Interviews with farmers and district administration officials revealed that one of the most pressing problems in recent years was the lack of storage capacity for agricultural produce. For example, towards the end of 2000, the FCI only maintained three storage facilities or 'godowns' in Kalahandi with a total storage space of 40,000 tonnes against the actual requirement of 100,000 tonnes.[8] In a few years' time, the demand for storage space was expected to increase to 150,000 tonnes. The civil supplies officer expressed concern over the lack of political interest to construct new godowns in the district and argued that if such constructions were not immediately undertaken, farmers of Kalahandi would face ruin in the immediate future despite surplus foodgrain production.[9]

As of late February 2000, all godowns in Kalahandi remained filled to the brim as there had not been any movement of food stocks out of Kalahandi since October 1999. Farmers were therefore forced to sell paddy at between one-third and one-quarter of the market price to petty (visiting) traders from outside the district and exploitative agents who procured foodgrains illegally by the roadside. The lack of storage facilities also resulted in the Orissa government failing to procure its target of 80,000 tonnes of levy rice from Kalahandi in 2000. The district agriculture department had chalked up plans to procure paddy through 13 so-called RMC (Regulated Market Committee) yards located throughout the district with the purpose of ensuring that farmers received the official support price fixed by the district administration.[10] However, millers' agents seldom showed up at these venues on the scheduled dates with the result that farmers often returned to their villages without selling their produce. Farmers alleged that despite their protests they had not succeeded in getting the district administration to force miller agents to procure foodgrains from these yards. The problem was not limited to paddy stocks but also affected vegetables and oilseeds which, like paddy, were sold at very low prices immediately after harvest. For instance, tomatoes, aubergines and potatoes were sold off immediately after harvest at only 40–50 paisa per kilogram and onions at Rs 1 per kilogram. Since there were no cold storage facilities in Kalahandi, traders and procurement agents from neighbouring regions purchased vegetables in bulk, keeping these in cold storages locally and then bringing them back to Kalahandi for sale at much higher prices. For the major part of the post-harvest period, almost 80 per cent of all vegetables consumed in Kalahandi originated from neighbouring Madhya Pradesh and Andhra Pradesh.[11] The high prices of these products remained beyond the reach of the majority of the population.

Employment programmes

In anticipation of drought and resulting increase in unemployment, the district administration focused on implementing two major employment generation programmes in Kalahandi – the Employment Assurance Scheme (EAS) and the Jawahar Rozgar Yojana (JRY). The EAS aimed to provide a minimum of 100 days of employment to BPL groups in order to check widespread out-migration from Kalahandi, and priority was given to the construction and repair of roads, buildings, bridges and water tanks. Under the JRY programme, funds were supposed to be distributed directly by the district administration to Gram Panchayats for the development of local infrastructure, the provision of clean drinking water and electricity and the improvement of roads and sanitary facilities. In accordance with the Minimum Wages Act, the wage rates for both EAS and JRY in 2000–2001 were Rs 35 and Rs 60 for unskilled and skilled labour, respectively. Both programmes were, however, severely handicapped by lack of adequate funds and, instead of a minimum of 100 days of EAS employment every year, the Collector and other officials claimed they could finance a maximum of 15–17 days of work per individual per year. Interviews with villagers in the study villages revealed that even this figure was highly inflated. Given the large number of people registered as beneficiaries of labour-intensive programmes in each village, very few were in reality able to secure more than 5–7 days of paid labour every year.

Table 4.6 shows government expenditure on labour-intensive programmes in Kalahandi based on funds received for overall drought relief. In 1996–97 and 1997–98, over 350,000 'mandays' were generated, whereas only 250,000 days of employment were possible in 1998–99 and 2000–01. Figures provided by the Dis-

Table 4.6 Government of Orissa relief allocation and expenditure (from Drought Relief Grant) on labour-intensive works in Kalahandi, 1993–2001

Year	No. of works completed	Allocation (Rs million)	Expenditure (Rs million)	'Mandays' generated
1993–94	–	1.8	1.8	36,000
1994–95	–	No allocation	–	–
1995–96	–	No allocation	–	–
1996–97	–	17.90	17.90	358,000
1997–98	–	20.00	20.00	400,000
1998–99	247	12.43	12.43	248,700
1999–2000	–	No allocation	–	–
2000–2001	221	10.00	10.00	250,000

Source: Office of District Collector, Kalahandi district.

trict Rural Development Agency (DRDA) showed that over 200,000 people were registered as EAS card-holders (and hence eligible for work) by the end of 2000. Hence, using simple arithmetic, it was clear that the district administration was seldom able to provide more than one or two days of employment in a calendar year to EAS cardholders.

Even when money was allocated by the central and state governments for the EAS and JRY programmes, they usually arrived in several instalments and only following the submission of so-called 'utilisation certificates' documenting that the earlier allocation was properly (and completely) spent. In addition to frequent delays that this caused in initiating and completing projects, officials also complained of cumbersome central and state government rules which required a host of separate reporting procedures. To further add to the problem, there was an acute shortage of Junior Engineers who were instrumental in planning and executing labour-intensive projects. Several BDOs argued therefore that additional EAS and JRY funds to their areas would make little difference given the limited number of staff at their disposal. The engineers alleged the choice of project location was more often than not dictated by political pressure, with local politicians keen on providing some form of employment to key supporters. A few local officials also complained that not all projects (e.g. road construction) were very labour-intensive in character, and argued for an increase in the construction of tanks and other water harvesting structures which would engage greater numbers in the population. Besides, road construction – the favourite of virtually all political leaders – was allegedly the most corrupt form of employment activity. Not only were contracts were awarded without a public tender process, contractors employed fewer people than required, paid wages lower than the official rate and purchased poor quality construction material. Politicians were also known to receive kickbacks for each contract awarded.

Nutritional interventions

A large majority of Kalahandi's population suffers from poor nutrition and the district has extremely high infant and maternal mortality rates. Malnutrition-related diseases are widespread and result from the consumption of food items that do not supply an adequate amount of calories, proteins, vitamins and minerals. During the study period there were three major interventions aimed at improving nutritional standards in Kalahandi – the PDS, the ICDS and the NMMP. A 'gratuitous relief' programme was also in operation, targeting those not covered by any of the above-mentioned interventions.

The Public Distribution System (PDS)

The PDS provides price support to producers and subsidies to consumers and is the most expensive and far-reaching of safety-net-oriented programmes in India. The central government – primarily through the FCI – procures rice, wheat, sugar and other essential commodities at pre-announced prices from producers spread across the country. After a period of storage, these commodities are sold to state governments at a uniform 'issue price'. After adding handling charges, states then distribute the commodities through a network of 'fair price shops'. The programme in Orissa was aimed at improving food security among BPL households by subsidising rations of rice, sugar and kerosene oil. Towards the end of 2000, over 4,000 shops distributed PDS rations to over 8 million 'ration card' holders in Orissa (Government of Orissa 2001).

In Kalahandi, the programme covered all 13 blocks, with over 800 shops providing rations to around 300,000 households.[12] Private agents appointed by the district administration transported rice, sugar and kerosene from the FCI godown in Kesinga to the headquarters of the Gram Panchayat (GP) from where shop owners collected their quotas. At the same location, a *Maitri* shop was open every day for direct purchase of rations. In 1996, the district civil supplies department started distributing rice through 29 'mobile vans' with the aim of providing PDS rations to areas without shops or where the nearest shop was more than 6 kilometres away. Each block, and all GPs within it, was notified of the mobile van's arrival schedule and Panchayats communicated this information to all villages under their jurisdiction. Parallel to the PDS, a targeted version – TPDS – was further implemented in six drought-prone and tribal blocks of Kalahandi and covered households with an annual income below Rs 6,000. The quotas and prices of rice, sugar and kerosene under these two programmes are provided in Table 4.7. Starting in the year 2000, annual village assemblies (*pallis sabhas*) in TPDS blocks selected the recipients for two additional programmes – Antodaya (25 kg of rice per month at Rs 3 per kg) and Annapurna (10 kg of free rice per month for senior citizens over 65 years without any income).

Although the PDS was an intervention for the reduction of food insecurity in Kalahandi, evidence from fieldwork shows that there were a number of problems which prevented the PDS from achieving even better results. For example, the numerous difficulties in compiling and updating BPL lists (discussed in Chapter 3) meant that many non-poor households were classified as BPL and given ration cards instead of genuinely poor households. The district civil supplies officer claimed that attempts by his staff to verify the authenticity of ration card holders was often resisted by local politicians and Panchayat representatives. Even when households did possess a ration card, they either were not aware of the benefits they were entitled to or could not afford to buy the commodities even at reduced prices. Another problem related to the arbitrary categorisation of 'drought-prone'

Table 4.7 PDS and TPDS allocations to BPL households, 2000

Commodity	PDS	TPDS
Rice	20 kg @ Rs 6.30 per kg	20 kg @ Rs 4.75 per kg
Sugar	1.5 kg @ Rs 12 per kg	1.5 kg @ Rs 12 per kg
Kerosene	3 litres @ Rs 3.50–9.00 per litre, depending on transport costs	3 litres @ Rs 3.50–9.00 per litre, depending on transport costs

blocks (eligible for the TPDS) based on unreliable rainfall data and rough estimates of crop loss. For example, a TPDS block could border a non-TPDS block, separated from each other by a stretch of road. A BPL household on one side of the road (in the TPDS block) could buy rice at Rs 4.75 per kg while the household on the other side (which was just as poor but located in a non-TPDS block) bought the same rice at Rs 6.30 per kg. NGOs and block-level officials thus argued that administrating the PDS was nightmarish since the programme did not take into account local poverty and deprivation levels and relative purchasing capacity. In addition to poor quality rice resulting from poor storage facilities, the PDS in Kalahandi was also hampered by inadequate transport facilities. For example, the civil supplies department owned only five mobile vans and hired the remaining twenty-odd vehicles from private owners, many of whom were unhappy with low government rates and were reluctant to lease their vehicles. The poor condition of Kalahandi's roads, particularly during the monsoons, further prevented the mobile vans from covering remote areas and the demand for rice rations often exceeded the carrying capacity of these vehicles. Several NGOs complained that there was widespread theft of PDS supplies, which were often diverted to the open market where rice, sugar and kerosene fetched much higher prices and provided shop owners with increased profits.

The Integrated Child Development Services (ICDS)

Started in 1975, the ICDS is India's longest running nutritional programme and the world's largest, covering over 29 million children and 5 million women. The programme aims at improving the nutritional and health status of children below 6 years of age by reducing the incidence of mortality, morbidity, malnutrition and school dropouts. The ICDS therefore provides a range of services to women and children including supplementary feeding, monitoring of child growth, immunisation against preventable childhood diseases, and health and nutrition education. The main unit of the ICDS is the 'Aganwadi centre' manned by 'Aganwadi workers' (trained women) and their helpers. Until December 1997, the World Bank assisted the ICDS programme in Orissa with Rs 30,000 per project every year. When this support stopped in 1998, the Orissa government undertook a survey of nutritional status among children in over 200 ICDS blocks using GIS data and launched a Rs 40 million plan to strengthen the programme.

Towards the end of 2000, Kalahandi's social welfare department ran over 1,200 (Aganwadi) centres and the programme covered around 185,000 children in the age group 0–6 years, over 11,000 pregnant women and over 12,000 nursing mothers. Although there was a formal requirement of a minimum of 10 years of schooling, tribal women qualified as Aganwadis with seven years of schooling. Salaries varied between Rs 400 and Rs 500 per month depending on the area of posting. Children below 3 years of age were supposed to be weighed once a month and children 3–6 years of age once every four months. Weight-for-age (WA) growth charts and cards had to be maintained for all children below 6 years in order to detect growth faltering and to assess nutritional status. Children surveyed were either classified as 'normal' or placed in one of the following four malnutrition categories: Grade I (mild), Grade II (moderate), Grade III (moderate/severe) and Grade IV (severe).

Table 4.8 shows two main forms of food supplements provided to children and pregnant and nursing mothers at Aganwadi centres in Kalahandi. The largest group of beneficiaries were covered by the supplementary feeding programme (often referred to as 'CARE feeding' since the international organisation used to provide food rations to the ICDS in some states) which targeted children less than 6 years of age, pregnant women, nursing mothers and adolescent girls of low-income households. These groups were identified in occasional surveys conducted by Aganwadi workers and were entitled to food assistance for around 10 months each year. The aim was to bridge the gap between the nationally recommended caloric intake and the average actual caloric intake of children and women in local communities. There was also a special emphasis on reaching children below the age of 2 years, and on encouraging parents and siblings to either take supplementary food rations home or bring the children to the centre for supplementary feeding. The types of food supposed to be provided at Aganwadi centres in Kalahandi included a hot meal cooked at the centre, containing a varied combination of pulses, cereals, oil, vegetables and sugar/iodised salt. In practice, and given limited funds, the most common type of meal supplied to children at the centres was a mixture of corn and barley and soya blend. When available, powdered milk was provided to pregnant women and lactating mothers to take home. The so-called 'emergency feeding' programme in Kalahandi was started in 1996, and consisted primarily of a single cooked meal provided to a 'destitute' person – defined as an individual who has no other means of acquiring food – at the Aganwadi centre. The BDO was in charge of providing food supplies and programme coordination. As Table 4.8 shows, there was a steady increase in the number of people covered by this scheme, with over 30,000 beneficiaries in 2000–01.

The ICDS in India is a highly centralised programme, and Chatterjee (1996) suggests that its top-down approach may be a reason why the programme's intended community ownership and management are virtually non-existent. As in other parts of India, there was little coordination between policy-making and policy-implementing organs in charge of coordinating the ICDS in Orissa. This made the task of planning, coordination, and implementation of ICDS services difficult

Table 4.8 Number of beneficiaries covered by ICDS feeding programmes in Kalahandi, 1998–2001

ICDS programmes	No. of beneficiaries covered		
	1998–99	1999–2000	2000–2001
Supplementary feeding (CARE)	112,500	126,600	133,200
Emergency feeding	22,245	22,245	32,177

Source: District social welfare department, Kalahandi.

for Aganwadi workers, district-level officials and organisations like CARE which provided free food supplies. The general trend observed in Kalahandi was that urban areas and blocks close to urban centres were far better covered than remote areas where children were more likely to be severely malnourished. There was also very little contact between Aganwadi centres and the health system operating in the district. Like their PDS counterparts, ICDS personnel almost always highlighted the shortage of funds when confronted with details of poor ICDS coverage in tribal areas of the district. Adding to the poor quality of nutritional supplements, Aganwadi workers did not have financial resources to purchase items like milk powder and the centres lacked proper equipment like nutritional charts and instruments to measure weight and height among children.

Overall, the lack of adequate funds resulted in irregular food supply, irregular feeding and inadequate rations for programme beneficiaries. Based on interviews with Aganwadi workers and block-level supervisors of ICDS projects in the study villages, certain additional factors appeared to explain the failure of the ICDS to live up to expectations. For example, there are very few Aganwadi centres in remote areas of the district and owing to a range of factors – including low levels of literacy, lack of awareness and local superstitions – many tribal families did not bring their children to the centres to receive supplementary feeding, immunisation and health check-ups. Even when food rations were sent home with the mother, there was no guarantee that the food would be consumed by the children. Many poor households preferred to sell such rations in exchange for cash or essential commodities. Like other services in Kalahandi, the ICDS too was plagued by an acute shortage of key personnel (including Aganwadi workers and programme supervisors); towards the end of 2000, over 50 positions remained vacant in Kalahandi. Given the extremely low levels of female literacy in the district, it was also difficult to recruit Aganwadi workers, and those who were eventually hired themselves lacked the nutritional and health knowledge that was required to educate their clients. Moreover, there was virtually no emphasis on personnel training and little effort to educate the Aganwadi women in techniques for monitoring the growth of children. Thus, despite being an important programme, the impact of the ICDS on improving the nutritional status of women and children in Kalahandi is limited.

The National Mid-day Meals Programme (NMMP)

The NMMP was initiated in 1995 by the central government with the aim of increasing primary school attendance and to improve the nutritional status and 'learning capacity' of school children in the 6–11 year age group throughout India. Under this programme, the Ministry of Human Resources supplied free rice to primary schools (first to fifth grade) at 100 grams of rice per student per day for 10 months in an academic year. In Orissa, the programme was in operation until April 2000 and the primary emphasis was on providing a cooked meal (mainly rice and pulses) during school hours. In many instances, however, schools did not have the required ingredients to cook a proper meal, nor did they have cooks. In such cases, around 3 kg of rice per month per child was allocated that could be taken home. The NMMP is believed to have increased the school attendance of children at the national level, but its impact on nutritional status and cognitive development among children in Kalahandi was difficult to assess. The programme had only been in operation for a couple of years and suffered from a shortage of funds like the PDS and ICDS programmes. Since 1998, the programme had on average covered over 90,000 children, constituting 60 per cent of primary school children in Kalahandi.

Interviews in the study villages revealed that the programme functioned best when children received a cooked meal at school. When rice rations were sent home, there was no guarantee that the food would actually be consumed by the children. Particularly very poor households were tempted to sell their rations in exchange for other necessities. In other cases food rations were consumed by a family member other than the child. A further problem was that funds for the programme did not always arrive in time in Kalahandi despite their release by the central government. In several cases, cooks and helpers engaged at primary schools in rural areas had to be paid with money earmarked for employment generation programmes. Schools also faced regular shortage of fuel and cooking ingredients and the district social welfare department was unable to withdraw the entire food stock (88,188 quintals) allotted to Kalahandi in 1995–99 for distribution among schools because of lack of available transport and poor communications with the FCI. In the final analysis, the NMMP did not really have a chance to take off before it was terminated in April 2000 when the Orissa government claimed the programme adversely affected the education system with teachers and students spending too much time preparing meals. The government also accused teachers of misappropriating food rations, thus adding to Orissa's high financial burden.[13]

Provision of 'gratuitous relief'

Gratuitous relief – the provision of weekly rice rations – is targeted at those who are not covered by PDS and social security schemes. BDOs in Kalahandi were instructed to distribute so-called 'GR cards' to potential beneficiaries. The *Sarpanch* of a Gram Panchayat was provided with one quintal of rice for distribution among GR card holders, who were entitled to rice rations of up to 5 kg per individual for the duration of one week. BDOs could extend this period by a further two weeks, the Sub-Divisional officer by one month and the District Collector by more than two months. In rare cases of extreme destitution, BDOs had the authority to allocate a one-off assistance of Rs 200 per individual from the District Red Cross Fund. Ad hoc gratuitous relief to those without a GR card was occasionally sanctioned by the Kalahandi Collector to distressed individuals who approach him during his weekly 'Grievance Day' meeting held on Saturdays at the district headquarters. In general, the requirement for gratuitous relief in the district increased in the post-harvest period (February–September) which was when household foodgrain stocks were depleted and able-bodied males migrated to distant cities in search of work, leaving their families behind.

Despite its usefulness, there were numerous difficulties in enforcing the gratuitous relief scheme, particularly related to the identification of GR beneficiaries. For example, paragraph 168(b) of the Orissa Relief Code provides that GR provision should largely be limited to villages with over 50 per cent crop loss. This essentially meant that, in the initial list of GR beneficiaries, individuals residing in a village with less than 50 per cent crop loss were excluded. Moreover, when beneficiary lists were not regularly updated, recent instances of destitution were not identified. Further, the capacity of the *Sarpanch* to provide relief depended on the amount of rice at his disposal divided by the total number of GR card holders in the area. The rice stored with the *Sarpanch* was also known to rot because of poor storage facilities (especially during summer months) and on other occasions it was simply sold in the open market. Although rightful claimants to gratuitous relief could theoretically seek redress from the Collector, in practice it entailed travelling long distances to Bhawanipatna, which they could neither afford physically nor financially. Finally, there are no guidelines in the Relief Code for assessing 'actual' cases of 'distress' and 'destitution'. Interviews with various district and state-level officials also revealed that they had widely different understandings of gratuitous relief procedures including the duration of some assistance that *Sarpanches*, BDOs, SDOs and Collectors were empowered to sanction.

Drought response: concluding remarks

The Orissa Relief Code is indeed very impressive and provides detailed instructions to government officials regarding the provision of relief following a wide range of natural calamities. Specifically related to drought, it provides early warning indicators related to rainfall and crop loss and a set of guidelines on typical measures that must be implemented to provide drought relief. The impact of drought is not felt overnight – it is a slow-onset process and there is usually enough time to intervene. It is surprising that, despite such codified instructions and an emphasis on long-term planning, vulnerability to drought in Kalahandi remains very high. Is the Orissa Relief Code adequate? How can government response be more effective? In the following I will discuss a set of challenges related to definitions of key terms, declaration of drought, provision of relief and the relative importance assigned to the Relief Code by politicians and administrators in Orissa.

The Code instructs the government to intervene only in case of 'widespread' calamities (para. 3), which in practice means that the volume of 'distress' has to be sufficiently large enough to trigger government response. For example, virulent epidemics are seen as resulting in 'localised' and 'minor' forms of distress, which do not require immediate and government intervention. Drought is also considered to be a 'natural calamity' without mention of 'man-made' activities like deforestation, pollution, etc., which increase the impact of drought. And, without recognition of man-made causes of drought, a long-term perspective to combat the phenomenon becomes difficult. The term 'famine' is no longer used in the Code for the following reasons: 'With the development of quick transport and communication facilities and with improvements in the food production situation in the country, the conditions of famine could not be said to appear on any local failure of rains' (para. 3.2). As a result, 'the question of declaration of any area as "famine affected" does not arise' (ibid.). Instead of famine, the terms 'scarcity' and 'distress' are widely referred in the Code although they are not really defined. For example, 'scarcity' is simply identified with a marked deterioration of agricultural production due to lack of, or excessive, rainfall and there is no mention of the types of indicators that must be applied to assess the extent of resulting 'distress'. Further, while 'malnutrition' is mentioned sparsely in the Code, there is no discussion of its symptoms and measures to identify severe forms of the phenomenon and the necessary remedial actions to be undertaken in times of severe drought.

The Code defines drought exclusively in terms of meteorological (rainfall) and agricultural (crop loss) indicators. There is no attempt to operate with a more nuanced definition which distinguishes meteorological, hydrological and agricultural factors from socio-economic indicators. Consequently, drought is primarily understood as 'agricultural drought' caused by shortage of precipitation to rain-fed agricultural activity. There is thus an official obsession with the actual deviation of the annual amount of rainfall received in a district from the historical average. Such an approach, however, does not provide an accurate idea of the extent and severity of drought and contributes to the neglect of the more important fact that in Kalahandi it is not the total amount of annual rainfall that leads to drought conditions but rather the *timing* and *distribution* of the rains. It is thus possible for Kalahandi to receive above average rainfall during a year and yet face a major drought.

Moreover, drought is declared only after sample crop-cutting experiments are undertaken in various parts of the district. In practice, these experiments are not carried out systematically or in a representative manner. Rather, they are based on an eye-estimation of crop loss followed only in specific cases with crop-cutting experiments. This is problematic as eye-estimation of crop damage is highly unreliable. In addition, villages that may experience crop loss slightly below 50 per cent are not classified as drought-affected and are consequently not eligible for relief despite clear evidence of distress. An exclusive reliance on rainfall data and crop loss categories also neglects the importance of vital social indicators that cause distress, including out-migration, fall in employment opportunities, fall in purchasing power, distress sale of assets, etc. This contributes to a weakening of the early warning capacity of government institutions and results in delayed intervention. Finally, available funds for drought relief in Orissa are very limited and the use of rainfall data in classifying a district as 'drought-hit' is unfair when prosperous coastal districts of the state compete with Kalahandi for scarce funds. The severity and impact of drought is not equal in all areas of the state and there is therefore a need for special provisions in the Code for the funding of relief operations in chronically drought-prone districts like Kalahandi.

In tune with Amartya Sen's ideas on public action in preventing famine, the Code recognises that the main responsibility for ameliorating distress and providing relief rests with the government. Such responsibility is activated by the declaration of drought in paragraphs 29 and 30 of the Code. However, strangely, paragraph 32 contradicts the primary importance attached to such a declaration and consequential action that ought to result from it when it notes that 'The declaration of drought does not imply the assumption by Government of any new responsibility for combating distress'. This is confusing for practitioners, as an acute drought-induced crisis requires that, in addition to the normal social security schemes already in place, newer (more innovative) measures must be implemented. Hence, the Code is unclear on the precise distinction between long-term development programmes and relief operations. Most district officials in Kalahandi were further not aware of the detailed procedures specified in the Code, and BDOs had not even seen – let alone read – the document. Informal queries revealed that only three or four copies of the Code were available in the district and even these were in the hands of senior officials like the Collector and the Sub-Collector.

One of the most important aspects of providing drought relief relates to the selection of beneficiaries for various government interventions including the provision of additional employment opportunities. There are, however, no detailed provisions on this matter and the Code does not mention why some vulnerable groups, particularly the elderly, are excluded from social security programmes like Old Age Pension (OAP) and become so-called 'destitute'. As such drought relief programmes were largely planned and implemented according to individual interpretations of what constituted 'adequate and feasible relief'. Finally, the Code covers an entire (large) state with widely varying climatic conditions, occupational practices and socio-economic groups. This means that there is little incorporation of knowledge of the local conditions that cause distress. The Code is not updated regularly and the procedures specified are often cumbersome and require the involvement of a large number of officials at the block, district and state levels. These factors delay the provision of early warning and the allocation of urgent funds required for immediate relief operations. The analysis of the procedures for managing drought also reveals that the *curative* aspect is far more dominant than the *preventive* aspect. Most importantly, the Code functions as guidelines and is thus not enforceable in a court of law. As Currie (2000: 134) rightly observes, 'there is rarely any legal redress or significant punishment for government officers who do not fulfil their duties as specified in the relief code'. The investigations, if undertaken, remain internal and the public are seldom aware of the results, so it is almost impossible to hold officials to account for failing to carry out their duties.

5

LEGAL INTERVENTIONS AND ADMINISTRATIVE RESPONSE TO STARVATION

An important function of courts in India relates to 'judicial review'. The Constitution empowers the judiciary – Supreme Court in New Delhi and High Courts and other lower courts in each state – to protect the fundamental human rights of citizens and intervene when legislative and executive actions are found to be unconstitutional. In the past couple of decades, judicial activism has increased following the decision of the Supreme Court to accept 'public interest litigation' (PIL) that address 'matters in which interest of the public at large is involved'. Such PIL petitions 'can be moved by any individual or group of persons . . . highlighting the question of public importance for invoking this jurisdiction'.[1] Similar forms of petitions relating to damage or threat of damage to the public interest are also accepted as 'writ petition' by lower level courts throughout the country. Since the 1980s, the judiciary has repeatedly intervened on matters related to starvation deaths and the human right to food. Parallel to such interventions has been the role of institutions like the National Human Rights Commission which has not only investigated cases of alleged starvation deaths in various parts of the country but has also directed sharp criticism at the efforts of central and state governments to promote development in some of the poorest regions of the country. Media coverage of acute poverty and deprivation in Kalahandi increased radically following Prime Minister Rajiv Gandhi's visit to the district in 1985. Several concerned individuals and organisations sought the help of the judiciary to pressurise the Orissa government into action. Alleging starvation deaths and the general neglect of the district by the authorities, several petitions were filed in the Supreme Court of India and the High Court of Orissa. These petitions and the subsequent judicial interventions in the late 1980s and early 1990s further increased national interest in the Kalahandi story. The focus of this chapter is therefore first on these legal interventions and thereafter on the impact they had on administrative understanding of, and response to, starvation in Kalahandi.

Supreme Court and the Orissa High Court interventions

In October 1985, two social workers from Kalahandi filed a PIL, highlighting 'a specific matter of utmost urgency concerning the famine afflicted area of Kalahandi'.[2] They alleged that large groups in the district were facing starvation and destitution and that the Orissa government had failed to respond to the suffering caused by recurrent droughts and resulting food crises. In particular, the petitioners highlighted the failure of safety-net programmes and the general inability of the Kalahandi district administration to control exploitation of tribal groups by traders, illegal confiscation of tribal land by moneylenders and the distress sale of assets by people on the verge of destitution. Noting that the poor were 'beyond the pale of juristic justice', the petitioners sought the intervention of the Supreme Court in addressing the 'unlawful and oppressive system that has replaced the legitimate functioning of the state'. Emphasising that their aim was to draw public attention to Kalahandi's woes – and not to seek punishment for any particular individual – the petitioners requested the Supreme Court to instruct the Orissa government to carry out its legal duty of protecting its citizens from acute distress and starvation. A second PIL petition was filed in the Supreme Court in 1987 by the Indian People's Front (a breakaway faction of the Communist Party of India) which highlighted the recurrence of drought in Kalahandi and Koraput districts of Orissa and alleged that destitution and starvation deaths had become a regular feature of these areas because of the callous attitude and negligence of the Orissa government.[3] It requested the apex court to investigate the state government's inaction in these districts highly vulnerable to starvation.

Upon receipt of the two petitions, the Supreme Court appointed a district judge to conduct an inquiry. In his report submitted to the Court in 1988, the judge was largely supportive of the Orissa government's relief efforts and concluded that no starvation deaths had taken place (Panda Commission 1988). Rather, he suggested that the problems of the district were primarily due to the laziness of a majority of Kalahandi's inhabitants and their lack of interest in government programmes, which in turn made them excessively dependent on government handouts (Currie 1998: 427). Such news made the petitioners react with dismay. They were highly critical of the considerable delays in starting the investigative process and the fact that, because of heavy monsoon rains and the lack of proper roads, the judge had not visited areas hardest hit by drought and starvation. Hence, one of the petitioners branded the conclusions of the judge's report as 'rubbish, faulty and insulting'.[4] Similar views were expressed by several Kalahandi-based lawyers who alleged that the entire investigation was suspect since the judge had not paid enough attention to the 'real reasons' behind Kalahandi's suffering which included the effects of successive droughts on debt, nutrition and migration. Indeed, in its final report in 1989, the Supreme Court did not agree with its own investigating officer and observed, 'Although the learned District Judge's report is against the alleged starvation deaths, we are of the view that the happening of one or two cases of starvation deaths cannot altogether be ruled out' (Supreme Court of India

1989, paragraph 7). Without blaming any specific person or institution, the Court directed the Orissa government to be more active and responsive to Kalahandi's needs. This fuelled further media interest in Kalahandi although the petitioners were disappointed that the Supreme Court did not order a further investigation into the matter.

While the Supreme Court investigation was under way, two writ petitions were filed in the Orissa High Court. The first was filed in October 1988, highlighting cases of bonded labour and the exploitation of tribal groups by local moneylenders.[5] The petition further claimed that destitution, migration and starvation had become routine affairs in Kalahandi and that the district administration had failed to take remedial action. The second petition to the Orissa High Court was filed in 1989 by a lawyer from Cuttack, who also argued that occurrences of starvation deaths and child sale in Kalahandi had increased after successive droughts and large crop loss and that large groups, fearing imminent destitution, were being forced to migrate from the district.[6] In March 1990, the High Court appointed a retired district judge to conduct an investigation. The ensuing report – based on extensive field visits and interviews – confirmed widespread impoverishment, exploitation of tribals by traders and moneylenders and the failure of the Orissa government to protect illegal transfer of tribal land to non-tribals in Kalahandi (Mishra Commission 1990). The report also confirmed several instances of starvation deaths in Kalahandi. The Orissa High Court subsequently ruled in February 1992 that five instances of death by starvation had indeed taken place and instructed the Orissa government to pay compensation to the families of the deceased.[7] The Court criticised the implementation of poverty reduction programmes and observed that the amount of money the government claimed to have spent in Kalahandi was highly exaggerated. It further indicted two senior civil servants in Orissa for failing to investigate news reports of, and prevent, starvation deaths during their tenures as Collectors of Kalahandi (High Court of Orissa 1992).

The immediate impact of the judicial interventions was a drastic increase in media attention on Kalahandi and pressure on the Orissa government to react. Indeed, a public authority had concluded for the first time in history that starvation deaths in Kalahandi had actually occurred although successive ruling parties since 1985 had denied all such claims. Following the adverse publicity generated by the Supreme Court ruling in 1989, Chief Minister J. B. Patnaik's Congress (I) government was voted out of office in the 1990 elections. When the Orissa High Court confirmed starvation deaths in Kalahandi in 1992, the new Janata Dal (JD) government – formed by Chief Minister Biju Patnaik in 1990 – mainly attempted to blame the previous government for its failures instead of initiating radical change. Despite the fact that reports of starvation deaths in Kalahandi and other districts in Orissa continued to appear in local and national dailies right throughout the period this government was in office, it largely ignored judicial recommendations to radically reformulate guidelines for improving administrative response to starvation (Currie 2000). Finally, Biju Patnaik's government was also voted out of office in 1995 amidst public concern of corruption and administrative bungling.

This was followed by a return of the Congress party under J. B. Patnaik as Chief Minister of Orissa.

Enquiries by the National Human Rights Commission

Following a visit to Kalahandi and other drought-affected districts of Orissa in December 1996, the central government's minister of agriculture requested the National Human Rights Commission (NHRC) to investigate 26 cases of alleged starvation deaths on an urgent basis so that 'the real picture might emerge' (NHRC 1996: para. 1). The Commission also received a memorandum signed by seven opposition MLAs from Orissa requesting it to 'intervene and investigate all allegations of starvation deaths reported from some areas of the State' (ibid.: para. 3). The ensuing investigation by a NHRC team concluded that, owing to extensive crop damage, inadequate income, high levels of deprivation and malnutrition in Kalahandi, 'the possibility of some of the deaths having taken place due to prolonged malnutrition and hunger compounded by disease cannot be ruled out' (ibid.: para. 8). In particular, the NHRC report identified the elderly and the physically handicapped as those most vulnerable to destitution and starvation and observed that once able-bodied members of a household migrated to distant cities they maintained little contact with family members they had left at home. In the Kalahandi, Nuapada and Bolangir districts of Orissa, the team investigated 21 cases of alleged starvation and concluded that in 18 cases death had occurred from a combination of starvation and diseases like tuberculosis and malaria. Table 5.1 shows that in Kalahandi alone the team concluded that four of five cases investigated were starvation-related. In conclusion, the NHRC observed that its investigating team had 'witnessed human suffering and destitution of an alarming magnitude' and warned that 'unless large scale relief measures are expeditiously undertaken . . . and vigorously implemented, the situation in the coming months is going to further worsen thereby causing very acute distress and suffering to the hapless people of the area' (ibid.: para. 21).

The very decision of the central government to request the NHRC to investigate alleged starvation deaths in Orissa had angered the state government. Even before the NHRC report was published, the Chief Minister, J. B. Patnaik, wrote to the Prime Minister in December 1996 pointing out that he had earlier informed the central government that the allegations of starvation deaths were 'baseless'. He went on to write that his government was concerned by the precedent that had been set which gave 'more credence' to newspaper reports and other forms of allegations from vested interests 'without substance' than to the 'solemn words of an elected Government'. Raising fundamental questions on federalism and centre–state relations, he went on to write:

> Is not the lack of faith in the elected government implicit in such a unilateral action? . . . I wonder if the Government of India will entrust to the commission investigation of all deaths in different parts of the country based on such

unsubstantiated reports . . . it will be a sad day if the governance by rule of law is given a go by like this. I am sure such a development will bother you as much as it bothers me.[8]

When the NHRC report, confirming starvation deaths in Orissa, was finally made public towards the end of March 1997, opposition parties demanded the immediate resignation of the Chief Minister and his cabinet. The Orissa government, however, argued that the NHRC report did not apply a correct definition of 'starvation death' and hence could not have established their occurrence.[9] Instead, the government highlighted its own development efforts in Kalahandi which included the provision of new tube wells, the free distribution of food in rural areas and the introduction of a new system whereby 'squads of officers' were to visit vulnerable areas in their districts and provide assistance to the needy. Opposition parties termed such measures 'cosmetic', and further alleged that the Orissa

Table 5.1 Cases of alleged starvation in Kalahandi investigated by the NHRC team, December 1996

Case	Victim	Date of death	NHRC conclusions
1	S. Bhoi, Male, 55 years (Jorabandh village, Narla block)	3 October 1996	The deceased was reportedly undernourished, suffering from fever leading to death.
2	Sahadev Suna, Male, 50 years (Saplahara village, Golamunda block)	18 October 1996	Family well-off; had productive cultivation, adequate foodgrains. Appears natural death due to illness . . . The case could not be treated as one of starvation death.
3	Surya Bhoi, Female, 45 years (Talathanra village, Kesinga block)	5 October 1996	Husband is blind, villagers informed the BDO about the precarious condition of the deceased warranting immediate attention in September. No action taken. Death resulted due to prolonged undernourishment.
4	Panu Naik, Male, 55 years (Saurapadar village, Kesinga block)	8 November 1996	According to district authorities, death has taken place due to fever. Villagers who were present at the time of the Team's visit, however, asserted that he had left behind his wife and two small children and had become very weak due to malnutrition which ultimately caused his death.
5	Khetra Mohan Joshi, Male, exact age unknown (Tumura village, Dharamgarh block)	October/ November 1996	Deceased was working in an aided school and had not received his payment of salary over a period of 5 months. There was great economic distress in the family. Death was possibly due to undernourishment.

Source: NHRC (1996: Annexure II).

government's own inquiry provided details of only 6 of the 21 cases investigated by the NHRC, and that the conclusions of the government-sponsored study contradicted with the statements provided by the relatives of the victims of starvation.[10] The issue of whether (and how many) starvation deaths had taken place in Orissa soon led to a war of words between the central and state governments in the following months. Amidst the political mud-slinging, the NHRC stood firm in its conclusion that numerous starvation deaths had indeed taken place in 1996 in Orissa and urgent action was needed to prevent future deaths. However, citing the case of the British government – which at the height of the Bengal famine in 1944 officially maintained that there was no famine – an NHRC official lamented that no government was willing to admit to starvation deaths, even in a democratic country like India.[11]

Subsequent legal interventions on the right to food

Judicial activism in 1989 and 1992 and the NHRC report of 1996 encouraged others to keep up the pressure on central and state governments by filing similar petitions highlighting the incompetence and apathetic attitude of the authorities in regard to preventing starvation in the country. For example, an independent MLA from Bolangir filed a PIL in the Orissa High Court in November 1998 alleging that nine individuals in his district had died from starvation and that thousands were being forced to migrate because of a severe drought. The petitioner alleged that the Orissa government and the Bolangir district administration were not in control of the situation and that urgent legal intervention was required. The High Court subsequently directed both central and state governments to inquire into these allegations separately and submit a report within two weeks.[12] The conclusions of the central team are unknown, but as expected, the Orissa government's report denied all allegations of starvation death. A news report quoted the Collector of Bolangir who ruled out the possibility of deaths from starvation as the deceased had 'partly digested food' in their stomachs and various quantities of rice were found in their houses.[13]

The trend of seeking judicial redress in the interest of the public continued when in early 2001, major national newspapers reported that people were dying from starvation in several parts of India. The Rajasthan branch of an NGO – People's Union of Civil Liberties (PUCL) – submitted a writ petition to the Supreme Court in mid-April 2001, questioning whether the right to life guaranteed under Article 21 of the Indian Constitution also included the right to food.[14] The petition requested the Court to intervene to prevent starvation deaths that were taking place despite surplus food stocks in possession of the central and state governments. It further asked, 'Does not the right to food which has been upheld by the apex Court imply that the state has a duty to provide food especially in situations of drought to people who are drought-affected and . . . not in a position to purchase food?'[15] In subsequent correspondence with the Court, the petitioner demanded that state governments throughout the country should be directed to radically improve the functioning of employment guarantee schemes and social security programmes. Subsequently, and in several rulings in the period September 2001–October 2002, the Supreme Court ordered 16 states, including Orissa, to identify families in distress and to provide them with immediate food assistance. In particular, the Court issued an order for improving the implementation of food- and employment-related schemes like the NMMP and the SGRY. In October 2002, it ruled that chief secretaries (as heads of state-level civil services), were responsible for the overall implementation of the judicial orders and would be held accountable for any confirmed cases of starvation deaths within their respective states. In doing so, the Supreme Court firmly established that the right to food was a constituent aspect of the right to life and the corresponding government obligation to protect the right to food of its citizens. For the monitoring and implementation of its orders at the state level, the Court also appointed a commissioner in May 2002 (hereafter Saxena Commission).

After a detailed enquiry process – and in his third report to the Supreme Court in May 2003 – the Commissioner expressed frustration over the lack of urgency and the 'routine violation of Supreme Court's orders by the respondent governments'. Citing an 'overarching lack of state commitment to the prevention of hunger and starvation,' he went on to claim that 'The elimination of chronic hunger does not get anything like the priority it deserves in policy planning and budget allocations' (Saxena Commission 2003). For example, the Commissioner found that, a year after the deadline set by the Supreme Court had elapsed, several state governments had failed to provide cooked mid-day meals in primary schools and that coverage of the NMMP programme in the remaining states, including Orissa, was patchy. The same applied for employment-related schemes like the SGRY since 'the most deprived areas . . . often ended up getting a very small share of SGRY funds' and governments found it 'politically or administratively expedient to spend the funds elsewhere' (ibid.). In terms of Orissa, the report concluded that the general tendency of the state government was to 'solve problems by ignoring them'. And the report found that district administration in Orissa and Maharashtra 'often under-reports the magnitude of severe malnutrition'. The Commissioner thus concluded that, although Supreme Court intervention on the right to food was 'potentially effective', the 'initiatives have only made a small impact in the massive problem of chronic hunger'. Hence, he urged the Court to ensure that stronger accountability mechanisms were put in place for the monitoring and enforcement of its orders.

While the Supreme Court was addressing the PUCL petition in late August 2001, newspaper reports alleged that around 20 individuals in five villages of Orissa's Rayagada district had died from malnutrition. The reported list of inedible food items consumed by these individuals included porridge made from dried mango kernels and wild roots. When the NHRC asked it in September 2001 to submit a report on the matter, the Orissa government not only denied starvation deaths but its highest-ranked bureaucrat (Chief Secretary) claimed that the consumption of mango kernels was not only a common practice among tribals of the areas but in fact also nutritious.[16] This caused a furore among opposition parties and the issue was discussed at length in Parliament, although the Orissa government was not officially indicted on this issue.

Orissa Relief Code guidelines on starvation

Despite considerable judicial activism and the laudable efforts of the NHRC on the right to food and prevention of starvation deaths, progress has been limited. The general conclusion is that judicial interventions and recommendations of organisations such as the National Human Rights Commission are not taken seriously by the political leadership. The trend in most Indian states, including Orissa, has simply been to dismiss any advice provided by the courts or the NHRC. Although judicial interest attracts sensational media attention, the courts have not been able to hold state governments to account for failing to improve food and nutritional security within their territories. However, as a result of media attention and the rulings of the Courts in the late 1980s and early 1990s, certain guidelines provided in the Orissa Relief Code were modified to better enable Collectors and other district officials to 'react' to press reports of starvation. The current version of the Code (updated in 1996) recognises that, despite official measures to provide employment, emergency feeding and gratuitous relief to those unable to undertake physical labour, the frequency of press reports of alleged starvation deaths has increased. In such cases, district officials are instructed to consult paragraph 39 of the Code which stipulates:

> Whenever a report of death due to starvation is published and it comes to the notice of the Collector, he shall immediately cause an enquiry into the allegation. The enquiry shall be conducted by a gazetted officer in the presence of the Sarpanch, Ward Member or some gentleman of the village and the result of the enquiry reported in the Proforma in Appendix VI within 48 hours if possible. The Proforma is not exhaustive. The Collector should include such other information which he considers necessary to give Government a complete picture of the situation in which the alleged death has taken place. If all the information cannot be collected forthwith a preliminary report should be furnished immediately to be followed by a complete report soon.
>
> (Orissa Relief Code 1996: para. 39.i)

The Proforma referred to in paragraph 39 requires the officer investigating a starvation death to fill out detailed information on various matters ranging from basic information such as age, sex, date of death, etc. pertaining to the victim, to other factors such as the level of crop loss in the village, employment opportunities and social security benefits available and whether the victim's household is in economic distress. Upon receipt of the enquiry report, the Collector must undertake measures to 'alleviate distress in the area as far as possible'. This may also include personally visiting the affected area to 'take stock of the situation and be satisfied about the adequacy of labour employment, food position and other relief arrangements' (para. 39.iii). Paragraph 40 provides that all reports related to starvation, migration, epidemics, etc. appearing in the press must be verified by the Collector, who must also 'issue a contradiction, if any':

> The Collector shall take steps to get such reports immediately verified by proper enquiry or otherwise and if found true should take immediate remedial action. Proper publicity relating to the relief measures undertaken should be given. If on the other hand, the report is found inaccurate, exaggerated or incorrect a contradiction stating, the correct facts may be issued by the Collector immediately. Copies of such contradictions should be made available to the higher authorities.
>
> (para. 40)

In a separate chapter on health measures, the Code provides that in times of severe distress 'cases of mortality may be high not so much due to direct starvation but due to increased incidence of diseases' and the outbreak of epidemics (para. 204). In cooperation with the Chief District Medical Officer and the staff of the Health and Family Department, the Collector must ensure that both preventive and curative measures are undertaken. These include hospital treatment for patients, frequent inspections of disease-affected areas and weekly reports on diseases, number of patients treated and the total number of deaths (paras 205, 206, 207). Special emphasis must be given to mother and child care in villages affected by scarcity and distress conditions such that there is provision for 'health and nutrition needs of pre-school children, pregnant women and nursing mothers, who constitute nutritionally the most vulnerable section of the community' (para. 210).

In general, it appears that regular media reports on starvation combined with the actions of the Supreme Court and the Orissa High Court had a positive impact in Orissa in that administrative procedures were drawn up to enable district officials to cope with cases of alleged deaths from starvation. Despite this positive step, paragraphs 39 and 40 of the Relief Code are, however, more concerned with reacting to press reports of starvation deaths than with preventing them in the first place. In other words, it is only when reports on starvation appear in the daily press that the Collector and his administration are to suddenly wake up from their slumber. There is thus little incentive or instruction to the district administration to monitor nutritional status of vulnerable groups at regular intervals and long before the outbreak of a major crisis which can result in cases of starvation.

The Civil Service response to starvation

The standard bureaucratic response in Orissa was that starvation was a problem in the 1960s and the 1970s. Although most officials appeared reluctant to openly admit the continued occurrence of starvation deaths today, several readily agreed that the level of malnutrition was generally higher in Orissa than in other states of India. There was also consensus that, within Orissa, Kalahandi topped the malnutrition statistics. Some also claimed that the alleged starvation deaths were actually caused by the consumption of 'improper kinds of food' owing to factors like ignorance of the local population and traditional dietary patterns. Thus, a distinction was made between deaths due to 'starvation' on the one hand and what many termed 'malnutrition deaths' on the other. Indeed, there was a general feeling that the term 'starvation' was bad, and had to be avoided at all times. 'Malnutrition', on the other hand, was a safer alternative as its existence was 'an open secret' and politicians in power could not expect civil servants to deny the presence of widespread malnutrition in districts like Kalahandi.

Starvation and its causes

Officials were generally uncomfortable when asked to define 'starvation'. Some were candid enough to admit that they found the term difficult to apply in daily use, arguing that, given the high levels of poverty in certain vulnerable areas, it was natural to expect some form of premature death. However, as Kalahandi's Collector argued, assessing whether these deaths were starvation-related was immensely difficult:

> What is a starvation death? . . . It is difficult to define. Kalahandi has many pockets where acute poverty is present and deaths due to diarrhoea and lack of safe drinking water take place . . . old parents are sometimes not looked after by their children . . . This is a problem of the social structure.[17]

In general, the willingness of bureaucrats to admit or deny starvation deaths rested on their understanding of the term. A senior district-level official aptly summed up the dilemma in the following manner:

> The problem is that nobody really applies a universal criterion in defining starvation deaths. It is too politicised to be dealt with properly since accepting one particular definition of starvation may cause much embarrassment to the government, particularly when it may be something totally different and something that the government cannot be directly blamed for.[18]

Most officials understood and defined starvation deaths narrowly, in terms of food intake, although there was some recognition that lack of access to food was also a major problem in Kalahandi. For example a senior official claimed that death from starvation was likely 'if a person goes without food for ten consecutive days'.[19] He did not elaborate on how he had arrived at a figure of ten consecutive days, but he argued that excessive focus on definitions diverted attention from the district administration's capacity to intervene and prevent premature deaths whenever possible:

I agree that starvation and malnutrition are related but my ideas may be very different from what others think on this issue. I feel the problem in my area is more of malnutrition and I try my best to ensure that no one in the sub-division dies due to lack of government intervention no matter what the problem is. In this sense it is pointless to be concerned with what starvation is and what it is not.

A senior official in the district medical office (a practising doctor at Kalahandi's main hospital in Bhawanipatna) claimed to have long experience in dealing with cases of starvation and that the incidence of tuberculosis and other chronic illnesses present in most rural settings of Kalahandi often accentuated the problem.[20] The additional district magistrate, however, argued that deaths in the district were 'not due to food deprivation' but that 'old people die from old age, pregnant women die during childbirth, children die from infectious disease, and adults die from both non-infectious as well as infectious disease'. Accordingly, starvation deaths could only take place if 'a person has been deprived of food or edible items, there is no access to food for a prolonged period of time – not a sudden occurrence, and if there is no one to help the victim with food'.[21]

In Orissa's capital city, Bhubaneswar, a senior official in charge of drought relief in Orissa argued that 'all starvation deaths reported in the press are politicised and originate from a political tussle between local politicians in the Gram Panchayat or between the local MLA and the Panchayat'.[22] A health department official defined starvation very narrowly and in terms of 'a person without food and water for three consecutive days'. Despite 'a major problem of the high infant mortality rate in Kalahandi', he ruled out the possibility of starvation deaths in Orissa since his department 'constantly monitors the body mass index of vulnerable groups' and ensured that the ICDS system regularly surveyed malnutrition among children'.[23] However, by far the most nuanced understanding was offered by the administrative head of the health department (who had also previously served as Collector of Kalahandi):

> There is considerable undernourishment and many diseases are prevalent in the district. The situation is definitely not one of famine. There is always some food available – the key question is who has access to it and who does not. Is there a sharing of food in local society? Despite the availability of funds, drastic improvements in lifestyles of the people have not occurred and people still lack adequate purchasing power to buy the food sold in the market.[24]

She went on to observe that, although starvation deaths did take place in Kalahandi, they were not as many as reported in the media. Such reports, she added, were the result of opposition parties using the term 'starvation' to malign the ruling party – a phenomenon that 'has become a regular feature of Orissa politics'.

Local procedures for early warning[25]

Although the Orissa Relief Code does not contain separate procedures for early warning of cases of starvation, news of 'distress conditions' is supposed to be provided as part of the early warning procedures followed for identifying the onset and impact of drought. Each of Kalahandi's 13 blocks was assigned a 'squad officer' whose duties included regular interaction with villagers, Panchayat representatives and teachers in order to identify individuals and households in distress and oversee the implementation of welfare programmes and services. On the first Monday of every month a large meeting (with 150–200 participants) was held in Bhawanipatna with the participation of squad officers, BDOs, Tehsildars, medical officers, civil supply officers, etc. The meeting – presided over by the Collector or by his or her deputy – provided an opportunity for the district leadership to be provided with early warning information related to food shortage and cases of severe deprivation. In theory these procedures were capable of providing early warning information; in practice they functioned best for assessing macro-level conditions relating to lack of rainfall and extent of crop loss in the district. Further, there were no efforts to monitor the nutritional status of vulnerable groups and there were no surveys conducted on dietary patterns and nutrition-related illnesses. Although the ICDS conducted surveys on a monthly basis, these were limited to children in the 0–6 year age group. The absence of a department of nutrition at the district level also meant that in the period 1996–2000 only a single nutritional survey was conducted in Kalahandi, and that was by a team of visiting nutritionists from Bhubaneswar. Moreover, crucial early warning indicators – unemployment and migration, influence of moneylenders, 'distress sale' of assets – were noticeably not given priority.

Existing early warning procedures prescribed by the Relief Code and envisioned by the district administrative leadership were further handicapped by inadequate telecommunication facilities and staff shortages. For example, a remote block like Lanjigarh did not have a single telephone line and the only form of communication was the unreliable police wireless. And Lanjigarh's health centre did not have proper equipment or an adequate supply of medicines, and very few doctors and nurses were willing to be posted there. The district administration's capacity to respond was thus severely limited and a senior official observed:

> When we get reports from the BDOs of a diarrhoea epidemic or something similar, then we take necessary steps to combat the problem. However, if the BDO does not himself know what is going on in the different areas of his blocks or he cannot send information to the headquarters, then who is to blame if people die?

Many officials, at state and district levels, spoke of the media's obsession with painting a 'negative picture' of Kalahandi. Some felt that although some reports were accurate, media coverage of the district was unfairly hyped in comparison to other places in Orissa. Such views are borne out in the following two statements:

> The local media is very bad. This includes both Kalahandi papers and correspondents of state-level papers based in Kalahandi who continue to publish negative stories of the district. They must also publish some good things.[26]

> Journalists and others must ensure that whatever is reported is correct and accurate. All facts must come to the forefront. One must paint a picture of a man or a bullock with two eyes and only then can an artist say that the picture is complete. If the artist is not available, then one needs to find someone else who can replicate or provide information of the original intentions of the artist. One must pay attention to facts; if there is confusion, then a thorough investigation must be undertaken before publishing a report. All district officials are obliged to provide information to the press and we do. Yet, our version of the story seldom finds any buyers.[27]

Another official illustrated the typical roles played by civil servants and the media when he observed, 'they [the press] claim starvation deaths; we deny it.' Indeed, the general view among officials was that the media, which is largely controlled by influential politicians, sensationalises issues of starvation without proper investigation. Such an understanding also appeared to have influenced the formulation of paragraphs 39 and 40 of the Relief Code mentioned earlier, which concentrate exclusively on how to 'react to press reports of starvation deaths'. The title of paragraph 40, 'Verification of Press reports and issue of contradiction, if any', is particularly interesting as it was perhaps formulated in response to constant media focus on starvation deaths. Several district officials believed that reports of starvation deaths were simply a cheap trick by editors and proprietors to sell more of their low-standard papers. However, and despite his lack of confidence in journalists, the additional district magistrate was quick to add that, whenever allegations of starvation deaths appeared in the media, the district administration ensured that these reports were verified:

> Even when press reports are false, the administration needs to view them in a positive sense. All negative reports have a positive effect. If not anything else, it functions as a wake-up call . . . then the administration must verify using its own channels. One must always be prepared for the worst . . . if a false report can expose weaknesses in our ability to respond to a crisis, then we ought to say something positive about the media's role after all . . . but obviously, if this happens all too frequently, then the media loses its weapon of surprise.

Similarly, some senior state-level officials admitted that media attention on Kalahandi did have a positive effect. For example, one expressed a genuine desire to supplement information received from field officers with that provided in press reports. Another official argued that the government would benefit considerably if the media improved its routine and started providing information at an earlier stage than was currently the case. She also added that journalists could do a better job at providing investigative reports:

> We would definitely prefer quick information of a developing situation, especially in times of disasters and ensuing epidemics. However, these reports should be credible . . . most newspapers have become oriented towards sensationalism and do not bother to cross-check their facts before publishing a report. I make myself accessible to the print media by way of monthly meetings with the press. However, I have also experienced that they often manipulate my statements.[28]

Another senior state official, who had served in Kalahandi for several years, argued that excessive media attention on Kalahandi was actually quite positive:

> The positive feature of media coverage is that it leads to increased interest in the region followed by VIP visits – these are important for focusing attention and for the allocation of increased funds. The increased focus of the media has also resulted in good and competent IAS officers being posted to Kalahandi in contrast to the earlier practice of sending average officers.[29]

The same officer, however, also argued that a coverage of negative issues resulted in the introduction of ad hoc solutions. With all politicians constantly worried about re-election, issues like starvation deaths were easily politicised and long-term solutions overshadowed by the perceived need to demonstrate that something was being done:

> One example is the Emergency Feeding Programme which is a typical short-term intervention and cannot provide long-term sustainability to the beneficiaries. In a democracy, we cannot tolerate hunger and as such there is a need for such short-term measures. I am not saying this is bad . . . only that we cannot continue with such ad hoc interventions without having a long-term plan. How long are we going to feed the people of Kalahandi? Must they remain dependent on the government for the rest of their lives? We need to question our efforts to help them become self-reliant. Politicians are seldom willing to wait for ten years in order to see the fruits of current action and hence democracies in a way, with the help of haywire media coverage of issues like starvation, encourage ad hoc interventions.

The impact of measures undertaken to combat starvation

Kalahandi's Collector and the Collector's staff held weekly 'grievance day' sessions on Saturdays in Bhawanipatna where any resident of the district could seek immediate assistance from the district administration on a wide range of problems.

Further, during a crisis the District Natural Calamities Committee – according to a 1989 Supreme Court directive – was supposed to advise the administration. Evidence from Kalahandi, however, indicated that the functioning of this Committee was far from satisfactory. For example, even though five members associated with recognised NGOs had been nominated, a newspaper report alleged that several of these members were 'dogged by controversies' which included allegations of corruption and mismanagement.[30] Such allegations affected their credibility vis-à-vis other committee members. Another news report documented that the committee continued to meet only twice a year instead of the revised Supreme Court directions of once every two months.[31] Thus, during an emergency, the district administration did not receive the required assistance and inputs it needed from committee members. Similarly, during its investigation of starvation deaths in Orissa, the National Human Rights Commission criticised the role and functioning of this key advisory organ and recommended changes in existing procedures by encouraging more direct involvement of political parties to provide it with increased political influence (NHRC 1996: para. 15). The Orissa government, however, chose to ignore these recommendations.

The Orissa Relief Code (para. 39) further instructs the Collector to launch an inquiry as soon as he or she is made aware of reports of death by starvation. The investigating officer is required to submit a report containing a long list of details as discussed earlier. The NHRC Team visiting Kalahandi in 1996, however, questioned the credibility of such reports:

> Some of the villages where alleged starvation deaths have taken place have reported a very high crop damage [as high as 90 per cent crop loss] . . . The Tehsildar who inquired into deaths has stated 'no' to the question in the Proforma whether he considers that the village was in acute economic distress. The Team wonders as to what the economic profile of the village could be, if it is not suffering from economic distress with 90% crop damage. This instance is quoted only to stress the right level of sensitivity and awareness needed to report on conditions of distress prevailing in the rural areas and to recommend effective relief measures as also the importance of objective and effective scrutiny of these reports.
>
> (NHRC 1996: paragraph 19)

Many NGOs also alleged that doctors were never consulted and the investigating officer – usually a revenue officer or a BDO – was usually not competent enough to assess whether a death had taken place due to starvation. They also alleged that the process of inquiry was not initiated immediately and a report normally took several months to be compiled and submitted. This resulted in inordinate delays in providing assistance to the surviving members of the victim's household and others in need of immediate assistance. Such complaints appeared credible in the light of a letter issued by the Revenue Department to all district Collectors in 1992, in which the Orissa government expressed concern regarding delays in the inquiry process.[32] However, once again, there was no evidence that these instructions had been adhered to in Kalahandi, or for that matter, in any other district of Orissa.

Methodological difficulties in investigating starvation deaths

As discussed in Chapter 2, classifying whether or not a death occurs because of starvation is immensely difficult as the cause of death could be the combination of both undernutrition and disease. In Kalahandi, investigating officers tended to focus exclusively on the role of disease in causing death. Such a focus overlooked the very process of starvation which increases the likelihood of being vulnerable to a terminal disease. In addition, there was a considerable gap in time between the filing of a starvation death report by villagers through Panchayat representatives/the BDO, or via the media, and the start of an inquiry process by the district administration. Hence, post-mortems of the corpse could not be carried out as relatives had already completed funeral rituals. In many areas it was also customary to cremate the body of the victim immediately after death, and the police only intervened if they had grounds to believe that the death had occurred under suspicious circumstances. Even when the corpse was available, climatic factors and delays in starting the investigative process meant that it was badly decomposed, making it difficult even for seasoned medical practitioners to ascertain the exact cause of death.

Given these difficulties, investigating officers usually tried to construct a rough health history based on narratives from household members, relatives, fellow villagers and health workers in the area. There were attempts to uncover whether the family had any available foodgrain stocks and undertake an assessment of the general economic condition of the family of the victim including whether he/she was receiving subsidised PDS rations, old age pensions, etc. However, even such techniques were not without flaws. For example, the NHRC (1996: para. 8) observed that its team faced numerous difficulties while investigating starvation deaths in Orissa. It noted that the team had visited the houses of the affected families and interacted with family members, neighbours and village functionaries. Through these interviews it tried to ascertain the extent of crop damage in the village and availability of foodgrains, utilisation of ration cards for withdrawal of stocks from the PDS, level of wage employment in the family, impact of relief measures like the emergency feeding schemes, and the functioning of the pension system (ibid.: para. 6). However, when the team tried to cross-check information on alleged starvation deaths with government records, it faced a major hurdle as the district health department did not have the capacity to maintain records of all cases of death in villages, particularly those located far from local health centres.

There are thus obvious limitations to any attempt to diagnose and investigate a starvation death. Owing to a variety of factors discussed above, many genuine cases of death from starvation actually go unreported, and estimating the exact number of such deaths in a calendar year is almost impossible. In certain study villages which had reported starvation deaths, relatives of the victim and fellow villagers often claimed that the victim died from lack of food. The standard local statement often heard in Kalahandi was '*kichhi khaiba kuna pahi mori gole*' (having nothing to eat, he died). And a former Collector of Kalahandi recollected frequently hearing the following statement during his visits to rural areas of the district:

> *Ghar nein, Dih nein, Bada nein, Kam nein, Dhana nein, Po nein, Jhi nein, Khai bake nein, Gulgula hauchhe, Marijuche agyan.*
> [No house, no homestead land, no agricultural land, no work, no vocation, no son, no daughter. No food to eat, in a miserable state. I am dying, Sir.]

Indeed, it was difficult to establish when investigating officers believed and verified such stories. The difficulty was further accentuated by the fact that deaths may also have been caused by the consumption of non-edible items (e.g. poisonous herbs and mango kernels) and infectious disease. And without the corpse, an accurate account pinpointing the exact cause of death could not be constructed. This also provided the district administration and the Orissa government with an opportunity to dismiss any allegations of death from starvation. To make matters even more difficult, investigating officers were usually under tremendous pressure from the ruling party to deny the likelihood of starvation even when an individual officer may have been convinced otherwise. But allegations of starvation – irrespective of credibility – were also a useful way of maligning political opponents or discrediting the district administration. To illustrate this, an official recounted an episode he had recently investigated in Kalahandi:

> When starvation deaths have been alleged, I have investigated them and even video-filmed the houses and found that there is always some food available. For instance, in 1998 I received reports of starvation deaths in Jayantpur, a village 30 km from Dharamgarh. Villagers said that a person died from lack of food. However, doctors said that the patient had a tumour in the neck and died of tuberculosis. Apparently, the victim's father had also died from a similar disease. The victim's wife was, however, healthy. Now, when the *Sarpanch* of the village lives 50 metres from the victim's house and has one quintal of rice to distribute under the Gratuitous Relief scheme, how can a person die from lack of food? Even if we accept that such Gratuitous Relief was not given, what about the social duty and responsibility of the healthy neighbours? I found that an explanation for the allegation of starvation death was rooted in village-level Panchayat politics, i.e. a former *Sarpanch* wanted to discredit the present *Sarpanch*.

The methodological difficulties in diagnosing and investigating starvation deaths became even clearer during a visit to Nuapada village in Borda Gram Panchayat of Bhawanipatna block in January 2001. Villagers claimed that three days earlier Lakshman Pradhan, a 65-year-old male, had died after a prolonged period of undernutrition. Bira Pradhan, the victim's son, claimed that, without the possibility of buying food, his family had, for the past six weeks, eaten rotten rice and leftovers from neighbours. When Bira and fellow villagers informed the Borda Panchayat representatives and the local BDO of his father's death, he was told that a doctor from the local health centre would be able to visit his village only in a week's time to investigate his father's death and issue a death certificate. Fearing decomposition, Bira was not willing to wait that long and had already cremated his father in accordance with traditional customs and rituals. Subsequently, the investigating officer attributed the death of Lakshman Pradhan to natural causes. Officially, this was not a starvation death. The situation looked particularly critical for several elderly people in the village and a local farmer claimed that he and his fellow villages had become 'immune to starvation'. Having experienced months of food shortage, many in Nuapada village claimed to have become accustomed to the pangs of hunger, and even at the best of times a household could satisfy no more than 80 per cent of its daily food needs. With three successive crop failures in the village, their diet had been reduced by approximately 60 per cent and such reduced food intake was further aggravated by the lack of nutritious food. Whereas the majority of the households appeared to suffer from malnutrition and ill health, the village had several healthy-looking young men. They turned out to be either landlords or relatives of people working for the district administration (e.g. teachers, clerks, block extension officers, etc.) in Bhawanipatna.

The Kalahandi posting: frustration and demotivation in the civil service

Among district officials there was a general sense of frustration. Some argued that, no matter how well they performed, they would continue to face criticism for not preventing some death or the other. One official complained that despite good intentions and proper execution of projects, the results from Kalahandi were 'perpetually considered unsatisfactory and given the slightest excuse, political parties, organisations and the locals have become accustomed to saying that the administration had failed'. Similarly, a former Collector of Kalahandi claimed that whereas news of acute distress and starvation were invariably projected as government failure, it was not the politicians but civil servants who faced the major brunt of all criticism. He went on to emphasise that it was important to be 'thick skinned' and be able to 'take the heat', even when one felt that one had done nothing wrong.

An important strategy by which the political leadership rewards and punishes civil servants in India is a system of rapid transfers by which officers – after a brief stint in a post – are assigned a new job in a new area or department (Banik 2001). This applies particularly to IAS officers – to which Collectors and Sub-Collectors belong – and is a major cause of demotivation among officials posted to the districts. Given the sensitive nature of drought relief and frequent press reports of starvation deaths in Kalahandi, successive Collectors have fallen prey to frequent and arbitrary transfers that are vaguely formulated as resulting from 'administrative necessity'. Whenever the Orissa government faces severe criticism for failing to tackle drought successfully, it simply transfers the district Collector without making any significant changes in the mechanisms for delivering drought relief. Although the system of transfers is practised all over India, its frequency has been particularly high in Kalahandi. For example, between 1996 and 2000, eight officers were in charge of the district, seldom having enough time to settle down to do a good job. As it was remote (a 14-hour-long road journey from Bhubaneswar) and drought-prone, several current and former IAS officers posted to Kalahandi referred to it as a 'punishment posting'. They claimed that, despite a desire to play an important role in the development of the district, they were aware that they could be transferred at any time and at short notice. Some officers coped better with this uncertainty than others, but almost all had difficulties in remaining motivated in the face of recurrent crises and press reports alleging starvation deaths. As a senior official observed, 'no matter how much you try, you are never good enough . . . there is acute poverty everywhere . . . we cannot perform miracles . . . this is a thankless posting'. Thus, from the civil service point of view, not only did frequent transfers affect the implementation of long-term development programmes in Kalahandi, they were also a major source of demotivation.

Some officials also recognised the limitations of administrative response following severe drought and successive crop failures, particularly those related to the impact of short-term relief interventions like the provision of gratuitous relief. The dearth of administrative personnel, given the large number of vacant posts in government services in Kalahandi, was also an issue often mentioned by both state and district-level officials. The general view was that this adversely affected the early warning and crisis response capacity of the local administration. Low salaries and poor infrastructure in the district appeared to be the major reasons that deterred officers from coastal districts of Orissa from working in Kalahandi. For example, as of January 2001, 10 posts of senior medical officer were vacant in Bhawanipatna hospital (the main hospital in the district) and, out of a total of 168 doctors assigned to Kalahandi district, 70 posts remained vacant.[33] The problem was not just confined to doctors but also to other personnel and the district lacked over 50 health supervisors. The condition of health centres located in remote areas was even worse. For example, in February 1999, a fresh medical graduate was the only resident doctor in Thuamul Rampur, responsible for the entire malaria-prone block. The remaining two positions remained unfilled as no one was willing to work in the area. The only reason this lone doctor agreed to work here was because he had received a government scholarship at medical school which obliged him to serve the government for at least three years. He argued that the lack of incentives (e.g. a salary of Rs 3,200) and the absence of proper equipment ('adequate only for first aid') and poor housing facilities ('I only have a chair, a cot and a kerosene stove') discouraged doctors from joining such posts.[34] Senior medical officers in Kalahandi argued that there should be greater incentives for young doctors to work in Kalahandi. This, they observed, could be easily facilitated by the introduction of a rotation system (e.g. two years of service in Kalahandi before being transferred to another district) and the provision of special financial and career incentives to work in health centres located in remote areas. For example, and in addition to a pay hike, they proposed that young doctors could be attracted to work in Kalahandi if they were guaranteed admission to (highly competitive) postgraduate studies. The district Collector also sympathised with the doctors and observed:

> It is a strenuous life for many officials since many posts remain vacant and they must do double duty. This affects the quality of the work. But whom do we blame? How do I blame a doctor for negligence when he his doing his best given the lack of resources and manpower? The Government of Orissa can solve this problem by providing incentives for postings to Kalahandi in the form of higher salaries, service benefits, better prospects of promotion, etc.[35]

Although some officials were willing to admit administrative shortcomings in managing drought-induced deprivation, others argued that the government could not always be the sole provider of assistance. The argument was that many deaths could be prevented if fellow villagers and relatives first provided assistance to the victim and then contacted the government for assistance. As one officer put it, 'There can never be an entire area or a village without any food . . . the main problem is that neighbours and family members or relatives do not react and sometimes fail to respond'. A similar view was expressed by a senior Orissa government official, who complained that during his tenure in Kalahandi, villagers would often travel long distances to the district headquarters to lodge a complaint of starvation death instead of immediately assisting the starving victim. He further added that it was 'peculiar' that the message of a likely starvation death 'spreads like wild fire' and the bonds of 'fraternity' only come to life after someone has died:

> I would often ask them: 'Why did you not provide food to the victim first instead of spending so much money to visit me?' They invariably could not answer my question. Thus, for me, these were clear cases of people wanting to sensationalise an event without doing their own bit first. The government is seen to be the Almighty and the provider of everything. The attitude in Kalahandi can be summed up by the following: Do nothing on your own – blame everything on the government.[36]

District officers and doctors also argued that, in addition to understaffing and poor infrastructure, a further problem in Kalahandi was that tribal groups often preferred to be treated by quacks and witch doctors rather than qualified medical practitioners. Indeed, a study by Behura and Das (1991) of villages in Kalahandi and Nuapada showed that villagers attribute sickness or loss of health to supernatural as well as natural/physical causes. Such tendencies were also observed in some of the study villages and there was an excessive dependence on the miraculous powers of the traditional healer/medicine man who prepared herbal medicines – pastes made from local herbs and plants. These healers appeared to have a wide repertoire of remedies for curing a wide range of illnesses and enjoyed high respect in village society. Respect, however, did not always translate into improved material benefits. For example, in a Lanjigarh village, the medicine man was just as poor as his fellow villagers although he lived in a hut that appeared to be better maintained than other huts. In fact, only in rare cases did the medicine man receive cash payment for his services. Instead, it was common to pay him in kind (food and non-food items and/or the offer of free labour for his field). Even if one accepted the limitations of these local healers, the main causes of ill health in the study villages could not, however, be ascribed simply to superstition, but rather a combination of lack of awareness and unhygienic conditions resulting from poor cooking and latrine facilities. Women, in particular, were exposed to poor living conditions as they spent the greater part of the day in dark kitchens without chimneys and did not inhale fresh air while cooking daily meals. Administrators, however, were keen on placing part of the blame for starvation and disease on the ignorance of the victims. For example, a senior health official in Kalahandi argued that, 'being ignorant and obsessed with superstition, many poor people do not make use of facilities available to them.'[37] The most stoic defence of government efforts, however, came from the additional relief commissioner based in Bhubaneswar who argued that the government should not be blamed when people died on account of their own ignorance:

> Let me tell you of a recent case of alleged starvation death. Pramia Bhoi, a middle-aged woman from Bolangir, died recently. Her husband apparently died of a disease two years ago and the family had been surviving by selling firewood. Suddenly Pramia fell ill and died. She did not make use of the option of working as a daily wage earner. When she fell ill, the doctors treated her, gave her medicines and recommended that she go to the hospital. But she did not do so. Whose fault is it then?[38]

6

THE VOCAL PRESS

Upon independence, India adopted a liberal version of press freedom; Article 19(1) of the Indian Constitution recognises freedom of speech and expression as a fundamental right. Although there is no specific constitutional mention of the freedom of the press, the idea of press freedom has gradually evolved through legislation and reports of various government-appointed bodies like the Press Commission.[1] The relations between the government and the press in the initial post-independence period were friendly and cordial, and the press was generally able to function without political pressure (Verghese 1978: 220). In the 1960s, however, the press became more critical of government policies and its adversarial role gained momentum in the period 1969–75, when Indira Gandhi's government introduced newsprint quotas and licence requirements for the import of printing machinery in an attempt to check the growing influence of the press (Dunnett 1988: 243). Things got worse during the 'National Emergency' (1975–77) when the government suppressed individual freedoms, censored the press, curtailed the jurisdiction of the courts and rendered the Constitution invalid (Bhaskar 1989: 71). Even after the end of the Emergency in 1977, the government maintained a monopoly over the electronic media, with state-run radio and television channels. It was also during this period that the circulation of newspapers and periodicals increased by leaps and bounds.[2] However, with the advent of satellite television and the Internet in the 1990s, the government's control over news coverage began to decrease gradually and the Indian media today is generally regarded as plural, independent and a role model for the Third World. After a general overview of the press in India, this chapter goes on to examine the nature and extent of coverage of drought and starvation deaths in Kalahandi in the English-language (national) and Oriya (local and regional) press, respectively.

A brief overview of the Indian press

English remains the language of the elite and ruling classes in India, and several studies conclude that English newspapers enjoy high status and are instrumental in setting the agenda in the political arena (Haque and Narag 1983; Prasad 1992;

Bathla 1998). Given the large number of languages and dialects spoken in the country, English has always performed an important function in national politics by providing political and administrative leaders from all parts of the country with a common medium for communication. As a result, some of the largest circulating English dailies in the country are published from the cities of New Delhi (e.g. *Hindustan Times* and *Times of India*), Mumbai (e.g. *The Indian Express*), Kolkata (e.g. *The Telegraph* and *The Statesman*) and Chennai (e.g. *The Hindu*). This trend is, however, changing with the increased regionalisation of politics, and social groups and political parties, strong in specific areas of the country, are increasingly becoming crucial actors in national politics. A study of the English press made the following observation:

> In recent times, there has been a decided shift away from English dominance in national politics. Caste groups uninfluenced by western education, and therefore not fully conversant with English, have succeeded in capturing political power, particularly in the 'Hindi belt'. Yet, even non-English speaking politicians cannot, or at least do not, ignore the English language press – as is obvious from their frequent references in Parliament to stories from the English press.
>
> (Joseph and Sharma 1994: 17)

Indeed, English-language dailies remain highly influential in India despite the disproportionate size of their readership in comparison to the increasingly popular vernacular press. The ownership of these newspapers also reflects the fact that they are run by the 'same dominant group to which it primarily caters' (ibid.). Consequently, 'the traditional definitions of news, accepted by the mainstream English language press in India, conform to the generally liberal, yet elitist, values espoused by the relatively affluent, upwardly mobile, university educated, upper caste urban male' (ibid.). This very aspect has had an impact on the coverage of minority interests and the plight of marginalised groups in the population. Although most English dailies do not actively intend to ignore such issues, the actual news coverage appears to cater to the interests of the fast increasing middle-class readership. For example, a study of news coverage on women's issues by the English-language press concludes that, 'although there is increasing coverage of human rights violations and struggles for social justice, this perspective is not always integrated into news coverage or editorial content' (ibid.).

The vernacular press in India has grown by leaps and bounds since the 1970s. While there was a reduction in the number and circulations of dailies in most industrialised countries, the circulation rates of Indian language newspapers grew by 140 per cent in the period 1976–88. As Jeffrey (1993: 2004) notes, 'No other country – indeed, no other continent – in the world has a newspaper industry as complex and highly developed as India's.' The growth of the vernacular press continued in the 1990s and the major languages of the industry include Hindi, Malayalam, Marathi, Bengali, Gujarati, Tamil, Kannada, Telugu, Oriya, Punjabi and Urdu. According to Jeffrey (ibid.), this expansion was helped by five sets of factors. First, radical improvements in printing technology have helped to produce attractive layouts and faster copies while improved roads and transport facilities have helped distribution. Second, literacy levels in India have improved greatly, increasing the potential readership base. Third, with increased purchasing power, more people can now afford to subscribe to newspapers. Fourth, owners and publishers have increasingly realised that the newspaper industry can be profitable, not least thanks to increased revenues earned from advertisements. Finally, literacy and purchasing power has increased interest in politics and there is a great demand for information. This is particularly a trend in Hindi-speaking areas and politically conscious states like Kerala and West Bengal.

While the overall growth of the vernacular press has been impressive, not all newspapers have managed to wrest free of political control. In several parts of India, political leaders actively own and edit newspapers and thereby promote their own political views and interests. In other cases newspapers are overly reliant on government advertisements in order to survive financially, seriously affecting their ability to be critical of official policies. In general, Indian language newspapers appear to do well in major cities and coastal areas of the country where the large readership potential guarantees the existence of several competing newsgroups.

Coverage of drought and starvation

In a seminal study of the role of the English-language press and anti-hunger strategies in India, Ram (1990) writes of how Indian newspapers began to voice views on hunger starting from the 1887–88 famine. In editorials, newspapers like *The Hindu* were able to criticise the lack of relief response by the British authorities. Press reporting assumed a new role in 1918, with coverage of food riots and related disturbances in South India following the failure of the monsoon rains. This was not a case of famine, but a 'food crisis' that led to widespread looting leaving hardly any area untouched (Arnold 1979: 111). In the years leading up to independence, the press was instrumental in bringing to the forefront issues connected with high prices, artificial shortages, hoarding, etc., which forced the colonial authorities to undertake countermeasures. In particular, the role of newspapers in covering the Bengal famine (1943–44) – particularly the adversarial role played by the Calcutta-based *Statesman* – has been subject to widespread praise (Aykroyd 1974; Sen 1981; Ram 1990). The nationalist press also played its part in criticising the government's callousness, with newspapers like *People's War*, *Amrita Bazar Patrika*, the *Hindustan Standard* and the *Eastern Economist* actively highlighting the suffering of famine victims.

In the post-independence period – particularly during the two major food crises in the mid-1960s and the early 1970s that brought India to the brink of a major famine – the Indian press once again played a crucial role. Writing on the major food crisis in Bihar in 1966–67, Brass (1986: 253) notes how two English-language dailies, *Searchlight* and the *Indian Nation*, played an important role in 'framing the whole drama' and then 'commenting on it'. Similarly Berg (1971: 115) highlights how, in the early stages of the Bihar crisis, various national and local newspapers repeatedly described the Bihar administration as 'incompetent', 'bungling', 'unimaginative', and 'unresponsive'. During the severe drought that affected Maharashtra in 1971–73, the national and local press covered the food crisis more actively and with a 'greater sense of sophistication and nuance' than was the case in Bihar (Ram 1990: 177). When large parts of the country were again affected by severe droughts in the 1980s and 1990s, the vernacular press, in particular, was instrumental in providing useful field-level reports that challenged official claims regarding the implementation of relief operations.

A focus on Kalahandi began in the Oriya press during the drought in 1965–66 and the severe food shortage that followed. However, the district did not receive much attention otherwise until the mid-1980s when sensational reports appeared in both Oriya and English-language newspapers on drought, starvation deaths, sale of children, large-scale out-migration and the exploitation of tribals by moneylenders. However, what really caught the public imagination was the story of the widow and mother of two small children, Phanas Punji, who was forced by poverty and near-destitution to sell her 14-year-old sister-in-law, Banita, to an old, blind and exploitative landlord for the paltry sum of Rs 40.[3] Following this report, the Prime Minister, Rajiv Gandhi, visited Kalahandi and met Phanas Punji, promising that both she and Banita would be given government jobs. This story, and the ensuing visit by the Prime Minister, led to a procession of regional and national reporters heading for Kalahandi. There was, in particular, an increased interest in sensational human-interest stories of poverty, destitution and government neglect, and Kalahandi took its first steps towards being projected as the starvation capital of India. Almost 15 years later, the President of the Kalahandi Journalists Association observed that, after the Phanas Punji story provided national attention to Kalahandi's problems, visiting media persons began treating Kalahandi as an exceptional case, as if 'poverty, starvation and squalor were for the first time being discovered in India'.[4] The sensational nature of the stories also substantially increased the circulation rates of Oriya dailies. Jeffrey (2000: 104) notes how, in the mid-1980s, *Prajatantra* began to cover rural news increasingly, both providing crucial early warning information of deprivation and performing an adversarial or 'raising hell' role. In doing so, its circulation rates increased from 57,000 copies in 1984 to 77,000 copies by the end of 1986. Facing recurrent drought and related deprivation, Kalahandi continued to receive attention in both Oriya and English dailies throughout the 1990s.

News coverage on Kalahandi in the English press

All major English language dailies of India have correspondents based in Orissa's capital city, Bhubaneswar, and there is considerable cooperation within groups of correspondents. They often socialise together and exchange information. Most spend considerable amount of time covering stories related to government policy and implementation, important debates in the legislative assembly, conflicts within political parties and factions, and visits by central government ministers and other high-level officials. In general, the dailies do not prioritise so-called 'human interest stories' unless a crisis is visible and sensational enough to warrant attention. A preliminary study of six major English dailies revealed that *The Hindu* and the *Indian Express* were the most active newspapers in terms of their coverage of Kalahandi during the severe drought of 1996–97. The *Indian Express* provided considerably coverage of news from rural Orissa and had the advantage of a local edition published from Vishakapatnam in neighbouring Andhra Pradesh and a local correspondent based in Kalahandi. Although *The Hindu* did not have a local edition, it regularly featured a section specifically dedicated to news coverage of the eastern states of India, and Orissa figured prominently in these reports. In the following sections, I will briefly discuss some of the main characteristic features of news coverage and editorials in these two newspapers in the period August 1996–August 1997.

The Hindu

During the early stages of the drought in Orissa, *The Hindu* focused its attention on the proceedings in the Orissa Legislative Assembly and the actions and statements of opposition leaders on the state government's efforts to manage the drought. For example, in September 1996, the paper carried a story regarding the demand by opposition parties urging the state government to convene an emergency session of the Legislative Assembly in order to discuss the government's 'failure' to provide adequate relief.[5] Around a month later, there was a report on an attempt by a group of opposition party legislators to force the state government to declare Kalahandi and certain other districts as 'famine' areas:

> Seven MLAs of the Janata Dal met the Governor of Orissa . . . demanding that the Governor immediately intervene and ask the State Government to declare the districts of Koraput, Kalahandi, Bolangir and Nawapara as famine area and sanction Rs. 300 crore for providing relief to the people. In the memorandum they said that they had visited the four districts and found the situation fast deteriorating and urgent steps need to be taken to combat the acute drought conditions. They stated that this year's drought was worse than what was witnessed in the districts of Kalahandi and Bolangir in 1965–66.[6]

In the weeks that followed, the attention shifted from the drought in Orissa to the sensational devastation caused by floods in neighbouring Andhra Pradesh. Kalahandi was, however, again back in the headlines starting mid-November when a report criticised the central and state governments for not implementing a long-term plan to avert drought:

> The Congress (I) and the Janata Dal, which have been in power during the last two decades, have not failed to make the sufferings an issue whenever drought occurred in this region. This year the situation is grim in the undivided

Bolangir and Kalahandi districts and migration from these regions has been very high. Though the Government has been repeatedly denying that starvation deaths occurred, the people in the area and the Opposition leaders are claiming that such cases have been reported. There is also going to be an acute shortage of drinking water and fodder for cattle.[7]

Four days later, an article headlined 'Noisy scenes in Orissa Assembly over drought' described the mayhem that occurred when opposition parties disrupted proceedings and demanded that all other legislative business be postponed until the conditions of drought were debated properly.[8] Subsequently, a debate ensued and the leader of the opposition demanded that the government set up a committee to monitor government efforts to tackle the drought. In the same edition, the paper published an editorial, 'Orissa's travails', questioning the real impact of central and state government commitment to tackle the drought:

> It is ironic that a resource-rich State like Orissa should witness so much human misery in its drought-prone districts for want of a long-term programme ... Conflicting reports on starvation deaths and migration of the marginal farmers ... point to a grim situation. Shortage of drinking water and fodder for cattle may become worse in the coming months to add to the woes of the villagers in the affected areas.[9]

The editorial further noted that there were demands to declare Kalahandi as 'famine affected' but went on to argue that the centre–state blame game over relief funds was only delaying long-term efforts to prevent human tragedy. Claiming that the administration did not have a 'clear picture of the distress in the affected districts', the report argued that the suffering in Kalahandi was being 'exploited as a political weapon by vested interests'. The editorial concluded by noting that the political leadership should view the Kalahandi case as a 'national problem'. Two days later, the paper's correspondent filed a report, 'Orissa's tale of woe', describing the condition of rural households which had 'empty vessels in the kitchen'.[10] The report noted, 'There are allegations that 100 starvation deaths have occurred' and went on to highlight the severe shortage of both relief funds and administrative personnel in Kalahandi. This story was followed by an insightful editorial in late November, 'India's Africa: Orissa – Chasing virtual food', in which the paper questioned the impact of political commitment in preventing starvation deaths:

> Over 25 million tonnes of foodgrains in the nation's silos and 180 starvation deaths in Kalahandi. A more devastating comment on administrative callousness is difficult. Have things come to such a pass that districts like Kalahandi ... no longer figure in the national consciousness? Have they, like Sub-Saharan Africa, fallen off the Indian map?[11]

Noting that almost all plans to develop Kalahandi and neighbouring areas invariably fail owing to administrative indifference and centre–state bickering, the editorial made a couple of suggestions that required urgent attention. These included channelling buffer stocks of foodgrains to starving areas, creating employment in support of rebuilding the economic base of affected communities, and the protection of forests for the maintenance of ecological balance. The editorial advocated a policy of 'targeted governance' which entailed implementing long-term measures rather than 'merely pouring state funds into a bottomless pit'. By the second week of December 1996, the situation in Kalahandi was getting out of control and there were reports that opposition parties in New Delhi were planning to send teams of politicians to the Kalahandi region to inquire into government lapses in the provision of drought relief.[12] Following a visit by a National Human Rights Commission team probing into starvation deaths in Orissa, a lengthy article, 'Spectre of hunger deaths again', commented on the political response to allegations of starvation:

> Starvation deaths, a ticklish issue, have once again started haunting the J. B. Patnaik Government this year as it had done in 1986. As has been the practice of Mr. Patnaik, the reports are being denied . . . One thing is certain that no amount of government denials can hide the basic fact that there have been deaths, if not due to starvation, at least because of lack of basic health facilities.[13]

The article further highlighted the early warning function performed by opposition parties in July–August, when they had warned the state government regarding the failure of the monsoons and the impending drought:

> What is really unpardonable is that in spite of the claims being made by the Opposition leaders, the Government has not yet felt the need to pull up the district administration in the affected areas for failing to enquire about such deaths taking place when it was given information.[14]

Three further reports were filed towards the end of December. The first related to the Prime Minister's criticism of the Orissa government's handling of the drought and its inability to utilise all available funds.[15] The second report was somewhat more sympathetic to the Orissa government's plight and pointed out that, despite promises by the Prime Minister and the central government, Orissa had not received any additional funds to meet the drought crisis.[16] The final report, published on New Year's Eve 1996, reported on how legislators in Orissa cut across party lines to jointly criticise the central government's 'indifference' to helping areas like Kalahandi with additional financial assistance.[17]

In the first two of months of 1997, the focus on drought and starvation in the columns of *The Hindu* dried up. Rather, priority was given to covering the upcoming Panchayat elections in Orissa which were to be organised for the first time in several decades. However, in March 1997, the paper published two reports specifically related to drought and starvation. The first report highlighted the statements by the leaders of Lok Mandal, an organisation of rural workers in

Orissa, which expressed concern over the 'man-made tragedy' resulting from the scarcity of potable and irrigation water in Kalahandi and several other districts of Orissa.[18] The second report, which was based on a visit to Kalahandi by the correspondent, focused on the delay in the allocation of central government funds and the imminent shortage of safe drinking water:

> Kalahandi, black spot of Orissa, which is reeling under acute drought conditions, is eagerly awaiting Central clearance of the third instalment of Rs. 4 crore under the Employment Assurance Scheme (EAS) . . . In November last, the Prime Minister . . . promised an immediate ad hoc assistance of Rs. 50 crore. But the State Government has yet to receive the full amount. In fact, the administration appeared a worried lot, for the situation would worsen if it failed to provide employment opportunities when they were needed most.[19]

In the period April–August 1997, the interest in Kalahandi and the Orissa drought waned and the paper carried only two further articles. One reported on the plans by opposition parties in Orissa to organise a 'hunger week' in April to protest against the failure of the authorities to avert drought and starvation deaths in Orissa.[20] The other article focused attention on Oxfam's allegation that the drought in Kalahandi was 'man-made' and that starvation deaths were the result of 'the exploitation of the tribal population and neglect of traditional irrigation systems' rather than the official complaint of lack of rain.[21] Interestingly, this also appeared to be the first time a newspaper article discussed the challenges related to defining a 'starvation death'. For example, although Oxfam provided figures of severe malnutrition rates in Orissa, the report noted that 'Oxfam representatives were unable to categorically state whether the "starvation deaths" in the State were indeed due to starvation or chronic malnutrition.'

The Indian Express

As early as in October 1996, numerous critical reports on drought and starvation began to appear in the columns of the *Indian Express*. Such reports primarily covered lack of adequate rainfall, extent of crop loss and the ensuing large-scale migration from districts like Kalahandi to neighbouring cities in search of work. In the second week of October, the paper's correspondent based in Kalahandi reported, 'People have been making bee-lines to the nearby inter-State bus stops and railway stations . . . heading for Raipur, Durg, Rajkot and Mumbai'.[22] Two reports in early November 1996 expressed concern over starvation deaths in Kalahandi and the neighbouring district of Bolangir. The first was concerned with government apathy:

> In Orissa these days, starvation deaths and the misery that follows, cause no concern in the administration. In fact, they are promptly attributed to 'mis-

chief' by the Opposition. And like the proverbial ostrich, the officials go back to bury their heads in the sand.[23]

The second report criticised the continuance of deforestation which accentuated the severity of drought in chronically drought-prone regions. Although the administration was aware of this, the report argued that it was doing little to respond to the challenge, and further pointed out that routine administrative tasks were not being undertaken in earnest:

> Orissa has been in the news for starvation deaths in Kalahandi . . . a callous administration is still to wake up to its implications and seems more intent on shirking responsibility rather than tackling it on a war footing . . . The revenue department is yet to fully assess the losses and present a case to the Centre for extra assistance. The public distribution system is in a shambles. There are just no funds for undertaking labour intensive work to prevent mass migration . . . If things are bad now, they will be nightmarish in the months to come.[24]

Reports on out-migration from Kalahandi appeared frequently in the columns of the paper throughout the period and an article in December reported on how the elderly – who had been left behind by their children – waited in vain for the postman to come with money orders from family members who had migrated. After extensive field visits, the reporter found that, instead of the promised 100 days of employment per year under the EAS, villagers were offered work for at the most three days.[25] The report also highlighted widespread corruption in the implementation of the EAS and alleged that elected Panchayat representatives were donning the hat of contractors in several areas of the district.

Although *The Hindu* was most active in covering drought and starvation in November and December 1996, it did not publish many follow-up reports in the first six months of 1997. In contrast, the *Indian Express* was outstanding in its coverage during this period. There was a regular flow of news reports from Kalahandi facilitated by two factors. First, a local edition of the paper was published from the city of Vishakapatnam, which devoted considerable space to news from Orissa. Second, and most importantly, the paper had the advantage of enjoying the services of a local journalist, Uma Shankar Kar, based in Bhawanipatna, the district headquarters of Kalahandi. No other English daily had a similar arrangement. Being a native of Kalahandi – in addition to being a lawyer and a professional journalist – Kar was able to provide informative and insightful reports on nutritional status and drought relief operations in the district. Thanks to the above factors, the *Indian Express* also enjoyed the largest circulation for any daily in Bhawanipatna – approximately 700 copies per day.

The consequences of the 1996 drought were severely felt in the early months of 1997 and Kar filed a large number of reports with detailed information on starvation deaths, out-migration and the problems of implementing anti-poverty programmes in Kalahandi. In one report, for example, he provided a brief glimpse into the daily lives of the drought-affected population:

> When the Assembly was debating whether to probe starvation deaths or not, Bhojanath Das, a Brahmin from Kalahandi's Hatikhoj village . . . was walking from village to village with a torn bag. Unable to feed his family, he had turned to a new avocation – blessing others with flowers and seeking rice. Hit with the deadly drought, no villager was willing to part with even a morsel. Every day, Das walks to other villages with flowers in his bag and rice in mind.[26]

The article went on to provide a ground-level view of the impact of the drought, which appeared to get worse. It particularly highlighted the start of distress sales of children and assets like cattle, utensils and jewellery and the increasing trend of forced migration from the district.

> Clusters of deserted houses, pot-bellied malnourished children, and emaciated old men and women walking with the help of an old 'lathi' [walking stick] – this has been a common scene in most of Kalahandi's villages – the district which was considered the rice bowl of the State till yesterday. The tragedy has just begun. The sun has become more biting, and the land that cracked up first is splitting vigorously.

On the same day, another report in the *Indian Express* documented the problems of labourers in Thuamul Rampur – one of the poorest areas of Kalahandi, where labourers engaged in soil conservation works started by the government had not received their wages for six months. The flurry of reports from Kalahandi continued in April 1997. In one article, the reporter noted that, in addition to large-scale crop loss in most villages, rivers and tanks were absolutely dry and there was an acute shortage of drinking water.[27] People had started digging 6-foot-deep trenches inside the dry tanks in order to extract small quantities of water for themselves and their cattle. The report was particularly critical of the district administration's response noting that few new tube wells had been dug and mobile water tankers had not been pressed into service. It also pointed towards the non-functioning of the District Natural Calamity Committee, which was created as per a directive of the Indian Supreme Court in order to monitor the implementation of welfare schemes at the district level. According to the report, this committee seldom met and so was not able to hold the district authorities accountable for the inadequate response to the crisis. The issue of water shortage was followed up in another article 10 days later with details of areas severely hit by the scarcity.[28] The major problems identified were lack of funds and lack of personnel in Kalahandi's Rural Water Supply and Sanitation Department, the inability to repair defective tube wells and the failure to dig new wells. The article added that the Collector of Kalahandi could not hire water tankers to supply drinking water to rural areas as he was awaiting the release of money from the State Red Cross Fund.

There were several articles on drought, starvation deaths and out-migration in May and June 1997. The reports in July and August described how farmers were coping with the lack of rain water for irrigation and how erratic rainfall in July had dashed their hopes of early germination of seeds. Other reports warned that, given the situation, a good harvest was not on the cards.[29] Some articles also provided details of how certain development programmes were proving to be ineffective. For example, diesel pump sets provided by the district administration for river-lift irrigation in Kalahandi were sold by poor farmers to fellow farmers in neighbouring Madhya Pradesh.[30] Similarly, another report detailed the poor implementation of the Integrated Rural Development Programme's 'group finance scheme' introduced in 1996, under which groups of beneficiaries were given loans to purchase tractors. The scheme was plagued by poor monitoring activities, corrupt bank officials, and the lack of adequate institutional capacity to implement the scheme.[31]

The impact of reports in the English press

The English press was generally active in covering the drought in Orissa, and Kalahandi received its fair share of attention. Newspapers carried numerous reports on the functioning of safety-net-oriented programmes, drought relief operations, occurrences of starvation deaths, centre–state rows over the allocation of drought relief funds, petitions to the judiciary alleging government neglect towards drought-hit areas, etc. In addition to such reports, freelance journalists and social activists occasionally visited Kalahandi and contributed an article or two in a major national daily. Two such individuals are particularly worth mentioning, as their reports further raised national concern and outcry over acute poverty and destitution in Kalahandi. In an article in the *Times of India* in June 1997, Devinder Sharma described state efforts to provide drought relief:

> Faced with the worst drought in the past 30 years, the infamous Kalahandi belt of Orissa . . . is once again in the grip of acute hunger and chronic malnutrition resulting in misery and deprivation of the people . . . ground water – a precious natural resource that can mitigate human suffering to a large extent – remains grossly unexploited . . . Kalahandi is a case study in what mismanagement of water and rampant corruption can do to a resource-rich community . . . I was shocked to see the criminal waste of financial resources in the name of water conservation and dug wells.[32]

In a follow-up article the next day, Sharma questioned the Orissa government's commitment to secure a long-term solution to the problems of Kalahandi and wondered how people could die from starvation despite a surplus in national foodgrain stocks:

> The hunger and misery that stalks Kalahandi is known to everyone. But what remains unknown is that starvation and hunger exists amidst plenty. As the

piteous small and marginal farmers and landless agricultural labourers starve and wait endlessly for the rice they produce on the lands owned by absentee landlords, the harvest finds it way to the procurement centres.[33]

Another freelancer, P. Sainath, was an award-winning journalist, whose series of newspaper articles on poverty and drought from India's poorest districts were eventually compiled into a book with the apt title, *Everybody Loves a Good Drought*. On a visit to Kalahandi, he wrote:

> Drought relief . . . is rural India's biggest growth industry . . . Even when it goes to scarcity areas, those most in need seldom benefit from it. The poor in such regions understand this. That's why some of them call drought relief *teesra fasl* (the third crop). Only, they are not the ones who harvest it . . . we have several districts in India that have an abundance of rainfall – but where one section, the poor, can suffer acute drought. That happens when available water resources are colonised by the powerful. Further, the poor are never consulted or asked to participate in designing the 'programmes' the anti-drought funds bring.[34]

Such reports by freelancers were based on field visits and detailed interviews with drought-affected groups and starving individuals, and provided the nation with some hard-hitting and investigatory stories of what it was like to live in these regions. The reports also provided a welcome breather from the mundane articles appearing in the press which simply repeated official denials of drought-related suffering.

The English newspapers generally covered drought in districts close to Bhubaneswar – that were only a day's travel away – more frequently than districts like Kalahandi. In this sense, the *Indian Express* had a huge advantage over its rivals as it had a local and knowledgeable correspondent in Kalahandi who sent a regular stream of analytical reports from the district. By comparison, the correspondents of the remaining English dailies were based in Bhubaneswar and seldom travelled great distances unless important political leaders (e.g. the Prime Minister, ministers, and leaders of opposition parties) were visiting the area. A VIP visit invariably attracted a large contingent of journalists although some insisted that they tried not to give 'unnecessary publicity to undeserving political leaders'.

Given that travel to remote districts is seldom undertaken and that travel budgets are often modest, journalists tended to base their reports on hearsay information gained from interactions politicians and bureaucrats with whom they socialised during private parties and other social functions. As the correspondent for *The Statesman* observed:

> Many politicians of opposition parties provide us with information . . . sometimes they ask us to accompany them on a field visit. Depending on the merit of the information and newsworthiness we make a decision to travel. We

also evaluate the credibility of the person providing the information. I try not to give publicity to visits by prominent politicians but many others do. The reality is that politicians need us more than we need them.[35]

Politicians were usually accessible and personal rapport with prominent leaders was cultivated by virtually all correspondents of English dailies. The correspondents also maintained regular contact with a section of high-ranking bureaucrats, who were often observed on the sprawling lawns of the Bhubaneswar Club – an elite establishment where the crème de la crème of Oriya society socialised. Such rapport, however, did not come about in a hurry. It was cultivated over a considerable period of time and the reputation and influence of the journalist and his newspaper were crucial. English dailies and their reporters were generally treated with greater respect than the Oriya press. Thus, for example – and over a glass of whisky at the Club – a reporter could extract useful information from a bureaucrat who had recently returned from a tour of Kalahandi. This was then published the following day without independent verification of the facts. In other cases, the reporter simply got hold of a report by UNICEF or an NGO like Oxfam and tried to relate the conclusions to Kalahandi without actually having evidence from the field. Occasionally, a new story appearing in a local Oriya daily was followed up if it was found to be sensational enough.

Journalists generally agreed that the government did not have an institutionalised base and capacity to make use of the information provided in press reports. The correspondent of *The Hindu*, for example, argued the government generally lacked 'benefit-oriented business acumen' in the implementation of welfare programmes.[36] And the Kalahandi-based correspondent of the *Indian Express* noted that although politicians belonging to opposition parties did occasionally provide some useful information, some of this was politically motivated – particularly those involving allegations of corruption levelled against political rivals. He went on to note that there were 'good and bad politicians' and that 'those with important networks and backing within their own parties' were in a position to influence public policy on drought.[37]

The extent to which national dailies were able to hold the authorities to account, however, depended on the credibility of news content and the ability of opposition parties to sustain interest in these issues in newspaper columns and legislative debates. A major problem in this context was the manner in which journalists understood the terms 'famine', 'malnutrition' and 'starvation'. The correspondent of *The Hindu* was candid in his observation:

The issue of starvation deaths has become a question of definitions. How do we convince the authorities that starvation deaths take place? When I visit Kalahandi, I am convinced there is acute poverty and widespread starvation. However, the government's response to my news reports is simply to deny the occurrence of starvation deaths without even investigating them.

The correspondent of *The Indian Express* wanted the use of a nuanced definition of starvation deaths, including elements of malnutrition, chronic undernutrition and disease:

> If one is tied up and left in a room without any food then one eats anything.
> Starvation is not an event but rather the result of a prolonged process of acute
> malnutrition and undernutrition. Then many different diseases can set in.
> Starvation deaths occur simply because government intervention is not good
> enough and does not reach the really needy.

He went on to add that it was crucial to distinguish between factual and false
reporting and alleged that most correspondents of English dailies (based in Bhubaneswar, 'the outsiders') did not understand the real reasons behind Kalahandi's
suffering. Interestingly, a handful of these 'outsiders' were willing to take self-
criticism and agreed that there had indeed been a 'sale of Kalahandi's poverty'
by both politicians and the media. The regular overflow of negative reports from
the district had weakened the credibility and impact of news reports even in the
English-language press. As the correspondent of *The Statesman* put it:

> We are disgusted by the one-sidedness of the coverage equating Kalahandi
> with Ethiopia . . . Everything is politicised to such an extent that credibility
> of the reports have been lost . . . The media needs to focus on constructive
> reports on how natural resources – minerals, horticulture, and cotton produc-
> tion – can be and is being improved. There should be a critical focus on
> how politicians are becoming rich and why government interventions are not
> working. This requires critical investigative reporting.

Despite the above limitations, the English press did perform a crucial role and
was very influential given that the ruling elite actually read these newspapers.
Although most newspapers were unable to provide early warning regularly from
Kalahandi, their reports were largely informative, critical and analytical. The correspondents were professional and received attractive salaries and work-related
benefits. Their greatest asset, however, was the rapport they enjoyed with high-
ranking politicians and bureaucrats in Orissa, which gave them a certain amount
of political and administrative clout. Powerholders actively courted these journalists, cultivating friendly relations in order to ensure that no negative reports on
them or their parties appeared in the columns of these influential newspapers.

The Oriya press

The vernacular Oriya press has traditionally been one of the most backward in
India. With a daily circulation of only 60,000 and with a ratio of three dailies per
thousand people in 1961, it had the lowest circulation rate among the 12 major
Indian-language papers (Jeffrey 1997: 511). Throughout the 1960s and 1970s,

growth of the Oriya press was hampered by high levels of illiteracy in the population, backward printing technology and the lack of proper communications. During the early 1980s, however, a small but important newspaper revolution took
place resulting from an increase in literacy levels, urbanisation and advertisement
revenue and improvements in printing technology, which allowed for attractive
news layouts and the use of coloured photographs. Between 1981 and 1991, daily
circulation increased from seven per thousand people to 22 per thousand; by 1992,
Oriya publications had climbed up four places to being eighth overall among the
12 major languages in India (ibid.). The press continued to grow and in 1996 the
total audited circulation rate of Oriya dailies reached 422,000 copies. *Samaj*, the
oldest daily, established in 1920, leads the group with 130,000 copies, followed
by *Dharitri* (established 1974; 105,000 copies), *Prajatantra* (established 1947;
70,000 copies), and *Sambad* (established 1984; 65,000 copies).[38]

Newspapers in Orissa are not unlike their counterparts in other states in their
organisational structure. Depending on the size and importance of the district,
a paper employs one or two stringers who are primarily middle-class or lower
middle-class local residents based in district headquarters (small towns), and not
trained in journalism. They seldom receive fixed monthly salaries but are paid
on the basis of 'space rates' – depending on every column centimetre published
(Jeffrey 2000: 143) – and a percentage (usually between 10 and 15 per cent) of
the local advertisement revenue they are able to generate for their papers. In
some rare cases, a small retainer fee of a few hundred rupees may be applicable
although the amount is considerably higher in the politically important coastal
districts of Orissa (e.g. Puri). Since they are not organised into unions – and rarely
have contact with each other – stringers are unable to demand better benefits
from their employers. By comparison, salaried employees, including reporters
and editorial staff of various ranks based in large cities, enjoy pension benefits
and are occasionally also covered by health schemes. Since Oriya papers do not
boast large circulation rates, they are not great profit-making ventures and, an
editor observed, 'since advertisement revenue in Orissa is very small, there is not
much profit going around which can be used to improve the working conditions
of journalists'.[39]

The Oriya press is, however, quite unique in India since virtually every newspaper in the state has been owned and/or managed by a politician, including
former Chief Ministers, current cabinet ministers, past and present members of
the Orissa legislature and close relatives of prominent politicians.[40] As Jeffrey
(1997: 512) observes, this is 'a record unrivalled elsewhere in India'. Historically,
newspaper evolution was characterised by personal rivalry among competing
politicians. Until the 1980s, politicians used newspapers to bolster their influence
and some papers 'were run at a loss because their proprietors valued the prestige
and leverage within the tiny elite that dominated Orissa politics from the 1930s'
(ibid.). Since Orissa was economically underdeveloped, with low levels of literacy
and urbanisation (it lacked a major national city), no national chain bothered to
start publishing in the state until the late 1990s. Further, the primitive printing

technology – there was no mechanical composition of the Oriya type until the 1970s – used by the Oriya media proved to be an advantage for politicians who wanted to control what people read. Jeffrey (ibid.: 512–513) writes of how a single edition 'travelled in a leisurely way throughout the state, arriving in some places five days or a week after it left the pressroom'. There were seldom any original articles and news reports were generally taken directly from Calcutta-based dailies, radio broadcasts and circulars issued by the Orissa government's press office. This meant that 'Editorials could be the indulgence of the owners' (ibid.). From 1955, the central government clamped down on the free import of newsprint, and publishing houses had to apply for a quota every year based on their circulation rates. Many non-serious actors began to trade their quotas in the black market and earn a profit. For their financial survival, newspapers also became increasingly dependent on government advertisements as revenue from private sources was nominal until the 1970s. Newspapers owned by politicians were virtually guaranteed advertising revenue as successive ruling parties in Orissa were of the view that, 'even if one's foes were in power, they had to calculate whether it was less trouble to feed a moderately hostile paper with government advertising rather than provoke it by cutting off the flow' (ibid.).

The Kalahandi press[41]

In 1996–2000 Kalahandi did not have daily newspapers although several weeklies, fortnightlies and monthlies were published from Bhawanipatna. They relied on outdated offset printing technology and were published irregularly given their weak financial base. The district's readership base was miniscule given high levels of illiteracy, and each of the three largest weeklies sold between 1,000 and 4,000 copies. Although Kalahandi had a total of eight registered newspapers/periodicals, only five were active in the period under study. Given the infrequent publication of these papers and the lack of proper archives, it was not possible to undertake a detailed survey of the content and nature of news coverage on drought and starvation. However, interviews with editor, owners and stringers provided some useful information on how the local press in Kalahandi functioned. A loose network of stringers, located in various parts of the district, constituted the backbone of the local press. Without any professional training, local traders, teachers or unemployed youths sent in reports on an irregular basis. They were normally not paid a fixed salary but, since they also functioned as local distributors and agents for their respective papers, they were able to earn a commission depending on the number of copies they sold and the amount of advertisement revenue they generated. With almost no resources at their disposal, stringers were seldom able to visit the areas of the district where poverty and deprivation was most acute. As a result, reports were largely based on guesswork and hearsay information gathered from contact with visiting district officials.

Dibdibi – established in 1978 and with an audited circulation rate of 2,000 copies in 2001 – was the most influential newspaper. Its coverage of drought was generally critical and the editor claimed that his paper, in close cooperation with the Kalahandi MP, played a crucial role in highlighting starvation deaths in 1985–86. Such reports subsequently triggered interest on the issue among the larger newspapers, and since then *Dibdibi* has continued to provide information and assistance to visiting journalists from regional and national dailies. A recurrent theme in the paper's new coverage was the high level of unemployment in the Kalahandi, a problem that is further accentuated in drought years. The editor accused the Orissa government of callous disregard of the district and complained that there was a lack of transparency in the workings of the district administration. Despite financial difficulties, infrequent publication and low circulation rates, the general impression was that *Dibdibi* occasionally provided the administration with useful information from rural areas of the district.

Among the remaining publications of note, *Masiha*, which was started in 1994 by a member of the Congress party, sold a little over 2,000 copies every week. It shared the same fate as other local publications in terms of an unstable financial base which resulted in infrequent publication. Given its political leaning, it was not surprising that the paper was regularly published in the period immediately preceding local elections. As *Masiha* was generally not critical of the administration, rival newspapers accused it of functioning as the mouthpiece of the ruling Congress government in Bhubaneswar. The paper did, however, publish critical stories on drought relief in 2000–01, when the Congress formed the opposition in Orissa. Another Congress-friendly weekly was *Arji*, started in 1999 by a former minister and activist, which had a circulation rate of 2,000 copies. Like *Masiha*, it too appeared to be critical of the district authorities only when the Congress was no longer the ruling party in Orissa. The editor, however, claimed that his paper was truly independent although several stringers alleged that only those with Congress party leanings were employed by the paper.

In general, the capacity of the Kalahandi press to provide credible information on a regular basis was weak for three main reasons. First, stringers had neither the financial incentive nor the qualifications to submit analytical reports. Second, even when they occasionally did have reliable first-hand information on impending local problems, they were unable to communicate this quickly to their editors without access to telecommunications. Third, Kalahandi weeklies were not published regularly, and so there was no guarantee that reports filed by stringers would actually appear in time to warn local authorities. These features also had an impact on the ability of the press to perform an adversarial function vis-à-vis the district administration. In addition to the poor quality of news reports published, the political connections of most editors and proprietors resulted in allegations of bias and officials dismissed critical reports as being politically motivated. Given their low circulation rates, Kalahandi papers were unable to attract lucrative advertisements from the private sector and were hence excessively dependent on whatever little was offered by the district government. And most local officials and political leaders subscribed to regional Oriya dailies for information, thus severely limiting the capacity and influence of the local press in Kalahandi to perform early warning and accountability functions in times of drought and food crises.

The regional Oriya press

The major Oriya dailies with a strong presence in Kalahandi were *Dharitri*, *Prajatantra*, *Samaj*, *Samay* and *Sambad*, although it was difficult to establish the exact circulation rates of these dailies in the district. They appeared to each sell between 200 and 600 copies every day, with *Dharitri* being the most widely read paper. Newspaper distribution was handled by agents who, in addition to subscription fees and delivery charges, received around 30 per cent commission on copies sold. Stringers working for these major dailies were generally not paid regular salaries although *Dharitri* paid a monthly retainer of Rs 1,500. With very little income from local advertisements, they ran small businesses or worked part-time for voluntary organisations. Some stringers even worked freelance for two or more rival publications and, like their counterparts in the Kalahandi press, they had virtually no travel allowances. Despite these limitations, and given the high rates of unemployment in Kalahandi, the job was considered prestigious and most stringers were viewed as wielding considerable influence in local society. Possession of a press card was particularly useful for networking, not least in terms of interacting with politicians and senior district officials including the Collector and the police chief. These actors were in turn aware of the advantages of being accessible and, by providing small favours to stringers, were largely able to ensure that they and their activities received positive coverage.

During the 1996–97 drought in Orissa, all four major regional newspapers studied – *Sambad*, *Samaj*, *Dharitri* and *Prajatantra* – were active in covering cases of starvation and the implementation of drought relief.[42] For example, in the period before the expected start of the monsoon in 1996 and 1997, the dailies regularly published articles related to scarcity of rainfall, lack of drinking water for humans and cattle, extent of agricultural loss and forced migration. The frequency of such reports was highest in June and July, when the rains typically failed and when agricultural operations could not be started in time. The usual format of such reports, gathered from official sources, were 'x number of villages in y areas of z district were affected by drought and there is shortage of safe drinking water'. Occasionally, some reports provided some early warning information to the authorities with the format: 'because of x per cent deficit of normal rainfall, severe drought is expected in y district' or 'because of infrequent rains and uneven distribution of rainwater in x district, locals fear that their suffering will be heightened by the onset of a severe drought'. The lack of available drinking water for humans and cattle was highlighted by referring to dry village ponds and tanks and non-functioning tube wells which were either depleted of water or in need of repair. For example, *Prajatantra* reported in the third week of September 1996 that scarcity of drinking water was increasing the spread of water-borne diseases and that a large-scale epidemic appeared imminent. Another report, in December

1996, reported crop loss in excess of 75 per cent in Dharamgarh sub-division, the traditional granary of Kalahandi.

Another set of reports in the four dailies focused on forced migration and the distress sale of assets like cattle, jewellery and cooking utensils by the victims of drought. Such reports, in which Kalahandi featured prominently, generally referred to 'thousands' and occasionally 'hundreds of thousands' of unemployed individuals and their families migrating to areas in neighbouring states in search of work. When the rains failed to arrive in full force by July 1996, stringers from the districts bombarded their newspapers with reports of how drought had already set in even though an official declaration of the district being 'drought-affected' was not forthcoming. Typical reports provided general information on the amount of land (hectares) and crops (mainly paddy and vegetables) affected by drought, the inaccuracies of official estimates of crop loss and the amount of funds sanctioned for relief. A large majority of the reports contained statements by ministers and civil servants, and only rarely was there an attempt to document whether official claims were accurate. Moreover, the visits of VIP politicians, including the Prime Minister and the Union Minister of Agriculture, were given prominent coverage followed by their promises of emergency assistance.

Dharitri, *Samaj* and *Prajatantra* frequently reported on the views of opposition parties and their recommendations to the government on how to manage the drought. Such reports were critical of the government's neglect of Kalahandi and were primarily based on proceedings in the Orissa Legislative Assembly in the period September–December 1996. For example, a topic which received considerable attention in the columns of *Dharitri* in November 1996 was the resolution in the Assembly according to which opposition parties wanted the state government to pressure the central government into declaring Orissa as 'affected by a serious natural calamity'. Similar stories appeared with great frequency in *Prajatantra* in the period November 1996–December 1996. While some of these related to criticism of the government's handling of the drought and the Chief Minister's 'unnecessary foreign trips' during a major crisis, others covered the demand by MPs in New Delhi for a review of social security schemes and drought relief practices in Kalahandi. The paper also repeatedly attacked the central government's 'stepmotherly attitude' towards Orissa in relation to the non-availability of urgently needed calamity relief funds. *Samaj* was critical of the government's efforts to provide drought relief, particularly highlighting the meagre funds allocated for the repair of tube wells and the construction of lift irrigation points. It further demanded a reduction of water taxes and the suspension of land revenue in drought-hit areas.

When the consequences of drought worsened towards the first half of 1997, Oriya dailies began reporting actively on people's reactions, protests and demonstrations. *Dharitri* and *Prajatantra* published a series of reports from all over Orissa on local protests organised by farmers, opposition parties, interest groups (especially farmers organisations) and local voluntary organisations, demanding the immediate launch of relief operations in areas that had not been formally classified as 'drought-hit'. Such protests included blockades of roads and railways, strikes, disruption of public services, and *gherao*[43] of high-ranking district officials.

Despite coverage on a wide range of drought-related issues, the most sensational reports dealt with starvation. *Sambad* – given its close affiliation with the ruling Congress party – seldom mentioned the issue and, on the few occasions it did, it merely reported that opposition-party politicians were claiming starvation deaths without adequate evidence. In contrast, a flurry of reports on starvation deaths appeared in the remaining three papers. For example, in the period April–December 1996, *Prajatantra* alone reported 496 starvation deaths in Orissa. Of these Kalahandi's share was 301, having mainly taken place between the third week of September and the first week of October 1996.[44] Further, the paper reported over 100 deaths in Koraput and 52 in Bolangir. Similar reports on starvation deaths in the range of 1–15 also emerged from nine other districts in Orissa. The three papers also provided good coverage of the visit by the central government's minister of agriculture to Kalahandi in November 1996 and the ensuing investigations undertaken by the NHRC, which confirmed several starvation deaths. These events provided the press with considerable ammunition for use against the Orissa government during the first three months of 1997.

The impact of the Oriya press: some general conclusions

Once the drought had set in and its impact was assessed by the newspapers to be severe, a larger number of human-interest stories were published in the Oriya press focusing on lack of food and drinking water, the poor state of health services and the ineffectiveness of social security schemes (e.g. old age pensions) and safety-net programmes (e.g. PDS). The nature and extent of critical reporting, however, varied considerably. Among the dailies, *Sambad* was very pro-government in its reporting. This was not surprising as it was owned and edited by a Congress politician who also happened to be the son-in-law of the Chief Minister of Orissa. Indeed, it appeared to function as the government's mouthpiece. In contrast, a paper like *Samaj* – which was run by a philanthropic trust – was largely impartial and balanced in its reporting. *Samaj's* coverage of Kalahandi was, however, poor and perhaps related to the relative inactivity of its stringers in Bhawanipatna, who were frequently hired and fired. *Dharitri* published the largest number of reports on drought and starvation. With a competent reporter (based in Kalahandi), its reports provided considerable early warning information focusing especially on indicators like shortage of drinking water, forced migration, distress sale of assets and the exploitation of tribal groups by greedy moneylenders. It also reported widely on people's protests and its editorial columns on drought were numerous and highly critical of the government's 'indifference' and 'callousness'. *Prajatantra* not only prioritised drought-related stories but was also one of the few papers to cover starvation regularly. In its editorials, the paper was scathing in its criticism of the inability of the Kalahandi district administration to prevent starvation deaths despite being provided with regular reports on the worsening nutritional status of vulnerable groups. News editors of *Dharitri* and *Sambad* claimed that, despite their general inability to carry investigative reports on a regular basis, they prioritised human-interest stories.[45] The editor of *Samay* candidly admitted that his paper tried to air public grievances even though this was not undertaken on a regular basis.[46] Others questioned the very purpose of early warning information since it did not appear to influence government action. Thus the owner of *Prajatantra* claimed that Oriya newspapers 'lacked teeth' and that 'the press generally fails to extract accountability'.[47]

Indeed, the ability of Oriya newspapers to provide early warning and thereafter extract political accountability was severely limited by a set of interrelated factors which, taken together, compromised the credibility of news reports. For example, a large number of reports simply cited the views of government officials without proper verification. In other instances opposition leaders coaxed their contacts in the press to focus on particularly sensational stories despite the lack of credible evidence. Thus, most reports appeared biased and one-sided. This was intrinsically linked to the poor working conditions and lack of proper training of stringers working in districts like Kalahandi. With little or no money at their disposal for travel and in the absence of telecommunications, it was difficult for stringers to highlight rural problems. Several members of the Kalahandi Journalists Association complained of periodic disruption of telephone services and the delays and increased expenses incurred when courier services were used to deliver reports to Bhubaneswar and Cuttack.

Another difficulty was the frequent and arbitrary use of 'starvation' by reporters to allude to a wide range of phenomenon, including sustained undernutrition and the effects of diseases like diarrhoea and malaria. Being on the perennial lookout for sensational stories, they found it difficult to resist the temptation of branding a case to be starvation-related even when evidence pointed towards other causes. Thus, although the use of 'famine' and 'starvation death' guaranteed a front-page article, it simultaneously undermined the credibility of these reports which were quickly dismissed by the authorities as being 'baseless', 'totally false' and 'politically motivated'. Fischer (1994: 25) suggests that the greater the emphasis on 'soft' versus 'hard' news, the greater the likelihood that myths will appear in the story. While several editors emphasised their preference for human-interest stories (or soft news), the confusion over definitions in the Oriya press also contributed to the popularisation of myths on tribal rituals and practices and inflation of the actual number of people dying from starvation. Moreover, depending on the 'interview incidence' of a news story, victims of starvation, and relatives of those who had died, sometimes exaggerated and misinterpreted the actual causes of the problem and related events. In other cases such statements were misinterpreted on purpose by journalists to add a sensationalist twist to a story. There was also a general trend to jump on a story after it had been reported in a rival publication. In this way, most reporters covered an event that had already taken place and stringers could not reach the site until well after the event.

In a study on the political economy of government responsiveness in India, Besley and Burgess (2002) conclude that both circulation rates and the credibility of news reports are greatly reduced when political parties or the government control the media.[48] Indeed, the general trend in Orissa was that opposition-controlled dailies reported starvation deaths in Kalahandi and the ruling-party-controlled dailies either avoided the issue completely or blamed such reports as being politically motivated. Thus the Oriya press was not perceived by the ruling party or the civil service as being 'neutral'. The editor of *Samay* admitted that, although 80 per cent of news coverage was independent of political control, 15–20 per cent of news items in the period leading up to elections focused positive attention on the paper's owner and his election campaign. Most editors and owners, however, did not view their political ties as being a particular problem. The Lok Sabha MP and editor of *Dharitri*, for example, claimed that he was comfortable 'wearing two hats' as his political position was 'at best a temporary one while the editorship was more permanent'.[49]

7

THE POLITICS OF STARVATION
AND CALAMITY RELIEF

One of the most important functions of political parties in a democracy is the aggregation and articulation of the interests of their supporters. The issue of starvation deaths in India is highly politicised, and has become a potent political weapon that parties and their representatives use against each other. In theory, politicians – especially those in opposition – have opportunities both to provide useful information to the authorities in terms of difficulties facing their constituents and then to hold the ruling party accountable for failing to adequately respond to such problems. A general issue of interest in this chapter concerns how elected representatives (political leaders and Panchayats) understand the concept of starvation together with its causes, and how they represent the interests of their constituents. Similarly, it is important to examine India's federalism and the recurrent centre–state disputes over drought and calamity relief. In this political blame game, state governments tend to claim that the centre ignores states governed by opposition parties, while the centre argues that states make unrealistic claims and do not utilise already available funds properly. How does this affect public action in preventing starvation?

Politics in Orissa since the 1950s has been dominated by an upper middle-class elite. As a result, in large parts of rural Orissa, people hold the view that the 'son of the king can rule', and even today one finds tremendous political support for former princes and Zamindars. This has meant that, in order to be elected to office, politicians feel the need to underline their identity as belonging to the traditional ruling elite, in addition to publicly displaying their wealth and power – giving the impression that they are capable of redistributing scarce resources among loyal supporters. Political parties, therefore, continue to nominate candidates from an elite group of well-known families for elective positions, although in recent years an increasing number of SC and ST politicians have successfully contested the elections and become influential within their own parties. Despite widespread deprivation in districts like Kalahandi, the formal trappings of democracy are in place in Orissa, with political parties contesting regularly to gain power. Left-wing parties have generally not been successful in Orissa, and consequently the large number of SC and ST groups in the state have not been politically mobilised

(Harriss 2000: 14). Related to this, Mitra (1992: 50) observes that, instead of 'class differentiation or political mobilisation from below', the main characteristic feature of Orissa politics has been 'occasional collaboration, alternating with confrontation, between leaders of the Western Hill districts and the Eastern Coastal districts'.

Historically, the dominant Congress party regularly shared power with smaller (often regional) parties in Orissa, and in doing so it managed to prevent others from encroaching on its power base (Mohanty and Mishra 1976: 240, cited in Mitra 1992: 50). However, and increasingly since the 1980s, the electoral landscape in the state has witnessed a challenge on Congress party dominance, with stiff competition provided by its major rival, the Janata Dal. As a result, government formation in Orissa has alternated between these two parties, with voters regularly adopting an anti-incumbency stance. The growth of both parties also largely evolved around the cult status and personalities of its leaders – the poet, novelist and journalist J. B. Patnaik of the Congress and the fighter pilot hero Biju Patnaik of the Janata Dal. Indeed, citing the influence of individual personalities and intra-elite competition operating from the same social base in Orissa, Harriss (2000) argues that it is unlikely that a change of political regime is of much significance for policy formulation or its implementation. Similarly, Mohanty (1990, quoted in Harriss 2000: 14) argues that the Congress and the Janata Dal have managed to monopolise the 'competitive arena' and keep 'alternative popular forces from acquiring political significance'. Thus, despite regular shifts of power after elections, there has generally been little change in policy formulation and implementation in terms of tackling drought and combating starvation in Orissa. For example, J. B. Patnaik's Congress government was voted out of office in 1990 amid allegations of child sale, government neglect and starvation deaths in Kalahandi and adjoining districts. The new Janata Dal government formed by Biju Patnaik did not initiate radical changes in its drought policy and mainly attempted to blame the previous government for its failures (Currie 2000). The Congress returned to power in 1995, and in the period under study (1996–2000) it controlled 80 of 147 seats in the Orissa Assembly. The Janata Dal spilt in 1997 following the death of its leader Biju Patnaik, and a faction led by his son, Naveen Patnaik, formed the Biju Janata Dal (BJD) in 1997, which became the main opposition party with 46 seats followed by the BJP with nine seats in the Assembly.

The ruling party

Under the leadership of J. B. Patnaik, the Congress party held power in Orissa throughout the 1980s and the second half of the 1990s. Following the diktat of the central party leadership in New Delhi, Patnaik was replaced as party leader (and hence had to relinquish the office of Chief Minister to a party colleague) in 1989 and 1998. This followed political scandals and the prospect of immediate defeat at the polls, which further institutionalised factionalism within the party. The bitter feuds between rival factions was glaringly evident in the late 1990s when the

Chief Minister, although the dominant personality in the party, had to contend with two other rivals. The bitter rivalry between the Chief Minister and his deputy was particularly well known in administrative circles, with hardly any contact between the two, each holding his own fort surrounded by loyal civil servants. A third faction, led by the President of the Orissa Congress party, was in opposition to both the Chief Minister and the Deputy Chief Minister, and frequently lobbied the Congress leadership in Delhi to remove the sitting Chief Minister from office. Although disunity within the ruling party affected daily matters of governance and had a negative impact on the party's electoral prospects in 2000, it did produce some useful internal criticism of government functioning. This was particularly apparent on the issue of starvation deaths and the government's handling of both long-term development and immediate crises in districts like Kalahandi.

Chief Minister J. B. Patnaik, whose government was earlier indicted on starvation deaths in Supreme Court and High Court investigations and rulings in 1989 and 1992, vehemently denied that starvation deaths had occurred on his watch:

> All reports of starvation deaths are exaggerated and meant to discredit my government . . . This is not in the interest of the people of Kalahandi. They should speak out and tell journalists to publish the truth. Journalists must base their reports on facts, not on myths . . . The positive aspects of development in Kalahandi are not highlighted . . . isolated instances of people dying of disease cannot be ruled out, but no one dies from starvation. I am sure of this and therefore have nothing to be ashamed of. I can guarantee that no starvation deaths have taken place during my tenure as CM.[1]

In particular, the Chief Minister lamented that the media largely ignored his efforts to improve irrigation, health services, infrastructure, literacy and schemes to reduce unemployment. Criticising the credibility of critical news reports originating from Kalahandi, he complained that the press used the Kalahandi story to discredit his government at the slightest opportunity. For example, he claimed that as soon as drought was declared the press assumed that his government was not in a position to tackle the problem:

> Just because there is a severe drought does not mean that things will be bad. Most opposition parties and journalists play a guessing game and wait for the government to make a mistake. And even when we do not make mistakes, we are at the receiving end. So the only way to tackle the situation is to ignore these baseless allegations.

The President of the Orissa Congress insisted that the problems of tribal groups in Kalahandi were real and serious and deeply rooted in the district's historical background as a princely state during which the seeds of inequality were sown.[2] Being a tribal leader, and heading a rival faction in the party, he was more willing than the Chief Minister to admit to lapses in the implementation of anti-poverty programmes in tribal regions. Nonetheless, he ruled out starvation deaths in Orissa, arguing that journalists did not really understand problems of starvation and migration and revelled at hurling accusations of government failure without being aware of the facts.

A cabinet minister – elected to the Orissa Legislative Assembly from Kalahandi – neither confirmed nor dismissed the allegations of starvation deaths from his native district. Rather, he preferred to highlight attempts by the Gandhi family – especially the former Prime Ministers Indira and Rajiv Gandhi – to address poverty and drought in the region. In contrast to party colleagues, a very vocal and influential Congress MLA – who was Chief Minister of Orissa in the 1970s – had no problems accepting that recurrent conditions of extreme distress in Kalahandi could well lead to starvation deaths. Blaming the rulers of princely states for the 'historical impoverishment of the locals, especially the tribals', she criticised current development efforts and the failure of politicians to check the activities of incompetent district officials:

> The bureaucracy is a machine, and politicians must utilise this machinery in a proper manner. It is important for the politician to hold the steering wheel and move the bureaucracy in the right direction. During my stint as Chief Minister, I would pay 'surprise visits' to the districts without informing the Collectors, thus making the bureaucracy 'afraid' of me.[3]

Successive ruling parties in Orissa have long practiced the appointment of preferred civil servants to important posts in the administration, irrespective of merit. The strategy is particularly important at the district level as the party feels it must have 'loyal' bureaucrats in place in 'sensitive' districts and posts, rather than someone owing allegiance to the opposition. The Chief Minister supported this practice, arguing that it was important for early warning and response to crises. Two former Chief Ministers complained that, with frequent shifts in power in Orissa, programmes initiated by the previous government were invariably discontinued. There was often the pressure to initiate a package of reforms entailing something 'new and exciting', and continuing with old programmes did not add a feather in the cap of a new Chief Minister and his cabinet. Hence there was a preference for ambitious and expensive projects even when the possibility of these being implemented successfully were understood to be slim. The Congress president also added that government programmes were failing in Kalahandi with the increase of 'decentralised' administrative corruption.

Along with civil servants, NGOs were at the receiving end of the blame game with ruling party leaders accusing voluntary organisations of being run by 'frauds', whose main intention was to project a negative image of districts like Kalahandi in order to attract funding from foreign donors. This money, it was alleged, was 'seldom spent for the upliftment of the poor', and there was no one to hold the organisations to account for the misuse of development funds. A senior leader went as far as to claim that she had requested the Chief Minister to bring all development NGOs under state control. Others claimed that a large majority of the NGOs did not possess relevant knowledge or expertise to carry out their functions and were, in addition, poorly informed of local conditions. For example, a local Congress leader in Kalahandi claimed that NGOs would often start the construction of buildings and the digging of wells only to abandon such projects midway. Most Congress politicians also believed that the bitter rivalry and competition among the large number of NGOs working in Orissa also meant that organisations seldom cooperated with each other, thus preventing large groups of people from access to their services. Thus, the overall impact of NGOs in developing districts like Kalahandi was considered to be miniscule.

The opposition

In the 1995 Orissa Assembly elections, Chief Minister Biju Patnaik and his Janata Dal party lost the elections having managed to win only 46 of the 147 seats. With increased factionalism within the party following the death of Biju Patnaik, a majority of legislators formed a separate party in 1997 – the Biju Janata Dal (BJD) – under the leadership of Patnaik's son, Naveen Patnaik. The other main opposition party in 1996–2000 was the Bharatiya Janata Party (BJP) with nine seats in the Assembly. The Left parties – CPI and CPI(M) – have never been strong in Orissa; although the former managed to win one seat in the Orissa Assembly in 1995, the latter remained unrepresented. From Kalahandi's quota of six Assembly seats, five were held by opposition parties and one by a Congress MLA who also was the Orissa government's minister of information.

Despite factionalism within – and disunity among – opposition parties, the issue of starvation deaths functioned as a useful tool to unite rival parties in their quest to discredit the Congress and demand the dismissal of the government. Indeed, although the existence of poverty was tolerated, starvation deaths were understood to symbolise the worst form of government failure in a democracy, and opposition parties made use of several strategies to create pressure on the ruling party. These included state-wide rallies, strikes and blockades of government services (e.g. squatting on the railway tracks and disrupting train services). In addition, on the floor of the Assembly, opposition leaders repeatedly demanded that the government convene all-party meetings to discuss drought relief measures, and strongly criticised the Congress for callousness in not providing emergency relief and for underutilising relief funds allocated from Delhi. The main opposition party until 1997, the Janata Dal, was particularly active. In one instance, seven legislators from the party presented a memorandum to the Governor of Orissa in October 1996, requesting him to pressure the Congress government into declaring Kalahandi and three other districts as 'famine-affected' and to sanction additional funds for immediate relief measures. In another instance, chaos erupted in the Assembly in November 1996 when the leader of the opposition demanded a special Assembly session on the drought and argued for the setting up of a special committee to monitor relief and to check corruption. Congress MLAs did not agree to this proposal, resulting in numerous disruptions in Assembly proceedings which lasted for several days. These disruptions, however, led to widespread local and national media attention on drought and starvation in Kalahandi.

Following the split of the Janata Dal in 1997, the BJD took over the responsibility of the main opposition party. When the Congress fared very poorly in the national parliamentary elections in 1998 – winning just five of 21 seats to the Lok Sabha from Orissa – the BJD launched a major campaign demanding the resignation of the Chief Minister for failing to respond to the needs of the poor. And the BJD president wrote to the Prime Minister in September 1998 alleging that the Orissa government failed to react amidst reports of 29 starvation deaths and mass out-migration from the state. In an interview in December 1998, the BJD President, who was also a cabinet minister in New Delhi, observed:

> The Congress has ruled Orissa for so many decades and yet reports of starvation deaths continue. What have they done for all these years? They have no excuses . . . their strategy has always been to ignore such problems, dismiss them as not being true and then sit back and let this happen all over again whenever there is a drought. There is absolutely no long-term strategy to fight drought and starvation deaths.[4]

Mentioning that he had repeatedly raised the issue of drought relief in Parliament, he claimed to have succeeded in pressing the central government into finally allocating to Orissa calamity relief funds earmarked for Kalahandi and other drought-hit districts.

Although the political scene in Orissa in the late 1990s was largely dominated by the Congress and the BJD, the BJP was making slow but steady progress in the popularity charts. In October–November 1996, the BJP's central leadership sent a team to investigate drought-related distress in Kalahandi. The team subsequently concluded that 180 starvation deaths had taken place in Orissa within a span of two months. It also claimed that the PDS had failed to provide the poor with access to subsidised rice and that the collapse of irrigation facilities had resulted in a drastic increase in unemployment. Following this report, the BJP unit in Orissa – which had thus far been relatively inactive – began to vocally criticise the government for administrative lapses and warned that food riots were imminent unless urgent remedial action were taken. In August 1998, two MPs from the party – representing Kalahandi and Bolangir districts – jointly wrote to the Chief Minister demanding that their districts be declared 'famine affected' and that relief measures be implemented on a 'war footing'. In an interview in early 1999, the Kalahandi MP argued that people in democratic societies could not be allowed to die from starvation and that the 'lack of proper nourishment' in Kalahandi could be solved if the Orissa government demonstrated adequate commitment to improve nutritional interventions.[5]

Other smaller opposition parties began to increasingly follow the lead provided by BJD and the BJP. Although it did not have a single seat in the Orissa Assembly, the CPI(M) party was nonetheless very active in the public discourse, its tactics revolving primarily around protest rallies and disruptions of public services. It attracted widespread attention in September 1998 when it accused the Congress of violating its own election manifesto from 1995, according to which the ruling party had declared that it would guarantee freedom from hunger if voted to power. Following this, the CPI(M) launched a civil disobedience movement involving 40,000 party workers in various parts of Orissa in protest against the unprecedented rise in prices of essential commodities like rice, wheat and sugar. The state secretary of the party claimed that, given high levels of malnutrition, starvation deaths in Orissa should not come as a surprise to those in power.[6] He went on to argue further that the criteria employed to assess starvation deaths varied enormously in political circles. Whereas ruling party politicians tended to adopt a very narrow definition of starvation implying a total absence of food for several consecutive days, the CPI(M) leader argued for a wider definition, according to which 'continued hunger, the eating of harmful items together with the total absence of proper healthcare leads to death'. He also believed that, instead of simply raising the issue of starvation deaths, a far more effective strategy for opposition parties would be to start holding the government responsible for its failure to improve health services and for the general neglect of development in districts like Kalahandi.

As the impact of drought continued to claim lives, opposition parties in Orissa realised the benefits of increased collaboration. Starting in April 1997, a united opposition decided to observe a 'hunger week', during which protest rallies were held in all severely drought-hit districts. On the Assembly floor, the opposition also flexed its muscles, demanding special debates on drought and accusing the state government of failing to prevent starvation deaths and neglecting the development of Kalahandi. Opposition legislators alleged that funds sanctioned by the central government for anti-poverty programmes in Kalahandi remained underutilised and demanded an investigation by the Central Bureau of Intelligence on the increase in administrative corruption. Claiming that the PDS was not supplying regular stocks of rice to many drought-hit districts, the opposition further claimed that the Orissa government was 'forcing people into starvation'. A team of legislators from the BJD, BJP and JD parties also visited drought-hit Kalahandi, Bolangir and Koraput districts in September 1998 and concluded that despite the 'grave' situation, the administration was yet to start measures to manage the drought. They further alleged that, although a thousand people in these three districts had been diagnosed with 'malnutrition-related diseases,' the Orissa government remained unperturbed.[7] Such orchestrated activity in July–September 1998 was increasingly covered in the press and on a few occasions even ruling party legislators joined hands with the opposition in criticising their leaders for their failure to address drought-related distress.

Almost all opposition leaders claimed that they regularly tried to warn the appropriate political and administrative authorities on both factual and anticipated problems related to poverty and drought. Evidence from Kalahandi, however, showed that, although politicians indeed were in contact with district officials, they seldom provided any concrete early warning information to the government. Neither ruling nor opposition parties were well organised at the district and block levels. And, except for the CPI(M), there were no cadre-based political parties in Orissa; this limited the ability of most parties to receive feedback from party workers at the village and block levels. Even the cadre-based CPI(M) was unable to maintain a large local presence in Kalahandi given the lack of resources and low voter mobilisation. Moreover, there was little formal contact between opposition parties and the government in Bhubaneswar except when the Assembly was in session. Occasionally –when it suited the ruling party – 'all-party meetings' were convened to discuss drought relief, although the opposition complained that these interactions invariably took place in the final stages of a crisis, thus defeating the very purpose of such interaction.

Whereas the ruling party had little positive to say about the print media, opposition parties presented a more balanced view, praising certain sections of the media for courageous and investigative reporting and chastising others for being 'mouthpieces of the Congress'. For example, a former MP from Kalahandi argued that it was pointless to simply criticise journalists without taking into account their poor working conditions. He believed therefore that press influence in Orissa would increase when journalists were better trained ('they are often unable to present facts properly'), given adequate travel allowances and paid decent salaries.[8] Leaders in Bhubaneswar were generally more critical of the role of the press than their Kalahandi counterparts. For example, while his colleagues in Kalahandi were generally positive of press coverage, the state secretary of the Orissa CPI(M) was scathing in his criticism of the Oriya press, characterising it as 'pathetic' and 'perhaps the worst in India':

> All current newspapers glorify the political profile of their owners, editors and financial backers. Since the general political consciousness of the poor in Orissa is low, such newspapers continue to sell copies and brainwash the public. We have very little funds to counter the propaganda of the big parties, which have unlimited resources.[9]

Some criticism was also reserved for district officials in Kalahandi who were accused of lacking genuine concern for the poor ('no missionary zeal') and of not having the courage to speak up against ruling-party misdeeds. As one leader argued:

> The Orissa Relief Code is admittedly not clear on starvation deaths but this does not explain why bureaucrats in comfortable positions do not understand what starvation really is. Only the poor know how it is to go hungry for days on end. The government needs to do everything. It should not come up with excuses.[10]

Another local leader accused the district administration of a 'feudalistic mindset', in which 'officials were the rulers and the poor their subjects' and a select elite consisting of businessmen, officials and ruling-party politicians decided public policy without any input from the poor.[11] Administrative corruption was another issue that was frequently mentioned, and opposition leaders accused high-level officials of 'minting money' during their tenures in the districts. A part of the blame for increased corruption was also reserved for ruling-party politicians, who were accused of siphoning off large amounts of money allocated in the name of development. Indeed, it was fairly common in political circles to refer to drought relief as the most important source of corruption and black money.

Finally, opposition parties shared the ruling party's scepticism of NGOs, especially those working in drought-prone and poor districts like Kalahandi. Although there was recognition for the good work being done by a handful of organisations – especially in terms of raising awareness of rights among tribals – almost all major NGOs in Orissa were branded as 'useless'. NGOs in Kalahandi were further accused of functioning as instruments of the government machinery and sharing the elitist attitude of government officials. Several leaders further complained about the 'luxurious lifestyles' of NGO workers and argued that the dominant NGO motto was 'to earn, not serve'. Like government officials, NGO workers were generally accused of lacking a 'missionary zeal', and of being more interested in the 'financial incentive' rather than the 'idealism incentive'. Interestingly, a section of opposition-party politicians were unwilling to publicly criticise large NGOs as these organisations provided some employment to those who otherwise would be without work. In addition, many organisations exercised considerable influence on the voting patterns of the poor in their areas of operation. Thus, it was beneficial for politicians not to antagonise influential NGO workers and their organisations, especially those working in politically important constituencies.

The Panchayat system

The Panchayati Raj system of local self-government in India consists of three tiers of elected decentralised governance: Zilla Parishad (ZP) at the district level, Panchayat Samities (PS) at the block level and Gram Panchayats (GP) at the village level. These Panchayat bodies provide advice to the district administration and the state government on policy formulation, implementation of development programmes and the selection of beneficiaries for social security schemes in the district. Until 1997, a two-tier, non-party-based, system (i.e. only the GP and PS bodies) was in operation in Orissa, and elections to the highest Panchayat authority – the Zilla Parishad at the district level – were repeatedly postponed by successive governments. The major reason for this appeared to be that MLAs in Orissa, once elected, were not in regular contact with their constituents and feared increased competition from Panchayats. Thus it had taken 37 years for Orissa to implement the three-tier Panchayat system when elections were held for all three levels in January 1997 – and for the first time with the official participation of political parties. However, there was little evidence during the study period to indicate that district officials were genuinely interested in seeking assistance from Panchayat representatives in relation to the management of food and health crises. With very limited resources at his disposal, the *Sarpanch* of a GP generally did not have the capacity to provide any form of policy feedback to the district administration. Further, the highest Panchayat official in Kalahandi – the Chairman of the Zilla Parishad – argued that it was difficult for Panchayats to assess whether deaths taking place in their areas were due to ill health or starvation. Nonetheless, he added, all Panchayat bodies were under instructions to send information on acute poverty and destitution immediately to the Zilla Parishad.[12]

An innovative scheme was introduced in the late 1990s according to which the district civil supplies department provided two quintals of rice to each *Sarpanch* for free distribution to anyone in distress within their GPs. While villagers, especially the elderly, complained that they never received such assistance, *Sarpanches* invariably claimed that they seldom received fresh supplies of rice despite repeated requests to the district civil supplies department. In general, the Orissa government had little faith in the Panchayat system, and several district officials highlighted the high levels of illiteracy among Panchayat representatives and their general lack of awareness on social issues. There was also a general reluctance on the part of the district administration to train Panchayats and improve institutional capacity. Thus, Panchayats functioned as local bodies without local activism; although representatives were elected and formally recognised by law, they were, in reality, highly marginalised. This trend was confirmed by the administrative head of the Orissa government's Panchayati Raj department who admitted that empowerment of Panchayats in Orissa was far from satisfactory:

> Officially, empowerment of Panchayats in Orissa is one of the best in India. However, the reality is very different. Panchayats have been given powers without adequate funds and training, and without competent government functionaries. Funds and functionaries are outside the ambit of these institutions.[13]

Efforts aimed at empowering Panchayats in Kalahandi was primarily contractual in nature in that the Zilla Parishad was given a sum of money for allocation to block-level PS and village-level GPs for labour-intensive works and general development activities in the areas of primary health care and education. Several informants claimed that the Zilla Parishad was too far removed from ground-level realities and was hence not aware of the actual types of assistance required by the lower-level Panchayat bodies. There was thus a desire, even by district officials, to see to it that the real unit of Panchayat empowerment was the GP. Towards this end, the central government had proposed that GPs should plan and execute projects on their own – and be given the power to hire private doctors and engineers if they felt government personnel were not doing their jobs properly. However, such initiatives were not given priority in Orissa, and senior state and district officials believed that, even if Panchayats in Kalahandi were given additional money to hire private doctors, they would be unable to do so given the acute shortage of doctors in the district. And with the increased availability of development funds at their disposal, there were frequent allegations of corruption. Others, including local leaders and NGOs, argued that with increased powers and more money at their disposal, Panchayats had become an extension of the 'corrupt, rude, arrogant and inefficient government machinery'.[14]

The general impression in Kalahandi was that none of the three tiers of Panchayat institutions had performed well, and that the institutions needed to be more vocal in order to have a greater impact on government programmes and practices. However, several factors prevented the Panchayats from realising their full potential. For example, representatives at the GP and PS levels were poorly paid, often as low as Rs 300 per month, thus lacking the financial incentive to be actively involved in local politics and development. Moreover, a large number of those who did get involved were illiterate and their knowledge of available alternatives to promote development was severely limited. Although a quota system was introduced to involve women in the system, it had little impact as women generally suffered from higher levels of illiteracy and were heavily under the control of their husbands, without the possibility of making independent decisions. Panchayat representatives were further not trained for promoting economic and social development in their areas and had difficulty conducting routine administrative functions like making accurate estimates of projects, preparing budgets, maintaining proper office records and keeping track of expenses. And Panchayats at all three levels in Kalahandi did not have adequate to finance their activities on account of the unwillingness of the Orissa government to transfer the funds earmarked for Panchayats.

The election of the Kalahandi Zilla Parishad in 1997 – for the first time in four decades – resulted in the Chairman of the Zilla Parishad becoming, at least theoretically, the most powerful official in the district. The Collector, by virtue of his function as Secretary of the Zilla Parishad, was relegated to a subordinate role. In practice, however, the old practice of the 'Collector Raj' continued. In virtually all important functions, the Zilla Parishad Chairman was forced to rely on the Collector, including the disbursement of development funds. District officials seldom took Panchayat representatives into confidence or consulted them in planning and executing policy, and in this sense the pre-1997 system continued to function without much change. Finally, whereas district officials publicly welcomed the sharing of powers with Panchayat representatives, they were in private highly sceptical of the whole idea of empowering institutions which they felt had no potential for functioning effectively. The district administration, especially the Collector, did not relish the thought of relinquishing the enormous power they exercised in relation to every sphere of district activity. Similarly, there was a general lack of political will to fully empower Panchayats according to the provisions of the constitution as political leaders, MLAs and MPs – be they from the ruling or opposition parties – considered these institutions as political rivals.

Consequently, there was little desire by the established political elite to share powers with Panchayat representatives.

Calamity relief and the politics of the money trail

As mentioned earlier, civil servants and politicians in Orissa consistently complained about not having the resources to provide adequate drought relief in Kalahandi. Interestingly – as seen earlier in this chapter – both ruling and opposition parties in Orissa put the blame squarely on New Delhi for not allocating sufficient funds under various calamity relief programmes. The central government's typical response was to accuse the Orissa government of underutilising available funds at its disposal. Federalism in India was placed under severe strain when the two levels of government did not agree on the extent and nature of assistance required. Since competing political parties often hold power at the centre and state levels, there is a constant tug-of-war for all potential sources that can be tapped. This means that allegations of favouritism are hurled at the centre whenever a particular state does not get the amount it believes it is entitled to. It is therefore important to examine the formal rules and actual procedures in place for the provision of calamity relief in India and whether the centre's alleged discriminatory treatment of Orissa affected the ability of the state government to undertake relief operations in Kalahandi.

National funds for calamity relief

Financial assistance to states affected by widespread natural calamities has been governed through the awards of successive finance commissions appointed by the central government, which recommends the formula for the sharing of all resources between the centre and states for a period of five years at a time. Following the recommendations of the Ninth Finance Commission, a *Calamity Relief Fund* (CRF) for each state was started in 1990–91 to enable state governments to provide immediate relief following a natural calamity without having to seek assistance from the centre. The central and state governments were required to contribute in a ratio of 3:1, and in the period 1995–2000 the size of the CRF was 63.04 billion, with each state entitled to withdraw a fixed sum annually (Report of the Eleventh Finance Commission 2000: para. 9.2). When relief expenditures exceeded the corpus of the CRF, the state government was expected to 'make a contribution from its Plan for providing employment opportunities as a measure of relief' (Orissa Relief Code 1996: para. 8.c.ii). The exact amount of such contribution (not to exceed 5 per cent of the annual plan outlay) was to be assessed by a 'Central team deputed by the Government of India after completion of necessary formalities of presentation of a Memorandum approved by the State government' (ibid.). If the central team concluded that the amount required could not be met by the state, then the central government had to provide the extra assistance, half as grant and half as loan (ibid.). The CRF was administered by a committee constituted by the state government and consisting of the Chief Secretary (*ex-officio* Chairman) and officials normally associated with relief works in affected areas. The central ministry of agriculture collected information regarding investment and expenditures made from the CRF by each state and offered advice to the state-level committees. All unspent CRF funds at the end of the five-year period (i.e. at the end of the financial year 1999–2000) were to be made available to each state government for use together with future CRF allocations (ibid.: Annex IX).

In 1995, the Tenth Finance Commission recommended the creation of a separate central fund – the National Fund for Calamity Relief (NFCR) – in order to provide assistance to states affected by 'national calamity' of 'rare severity'. In its report, the Commission noted:

> if a calamity of rare severity occurs, it should be dealt with as a national calamity, requiring additional assistance and support from the Centre, beyond what is envisaged under the CRF scheme. Moreover, the national dimensions of such a calamity would entail assistance from other States too, both in terms of financial support and material help.
>
> (Report of the Eleventh Finance Commission 2000: para. 9.3)

Without providing a way of assessing 'calamity of rare severity', the size of the NFCR was fixed at Rs 7 billion, to be built up over the period 1995–2000, and to which the centre and states would contribute in the ratio of 3:1. The National Calamity Relief Committee chaired by the central government's minister of agriculture decided whether a calamity qualified as one of rare severity and the size of ensuing relief allocations. Annual NFCR allocations to a state were generally limited to one-fifth of the total size of the Fund and recipient governments were required to submit periodic (quarterly) expenditure information to the ministry of agriculture in New Delhi.

Orissa's share of CRF and NFCR funds fixed by the Ninth and Tenth Finance Commissions in the period 1990–2000 are given in Table 7.1. In addition, for a seven-year period starting 1995–96, the Orissa government was allocated Rs 43 billion under the Long Term Action Plan (LTAP) earmarked for drought relief and development of the Kalahandi, Bolangir and Koraput (KBK) districts. After several years of neglect, Prime Minister Vajpayee's government revised the programme (and renamed it RLTAP) in 1998 and promised approximately Rs 60 billion to the KBK region for the nine-year period 1998–2007.[15]

Table 7.1 Orissa's share of CRF and NFCR funds, 1990–2000

Year	CRF (Rs million)	NFCR (Rs million)
1990–95	470	–
1995–2000	2,580	51.7

Source: Orissa Relief Code (Annexure X, p. 307).

Centre–state disputes on calamity relief: November 1996 to May 1997

In November 1996, the Orissa (Congress) government requested the central (United Front) government to declare the severe drought in the state as one constituting a 'national calamity'. When the centre refused, Orissa accused New Delhi of adopting a 'nonchalant attitude' towards the drought-affected people of Orissa[16] and went on to demand Rs 5.8 billion from the CRF, based on the argument that the state had experienced a crop loss totalling Rs 7 billion. Such a claim was contested both by opposition parties in Orissa and by the central government; they jointly accused the Orissa government of being thoroughly unprepared to provide a response despite being aware of the nature and severity of distress in the affected districts. At a meeting convened in New Delhi in late November, the PM assured a group of politicians from Orissa that the central government's contribution to the CRF – Rs 367 million – had already been released.[17] Following accusations in the Lok Sabha relating to the central government 'apathy' about Orissa's problems, the PM visited the drought-affected districts of Orissa in December and subsequently announced an immediate ad hoc assistance of Rs 500 million. Towards the end of December, the PM wrote to the Chief Minister of Orissa expressing his willingness to provide additional relief funds from the NFCR if required. However, he also expressed concern over the fact that Orissa had not managed to fully utilise funds released by the centre under various centrally sponsored welfare programmes, including the LTAP.[18] When the central government's minister of agriculture – following a visit to the KBK districts in December – requested the NHRC to investigate allegations of starvation deaths and the nature of drought relief provided in the state, the Orissa government was angered. The Chief Minister claimed that his government had already started an inquiry into the starvation issue and his revenue minister complained of the 'grave fault' committed by the Tenth Finance Commission in terms of CRF allocations to Orissa. As a result, he argued that, although Orissa required over Rs 4 billion for the period 1995–2000, the state was allocated only Rs 2.5 billion in CRF funds.[19] The year ended with heated discussions in the Orissa Legislative Assembly on 30 December, when MLAs – cutting across party lines – severely criticised the centre for its indifference to the financial needs of Orissa. Several legislators demanded the PM's resignation when it was revealed that the Rs 500 million grant promised by the PM earlier in the month had not yet been transferred to the Orissa government's account. Legislators from the Janata Dal party (which supported the United Front government at the centre) threatened to organise state-wide protests against the centre's mishandling of the Orissa drought.[20]

As the drought worsened during the first three months of 1997, the PM appointed an all-party parliamentary committee to enquire into reports of starvation deaths and large-scale migration of people from Orissa. The central government insisted that it was providing 'extraordinary assistance' to the state since – in addition to the Rs 500 million sanctioned by the PM in December 1996 – it had released a total of Rs 1.4 billion under the LTAP programme without waiting for audited reports and the 'utilisation certificate' from the Orissa government.[21] Throughout March 1997, however, the Orissa government's position remained unaltered. It continued to claim that it had not received any money from the centre, not even the immediate ad hoc assistance of Rs 500 million promised by the PM. Towards the end of May 1997, the drought relief controversy resurfaced once again but by then the Prime Minister, Deve Gowda, had resigned and a new United Front government under I. K. Gujral had taken over in New Delhi. Recognising that cumbersome administrative procedures and lack of proper communication on drought relief had strained centre–state relations in recent months, the new PM appointed a 'working group' consisting of central and state government officials to sort out the differences.

In early May, the PM informed Parliament that his government had transferred a total of Rs 3.8 billion for drought relief operations in Orissa on top of the Rs 40 million granted for emergency feeding programmes in the KBK districts. He further indicated that, if required, additional funds would be made available to Orissa under the Integrated Rural Development Programme (IRDP).[22] A few days later an all-party parliamentary delegation submitted a three-page memorandum to the PM and urged him to immediately dispatch large stocks of rice and medicines to Orissa and launch an investigation into the state government's response to the needs of drought-affected groups. The delegation claimed that, although the Orissa government was aware, since mid-August 1996, of the failure of the monsoons in the western districts of the state, it started relief operations as late as November 1996. Moreover, they alleged that 'a lethargic and corrupt administration' in the affected districts had further contributed to the worsening of an already grim situation.[23] Taking a cue from this meeting, the PM launched a scathing attack on the Orissa government in mid-May 1997 for failing to fully utilise calamity relief funds already available at its disposal.

Drought relief and the political blame game

Several authors have argued that drought relief in India is particularly controversial since drought management and the financing of relief are the domain of the Finance Commission and not a part of general development efforts under the purview of the Planning Commission. As such, drought is viewed as an 'event' requiring 'emergency relief' rather than a 'process' to be seen in relation to annual development programmes (Dubashi 1992; Rangasami 1994). Based on a study of the 1987 drought in Gujarat, Katiyar (1993) argued that the fire-fighting or ad hoc nature of financing relief operations is a problem as both central and state governments politicise and tailor drought relief to suit their own purposes. Similarly Mathur and Jayal (1993: 119) observe that a state government may find it beneficial to use calamities to 'project itself as the guardian of public welfare' and the 'party in power attempts to emerge as the champion of the cause of the poor and the backward and uses relief measures to gain political mileage'.

Most Indian states contain large arid zones that have been classified as 'drought-prone' based on rainfall deficiency and average annual crop loss. In practice, the central government formally carries out the task of classifying drought-prone areas under the Drought-Prone Areas Programme (DPAP). However, centre–state relations most often dictate which areas (and in which state) are included under this lucrative scheme. It is generally beneficial for states to have as many of its blocks as possible classified as DPAP blocks since additional central government funds for drought-related projects can then be expected.[24] The PM is also empowered to sanction emergency funds under different centrally sponsored programmes in times of crises, and states additionally eye several other sources of revenue like the Prime Minister's Emergency Relief Fund. With limited funds available for social security programmes, most states operate under the belief that the declaration of drought is the sole means of reducing vulnerability to natural calamities. Hence it has become common practice for states to make exaggerated claims on the severity of the drought (e.g. 'worst drought of the decade/century') as there is competition to extract as much as possible from all possible sources at the national level. As Dubashi (1994: 2602) writes, 'While the administration wakes up only when droughts actually occur, the political leadership marks its success by the quantum of relief funds obtained from the Centre with little concern for long-term planning for dry regions and no understanding of ecological issues.'

In virtually all drought years, there is a set pattern in centre–state disputes – the centre insists it has sent the money while states claim not to have received any. More often than not, it is immensely difficult to assess who is speaking the truth since drought relief provides the arena for playing a rather popular political blame game in which the main players – central and state governments – accuse each other of lies, corruption, neglect, incompetence and mismanagement. Like Orissa, several states in the period 1995–2000 regularly complained to the centre that the size of the CRF allocated to them was inadequate, expressing strong reservations on the criteria employed to allocate CRF funds. Thus, for example, Andhra Pradesh insisted that the size of the CRF ought to be determined after taking into account actual expenditures incurred on relief and a state's proneness to various calamities like drought, cyclones and flood. While Karnataka argued for alternative criteria such as the proportion of a state's 'unirrigated area', Uttar Pradesh proposed that the main criteria ought to be the actual relief expenditure incurred together with inflation (Report of the Eleventh Finance Commission 2000: para. 9.5). Moreover, several states requested that their contribution to the CRF be reduced and that the central government's contribution be increased correspondingly. Other states argued that the entire CRF should be provided by the central government as a grant, without any contribution by state governments.

The perception of the severity of drought and food scarcity conditions together with the required amount of financial assistance varied widely among states and between them and the central government. Such differences were related to the amount of resources requested, the speed and reliability of central disbursement procedures, utilisation and monitoring of allocated funds at the state level, and the use of criteria to determine 'national calamity' and/or 'calamity of rare severity'.

Disbursement procedures and allegations of favouritism

Firmly believing that state governments exaggerated their claims of the impact of drought and required relief, the centre tended to allocate only a fraction of the total request. Such caution appeared further justified by the fact that the total amount of requests for assistance by state governments was normally three to four times greater than the corpus of the CRF fixed by the Finance Commission. However, states complained that, even after the public announcement of annual (and fixed) CRF allocations, funds did not reach them in time.[25] A test audit by the Comptroller and Auditor General (CAG 1999) confirmed such claims when it observed that, not withstanding the magnitude of the calamity, grants from the NFCR in 1996–99 were released with delays of 3–13 months. Therefore calamity relief funds 'failed in mitigating the suffering of the persons affected by calamities of rare severity' (ibid.: para. 1.8). Bureaucrats and politicians in Orissa were united in claiming that political considerations were usually the paramount determinants of which state gets how much relief and how soon. It was thus hypothesised that favourable relations between state and central governments – made possible by the same political party or allied or 'friendly' parties in power at both levels – ensured that calamity relief funds keep pouring into the coffers of 'friendly' state governments. In comparison, it was alleged, states under the control of opposition parties not only received less funds than originally requested but that the disbursement procedures were delayed such that funds were not available when needed most.

The events of September–October 1998, when various parts of India experienced food shortage and a scarcity of drinking water, provides an illustrative example of the problem. A coalition government – formed by the BJP party and its allies – held power in New Delhi and was involved in a heated debate with several states governments controlled by opposition parties. Table 7.2 shows the request for funds by these six states and the actual amounts allocated by the centre. A major controversy erupted when the governments of West Bengal, Bihar and Assam (with opposition parties in power) accused the centre of favouring the BJP

Table 7.2 Request by selected states for calamity relief funds, September–October 1998

State	Ruling party	Requested calamity relief (Rs billion)	Funds received by states (Rs billion)
West Bengal	CPI(M)	6.7	0.75
Bihar	RJD	15	0.75
Uttar Pradesh	BJP	–	5.5
Andhra Pradesh	TDP	5	2
Assam	AGP	5	0.41
Karnataka	JD	3	0.5
Orissa	INC	4.4	–

Source: Compiled from newspaper reports in *The Hindu, The Statesman, The Telegraph, Indian Express, Hindustan Times* and *Times of India.*

government in Uttar Pradesh and the Telegu Desam (an ally of the BJP) government in Andhra Pradesh. The trouble erupted after the Prime Minister, Atal Bihari
Vajpayee, after an aerial survey of flood-hit areas, declared a calamity of 'rare severity' and sanctioned Rs 5.5 billion to Uttar Pradesh. In comparison, West Bengal and Bihar – both ruled by opposition parties – received only Rs 0.75 billion
each, despite claiming to have been equally affected by floods as Uttar Pradesh,
if not more. The Assam government further complained that it had received even
less than its eastern counterparts Bihar and West Bengal. All three governments
accused the centre of 'playing politics with calamity relief' and neglecting the
country's eastern region in favour of Uttar Pradesh.[26] The situation was further
aggravated when the PM announced a grant of Rs 2 billion to the government
of Andhra Pradesh (in the hands of its New Delhi ally) without increasing the
allocations to West Bengal, Bihar and Assam. Not surprisingly, Andhra Pradesh
was pleased with this announcement as it had earlier (in the period 1996–97)
repeatedly accused the previous (United Front) government in New Delhi of discrimination in the allocation of cyclone relief. This time around, its ally – the BJP
– appeared to be delivering the goods.

A review of the literature on drought relief in India shows that successive ruling
parties at the centre have traditionally been eager to provide urgent assistance to
states controlled by them or their allies. For example, studies of the 1987 drought
in India suggest that the Congress government in New Delhi strongly felt that
holding back relief assistance from opposition-party controlled states was a useful
strategy for discrediting the performance of its rivals (Bhalla and Bandyopadhyay
1992; Katiyar 1993). Thus, the relief allocations made by the BJP government in
New Delhi in September–October 1998 appeared to be a continuation of policies
practiced by previous administrations. However, calamity relief is politicised not
only by the centre but also by states; a newspaper editorial aptly summed up the
situation as follows:

> the real issue is not BJP versus CPI(M) or RJD or even UP versus Eastern
> India. It is that abuse of relief funds has become institutionalised to such an
> extent that any talks of correctives are deemed as naïve. Additional cynicism
> comes from the craven to corrupt conduct of officials. Too scared – despite
> service rules that afford not inconsiderable protection – to protest or too eager
> to please, the *babus* have become the forward party for politicians hunting the
> human debris of a natural disaster.[27]

Utilisation and monitoring of allocated funds

A report by the Comptroller and Auditor General of India (CAG 1999) appeared
to substantiate central government claims that states generally demanded additional money without first spending what was already available to them. Thus,
in the period 1992–1998, implementing agencies in nine states delayed relief assistance to the victims of calamity by 1–80 months. The report further concluded

that states recipient of calamity relief spent almost 20 per cent of allocated funds in areas where no calamity had taken place (ibid.: paras 1.7, 1.8). Although the central government's ministry of agriculture was supposed to monitor CRF and NFCR expenses, state governments gave very low priority to submitting information on expenses incurred and details on the pattern of utilisation of calamity relief funds (CAG 1999: para. 1.9). The report particularly singled out relief operations in Kalahandi in the 1990s as being 'a stereotype instance of infective government response of the State government in the face of calamity' (ibid.: para. 1.7.2). Whereas several officials in Kalahandi regularly complained that they were unable to initiate or complete relief projects on the grounds of shortage of funds, the CAG report revealed that the Collector of Kalahandi managed to spend only half of the Rs 41.6 million available at his disposal during the drought in 1996–97. This inability to utilise funds appeared even more mysterious given that the district administration had originally demanded a total of Rs 322 million to combat the crisis.

The reasons for such underutilisation of funds in Kalahandi and other areas of the country are many and include poor local infrastructure, lack of long-term planning, administrative callousness and lack of communication between civil servants, politicians and civil society organisations. Cumbersome bureaucratic routines in Orissa, for instance, require that all district relief plans be approved by the State Relief Commissioner in Bhubaneswar. This process usually takes several months and can be even further delayed when the Collector does not submit his proposals in time. Thus, although the Orissa government declared Kalahandi as 'drought-affected' in February 1997, it took the Collector three months to submit proposals for labour-intensive programmes to the Relief Commissioner's office for approval. A further four months were needed by the Relief Commissioner to approve these plans, so employment programmes in the district could start only in September instead of February/March. Thus, even if one were to accept the views of ruling-party politicians in Orissa that the centre delayed the disbursement of relief funds to the state, the CAG report clearly highlights two major problems – time-consuming administrative routines and the hunger of state governments to clamour for relief funds without managing to spend what is already available.

Declaration of 'national calamity'

A major source of discord between central and state governments in 1996–2000 related to NFCR allocations, which – according to the guidelines framed by the Tenth Finance Commission – could be granted only to states experiencing 'calamities of rare severity'. Since there were no specific norms for identifying such calamities, administrating the NFCR was a particular problem. As noted by the Eleventh Finance Commission:

the [Tenth] Commission did not specify norms for identifying calamities of rare severity on the ground that any definition would bristle with insurmountable difficulties and was likely to be counter-productive. It felt that a calamity of rare severity would necessarily have to be assessed on a case-by-case basis by taking into account, inter-alia, the intensity and magnitude of calamity, level of relief assistance needed, capacity of the State to tackle the problem, the alternatives and flexibility available within the plans to provide succour and relief etc.

(Report of the Eleventh Finance Commission 2000: para. 9.18)

States were therefore quick to realise that they stood to gain large amounts of money once a calamity within their territory was classified as one of 'rare severity'. Not only would this entitle them to 100 per cent income tax exemptions on all donations made by individuals and organisations, but all other state governments in the country would be obliged to provide financial and other forms of assistance to the calamity-affected state. Towards this end, state governments realised that it was of the utmost importance to use the term 'national calamity' while describing the impact of an event within their territories. Interestingly, neither the CRF nor the NFCR guidelines had any mention of 'national calamity', even though the rules governing allocations from the NFCR spoke of calamities of 'rare severity'. Hence, any time that the central government appeared willing to use the term in certain cases and reluctant in others, it brought forth allegations of favouritism and discrimination. Although there were numerous controversies over the declaration of a 'national calamity', events relating to cyclone relief to Orissa in 1999 were particularly interesting and help illustrate the confusion in the usage of these terms and the resulting implications. Immediately after a major cyclone struck the coast of Orissa in October 1999, the state (Congress) government demanded that the centre (BJP-led coalition) declare 'a national calamity of rare severity'. In the months that followed, the central government provided large sums of money in numerous instalments but categorically refused to use the term 'national calamity'. Although repeated mention was made of 'severe calamity' and 'large-scale disaster', the Congress party's leader, Sonia Gandhi, was not pleased with the centre's efforts, arguing that 'Politics should not come in the way as far as such matters are concerned.'[28] To this, the central government replied that it had already declared the disaster as one of 'rare severity' and had sanctioned NFCR funds according to calamity relief guidelines. In addition, the most senior civil servant in the ministry of agriculture publicly declared that the debate on whether to brand the cyclone a 'national calamity' or not was of little use since there were no official provisions for such a term:

I would like to be educated on what a national calamity is. I would also like to know in which book it is written . . . Even if it is not being declared as a national calamity, there will be no lack of effort in providing funds or resources to the State government.[29]

Although the above observation was entirely correct, further confusion was added by a member of the Prime Minister's Office, according to whom there were 'technical' and 'legal' problems in declaring the devastation in Orissa as a 'national calamity'. These problems, according to this official, were related to the fact that a formal declaration of a 'national calamity' would force the whole country to be involved in the relief measures:

> Short of declaring it a national calamity, everything is being done by the Centre. Since the disaster is not being declared a national calamity, it does not become binding on the States to make contributions in either cash or in kind. The States which are helping in the relief and rescue operations are pitching in voluntarily.[30]

Even greater confusion followed when the PM observed in Parliament in April 2000, 'Without declaring it a national calamity, we did everything'.[31] Ironically, it was later reported that the Orissa government, while consistently complaining of the centre's reluctance to declare a 'national calamity', had itself failed to even declare the cyclone devastation as a 'state calamity', as required under Section 118 of the Orissa Relief Code. Thus the political leadership at both levels of government operated with a term that formally did not exist in administrative rule books. The only difference between a calamity of 'rare severity' (legally provided in the guidelines of the NFCR) and a 'national calamity' was the belief that the latter could force the entire nation (all state governments and organisations) to provide assistance. The widespread usage of 'national calamity' was also of enormous symbolic value since the slightest reluctance on the part of the centre to use the term led states to accuse the central government of 'apathy', neglect' and 'step motherly treatment'. In order to address this problem, the Eleventh Finance Commission recommended in 2000 that the NFCR should be discontinued because of both the difficulty in defining calamities of 'rare severity' and the general difficulty in providing adequate financial assistance to states with the limited amount of money available in the Fund. It further recommended the creation of a national centre for calamity management in the central government's ministry of agriculture in order to 'monitor all types of natural calamities, including calamities of rare severity, without any specific reference from the Centre or the State government'. It further noted that this body should be empowered to make recommendations 'to the Central government as to whether a calamity is of such severe nature that [it] would call for financial assistance to the affected State over and above what is available in the CRF or other plan/non-plan sources' (Report of the Eleventh Finance Commission 2000: para. 9.29n).

A complex set of factors characterise the politics of calamity relief in India, and the long-lasting war of words between the centre and Orissa in 1996–97 provided both governments with an excuse to avoid taking responsibility for the debacle. When the state government was formed either by the same political party as the one in power in New Delhi or by a political ally, there was increased central government urgency in disbursing calamity relief funds. On their part, states viewed calamity relief as an important source of supplementing the regular income they required for development and hence there was a tendency to exaggerate the nature of the crisis and the amount of resources required to combat it. The centre–state blame game has become strongly institutionalised in Indian federalism and the involved players refuse to budge from their favoured positions whenever drought and other calamities bring this exciting game of calamity relief to town.

8

PARLIAMENTARY ACTIVISM

While starvation deaths in Kalahandi were making headline news and the central and state governments were quarrelling over drought relief, the Lok Sabha[1] – the lower house of the Indian Parliament – was not sitting idle. Indeed, starvation deaths reported in the media figured prominently in Lok Sabha debates and questions, and MPs frequently pressured the government to improve both its attitude and its response to drought-related deprivation. But did such a focus on Kalahandi have a positive impact? And to what extent do parliamentarians actually influence public policy on poverty and drought? It is therefore important to examine the role and capacity of the Indian Parliament – and political articulation within it – in holding central and state governments to account for policy failures. In doing so, this chapter does not follow any particular method of discourse analysis but relies on Mathur and Jayal's (1993) recommendation of studying political articulation as a two-fold issue – the *character of representation* and *extent of participation* of MPs in parliamentary debates and questions and the *content of representation*, debates and questions.

There are relatively few studies on the role of the Indian Parliament and its legislators in influencing public policy. Pioneering studies by Lal (1956) and Morris-Jones (1957) placed considerable emphasis on analyses of legal norms, rules and parliamentary procedures; others have focused on how SC MPs influence decision-making (Narayana 1980), the role of Parliament in holding the executive accountable on electronics policy (Jain 1985a) and a study of the Parliament's role in promoting science and technology (Rahman and Haritash 1985).[2] These studies generally concluded that MPs played a limited role in expanding and influencing the scope of public policy. Another study (Jain 1985b) argued that MPs had a strong regional bias in development-related issues given the considerable influence of caste, heredity and religious factors. The study also noted that the extent of political integration and support or criticism of overall government policies by Indian MPs was difficult to ascertain empirically given the general lack of a national perspective in legislative deliberations. With a specific focus on drought in various parts of India during 1985–89, Mathur and Jayal (1992, 1993) analysed the influence of Lok Sabha MPs in relation to long-term development strategies and short-term drought relief interventions. The study concluded that MPs were particularly concerned with the immediate issue of drought relief, especially in relation to the amount of money that was allocated by the central government to their home states. Although the study found that MPs showed some interest in formulating a national drought management policy, it concluded that 'MPs rarely voice policy alternatives or grill the government on the failures of its long-term policy' (Mathur and Jayal 1992: 64).

Representation and participation

The period under review is September 1996–July 2002, during which the eleventh, twelfth and thirteenth Lok Sabhas were in session. Since the twelfth Lok Sabha period (March–April 1999) lasted only for a year and did not witness any major debate on drought and starvation in Orissa, the major focus here is on debates and questions in the eleventh Lok Sabha period (May 1996–December 1997), which corresponded with a severe drought in Orissa. For purposes of comparison, the character and content of representation of debates and questions during the first three years of the thirteenth Lok Sabha period (September 1999–July 2002) – during which Orissa again faced drought – are also analysed.

A first difference between the eleventh and thirteenth Lok Sabha periods relates to the severity of the 1996 drought in Orissa, which received far more media coverage than droughts in 1998–2002. Another difference relates to the regime in power in New Delhi and Orissa during the two periods as shown in Table 8.1. While two successive United Front governments (formed by the Janata Dal and its allies) held power at the centre in 1996–97, the Congress ruled Orissa and accounted for 17 of Orissa's total quota of 21 Lok Sabha MPs. The Kalahandi MP, however, belonged to the opposition camp, representing the Samajwadi Janata Party Rashtriya (SJPR) from Orissa. By comparison, the BJP and its partners in the National Democratic Alliance (NDA) held power in New Delhi in 1999–2002. In Orissa, the BJD formed a new government in alliance with the BJP following a resounding victory over the Congress in the 2000 Orissa Legislative Assembly elections. In the ensuing elections to the thirteenth Lok Sabha, the Congress managed to win just two seats in comparison to the BJD–BJP alliance's 19. The Kalahandi MP in the Lok Sabha during this period belonged to the BJP, and was thus a member of the ruling alliance in Orissa.

Table 8.1 Political representation in the Lok Sabha from Orissa, 1996–2002, by party

	Party representation				
Lok Sabha period	*Congress (INC)*	*Janata Dal (JD)*	*Biju Janata Dal (BJD)*	*Bharatiya Janata Party (BJP)*	*Samajwadi Janata Party – Rashtriya (SJPR)*
XI (1996–97)	17	3	–	–	1
XIII (1999–2002)	2	–	10	9	–

Source: Tabulated from statistical reports on the Lok Sabha, Election Commission of India.

Parliamentary debates

Debates in the Lok Sabha take place in four main formats – 'statement by minister' (which keep MPs informed of specific government policies and matters of public importance), 'short duration discussions' (which allow MPs to discuss matters of 'urgent public importance'), 'special mention' (which allows MPs to request a minister to respond to an urgent matter) and 'matters under rule 377' (which provide MPs with the opportunity of raising pressing problems specifically related to their constituencies). Tables 8.2 and 8.3 show the extent of participation of MPs – including cabinet ministers representing the central government – in debates in which drought and starvation deaths in Kalahandi were mentioned. Since there was only one instance of a 'statement by minister' that mentioned Kalahandi in the period 1996–2001, this category has been combined with the 'short-duration discussion' category.

From Tables 8.2 and 8.3, certain general observations can be made regarding the extent of participation of MPs in Lok Sabha debates. Since the Congress was the ruling party in Orissa in 1996–97 (and was not part of the central government), its MPs were free to criticise the minority United Front government for its general neglect of Orissa. This is reflected in the active participation of Congress MPs from Orissa who tended to dominate the debate on drought in the state. Furthermore, the second largest party in the Lok Sabha (after the Congress) in 1996–97 was the BJP – also not part of the central government and hence free to criticise the centre on drought policy. Thus the eleventh Lok Sabha period was unique in the sense that MPs from two of the largest parties in the country were free to attack the central government on drought, consistently putting the small minority of United Front MPs on the defensive. Although the BJP did not hold any parliamentary seats from Orissa, its MPs from Bihar, Rajasthan and Uttar Pradesh were quite active in debates, especially in the short-duration and special mention categories.

During 1999–2002, the BJP and its NDA partners provided political stability in New Delhi after several years of United Front rule. Corresponding to a change

Table 8.2 Participation of MPs in debates on drought and starvation in Kalahandi, 1996–97

Lok Sabha period	Type of debate	No. of debates	Total no. of participating MPs	MPs from Orissa	MPs from other states	Cabinet ministers
XI (15 May 1996–	Short duration discussions	5	29	12	14	3
4 December 1997)	Special mention	8	11	6	4	1
	Matters under rule 377	5	4	4	–	–
	Total	18	44	22	18	4

Source: Compiled from reports on eleventh Lok Sabha proceedings (various years).

Table 8.3 Participation of MPs in debates on drought and starvation in Kalahandi, 1999–2001

Lok Sabha period	Type of debate	No. of debates	Total no. of participating MPs	MPs from Orissa	MPs from other states	Cabinet ministers
XIII (13 September 1999–30 August 2001)	Short duration discussions	3	7	7	–	–
	Special mention	4	5	2	3	–
	Matters under rule 377	5	1	1	–	–
	Total	12	13	10	3	–

of government at the centre, state elections held in early 2000 resulted in the BJD forming a government in alliance with the BJP in Orissa. This meant that, for the first time in almost a decade, the very same political parties held power in both New Delhi and Bhubaneswar. The opposition from Orissa was represented by two Congress MPs; this explains why, for the most part, overall participation in debates on drought and Kalahandi was far less in 1999–2002 than in 1996–97.

Parliamentary questions

In addition to taking part in debates, MPs can make use of parliamentary questions – written ('unstarred') and oral ('starred') – to express concern on urgent matters of national importance and related to their state and constituency. Written questions elicit written answers and are used by MPs to acquire information on the nature of government policy and the functioning of various government-sponsored programmes. The answers provided by the ministers concern their departments and provide data that MPs can use to alert the government on matters that concern their constituents. In addition, such Q&A sessions enable MPs to 'continue to probe the Government's performance on other occasions' (Mathur and Jayal 1993: 87). Oral questions are used by MPs to elicit oral answers from ministers and, in contrast to written questions, they allow for supplementary questions to the responding minister. This allows MPs to extract further information on issues of policy implementation which can subsequently be used to monitor government performance.

Unfortunately, data on written and oral questions were available for only the 1999–2002 period and therefore the two Lok Sabha periods could not be compared. Nonetheless, the available data exhibit several interesting features. For example, between February 2000 and July 2002, a total of 30 MPs asked 17 questions on starvation deaths, eight of which specifically referred to Orissa and the KBK region. On three occasions, two or more MPs jointly asked a question and in a couple of instances MPs from two or more parties were involved. As Table 8.4 shows, MPs from 12 states and representing 10 political parties raised

Table 8.4 Participation of MPs in questions on starvation deaths, thirteenth Lok Sabha period, 1999–2002, by state

State	Total no. of MPs	No. of questions	Political party									
			INC	BJP	BJD	TDP	CPI(M)	AIMIM	PWPI	RJD	SS	SP
Assam	14	1	1									
Kerala	20	2	2									
Andhra Pradesh	42	5	1			3		1				
Orissa	21	3	1	1	1							
West Bengal	42	3					3					
Maharashtra	48	4	1	1					1		1	
Uttar Pradesh	80	1										1
Punjab	13	1	1									
Bihar	40	6		2			1			3		
Karnataka	28	2	1	1								
Madhya Pradesh	29	1	1									
Rajasthan	25	1	1									
Total	**402**	**30**	**10**	**5**	**1**	**3**	**4**	**1**	**1**	**3**	**1**	**1**

Source: Compiled from Reports on thirteenth Lok Sabha proceedings (various years).

questions related exclusively to starvation deaths. MPs from Bihar topped the list with six questions followed by Andhra Pradesh and Maharashtra with five and four questions, respectively. However, only 3 of 21 MPs representing Orissa raised questions on starvation deaths despite the fact that newspaper reports in the 1999–2002 period were filled with stories of starvation not just from Kalahandi but also from five other districts of Orissa. The reluctance to criticise the Orissa government in the Lok Sabha can be explained by the fact that only two MPs from Orissa belonged to the opposition (Congress) camp. However, it is interesting to note that, despite forming the central government, MPs from the BJP and its NDA allies – Telegu Desam Party, Shiv Sena and Biju Janata Dal – raised a few questions on starvation. The most active party on the issue of starvation deaths was, not surprisingly, the Congress with 10 active MPs. It was also the largest opposition party in the Lok Sabha.

Only two questions specifically related to Kalahandi were asked during the entire period under study, and both questions were raised by the Kalahandi MP. Table 8.5 shows that he was generally quite active, credited with a total of 59 questions on various topics. These were mostly general questions on issues affecting Orissa, and among them were 11 questions related to the overall development of the KBK region and four drought-related questions which concerned the provision of a new variety of seeds to farmers, loan assistance to Orissa and the need to improve irrigation facilities.

Given the dominance of the BJP and the BJD parties in the delegation of MPs from Orissa, it was not surprising that these legislators were unwilling to pose critical (and numerous) questions on controversial issues related to starvation. Nonetheless, it is surprising that the Kalahandi MP did not profile his constituency more actively, particularly since the district faced drought for two consecutive years in 1999–2000 and 2000–01. However, when compared with his colleagues who represented Kalahandi's neighbouring districts which were equally affected

Table 8.5 Parliamentary questions by selected MPs from Orissa, 1999–2002

Constituency	Political party	Total no. of questions	Questions on own constituency
Kalahandi	BJP	59	2
Bolangir	BJP	83	4
Balasore	BJP	27	2
Koraput	INC	54	2
Dhenkanal	INC	244	9
Cuttack	BJD	258	16
Sambalpur	BJD	5	–
Puri	BJD	8	–
Kendrapara	BJD	253	3

Source: Compiled from Reports on thirteenth Lok Sabha proceedings (various years).

by drought (e.g. Bolangir, Koraput and Sambalpur), the Kalahandi MP did not fare too badly.

It is normally believed in Orissa that politicians from the state's coastal districts – Puri, Kendrapara and Cuttack – are more vocal and active in parliament than those representing western districts like Kalahandi. Table 8.5 provides evidence of this in that, apart from the Puri MP, all others representing coastal districts of Orissa (especially Cuttack and Kendrapara) were comparatively more active than MPs from western districts. It is generally difficult to assess the level of participation and influence exercised by Orissa MPs in the Lok Sabha based exclusively on parliamentary questions. A closer look at the content of Lok Sabha debates, however, may provide a better indication of various perspectives on drought and the general ability of MPs to trigger government action on starvation.

Perspectives on drought and starvation deaths, 1996–97

The adverse effects of the 1996 drought in Kalahandi were first mentioned during the second (budget) session of the eleventh Lok Sabha period and were repeatedly highlighted by various Orissa MPs between September 1996 and August 1997. A chronological sequence of debates during this period is provided in Table 8.6.

Starting in September 1996, the Kalahandi MP was particularly concerned with the poor state of health services and the refusal of doctors to work in his constituency. He repeatedly urged the central government to ensure that an adequate supply of medicines was dispatched and doctors immediately recruited to fill vacancies in Kalahandi. However, it was only in the third (winter) session of the Lok Sabha that a major three-day-long debate on Kalahandi took place on 27, 28 and 29 November 1996. Following a statement by the Minister of Parliamentary Affairs on the acute drought crisis facing Orissa (made on behalf of the Agriculture Minister), four 'short duration discussions' followed with active participation by MPs from Orissa (in particular, the MP from Kalahandi) and other states. References to the 'famine-like' situation developing in Kalahandi were again made in the final days of the winter session in December. The remaining debates took place in the fourth (budget) and fifth (monsoon) sessions of the Lok Sabha and were characterised by repeated appeals by Orissa MPs to the central government for the immediate disbursement of drought relief funds.

In general, the debates during this period were frequently disrupted following MPs speaking out of turn and protesting loudly whenever opposition MPs directed harsh criticism at central and Orissa governments. There were also numerous complaints from Orissa MPs that they needed more time to debate drought-related deprivation in Kalahandi and to forward constructive proposals for a solution of the crisis. Some expressed anger over the fact that on several occasions the PM and his Agriculture Minister were absent during discussions on the drought in Orissa. The PM's reluctance to engage in the debate, they argued, showed a 'lack of respect' for Orissa's poor and proved that the central government did not consider the drought situation as serious enough.

Table 8.6 Chronological sequence of debates on Kalahandi, 1996–97

Date	Type of debate	Topic
9 September 1996	Matters under rule 377	The need for effective steps to eradicate poverty in Kalahandi and Bolangir
10 September 1996	Special mention	The need to provide relief in drought-affected areas
10 September 1996	Special mention	The need to release funds for backward districts of Orissa
10 September 1996	Special mention	Provision of adequate medicine and doctors
27 November 1996	Statement by minister	Drought in Orissa
27 November 1996	Short duration discussion	Famine and drought in Kalahandi
28 November 1996	Short duration discussion	Drought in Kalahandi
29 November 1996	Short duration discussion	Natural calamities, drought relief and rehabilitation in Kalahandi and Orissa
5 December 1996	Matters under rule 377	Famine situation and the need for early completion of irrigation projects
11 December 1996	Special mention	Non-receipt of drought relief funds by Orissa government
25 February 1997	Special mention	Non-receipt of drought relief funds by Orissa government, callous attitude of the centre
26 February 1997	Matters under rule 377	The need to release additional drought relief funds to drought-affected Orissa
7 May 1997	Special mention	Demand for making urgent arrangements for drinking water in Kalahandi
7 May 1997	Matters under rule 377	Demand for additional drought relief funds for Kalahandi region
14 May 1997	Special mention	The need to increase drought relief on account of to starvation conditions
24 July 1997	Matters under rule 377	The need to enhance quota of cereals for Orissa under the Public Distribution System
30 July 1997	Special mention	The need to provide financial aid and start relief measures in Kalahandi
6 August 1997	Short duration discussion	Heavy loss of lives and property due to droughts and floods in India

Source: Compiled from Reports on eleventh Lok Sabha proceedings (various years).

The 'angry man' from Kalahandi

Bhakta Charan Das – a former central government cabinet minister – was elected to the Lok Sabha from Kalahandi in 1996, and represented the Samajwadi Janata Party Rashtriya, an offshoot of the Janata Party. During his days as an MLA from Kalahandi in the Orissa Legislative Assembly (1985–89), he was known to frequently raise issues relating to Kalahandi and was widely referred to as the 'the Assembly's angry man' as he would often try to disrupt proceedings whenever he felt that the members of the Orissa government did not fully appreciate the difficulties facing his constituency. His participation in Lok Sabha debates was equally vocal and dramatic, and his SC background appeared to provide additional legitimacy to voice the concerns of the traditionally downtrodden people of Kalahandi. In fact, Das was largely credited as one of the major architects behind the campaign to highlight Kalahandi's problems at both state and national levels. As a result of his efforts the Prime Minister, Rajiv Gandhi, made a high-profile visit to Kalahandi in 1985. When interviewed in 2001, Das claimed that his greatest achievement was his ability to secure generous grants from the central government for the overall development of Kalahandi.

During Lok Sabha debates that focused exclusively on drought in Orissa, Das was one of the most active MPs. This was hardly surprising given that he was the only representative from Orissa who did not belong to the ruling party at either the state or the central level. Despite this, he enjoyed a good rapport with the large majority of Congress party MPs from Orissa who often supported Das in debates, especially when criticism was levelled against the central government. Throughout November 1996, Das consistently pointed out that the drought in Kalahandi and neighbouring districts was serious, regularly providing statistics relating to rainfall deficiency, extent of crop loss, number of people being forced to migrate in search of food and work and the large number of drought-affected villages. In a debate towards the end of November, he began by observing that the severe drought in Kalahandi had lead to an 'almost famine situation', and followed this up the next day by highlighting 'pitiable' situation of Kalahandi where 'people are dying of starvation in hundreds and hundreds'.

Das was also the only MP to highlight the fact that starvation was not related to total food availability in the region but rather a result of lack of access to food and low purchasing power. In subsequent discussions, he claimed that hundreds of starvation deaths were taking place in his district and that preventing these ought to be a matter of urgent priority in a democracy like India. Arguing that politicians in India's democracy had become 'masters of lip service', he observed:

> Why should the people remain in drought condition continuously in this independent nation when government after government is coming in the State as well as in the Centre? Are we going to discuss about the drought situation again next year or after five years or ten years in this House? . . . We should be honest to solve the problems of this area which is continuously and chronically affected by the drought.[3]

He went on to propose several concrete measures that the Orissa government could implement in Kalahandi. These included measures to check migration, supply safe drinking water, dig new wells, provide free foodgrains, waive loans and promote crop insurance schemes for farmers. The government was also criticised for not being committed to long-term economic development and the improvement of infrastructure and communications in the district. A matter of particular concern related to how he had provided the government with early warning information of Kalahandi's problems and yet the government had been slow to react:

> During the last Budget Session . . . I had warned the Government of Orissa as well as the Government of India about the drought situation in Orissa. At that time . . . I was the only Member who spoke . . . But no precautionary measures were taken in spite of that . . . it is not for the first time that Kalahandi district has been affected by drought . . . but no permanent measures have been taken . . . The governments at the State and at the Centre have been so much callous. The monitoring agencies have not shown importance at all so far as the permanent solutions to save the people from the drought are concerned.[4]

Speaking for hours at a time, the MP repeatedly attacked the central and state governments for failing to view the KBK region as a 'special case' in need to urgent action. Together with fellow MPs from Orissa, he also complained that certain states (e.g. Andhra Pradesh) were being given preferential treatment in comparison to Orissa. However, his criticism was also directed at the Orissa government which, he alleged, was not capable of spending money properly at the district level because of poor infrastructure and a severe shortage of government personnel as 40 per cent of government posts in the district remained vacant. Despite the insistence of the Orissa government that it needed additional funds – a matter frequently raised by Congress MPs from Orissa – Das was sceptical as to how such relief funds would benefit his district. Referring to widespread corruption involving bureaucrats and private contractors, he requested the central government to allocate funds directly to the drought-affected districts and appoint an officer to monitor the expenditure.[5] Despite being the lone opposition MP from Orissa who was active in debates on drought and starvation in Kalahandi, Das successfully managed to combine rhetoric with factual information and proposed several concrete remedial measures for the government to implement. And his criticism of central government response received widespread support from his fellow MPs from Orissa.

General participation of MPs in debates

Most MPs participating in the debates on drought expressed concern over Orissa's plight, and they generally agreed that Kalahandi remained severely underdeveloped. In addition, several MPs discussed the role of the media and early warning information, the regular occurrence of starvation deaths, the lack of central government funds for drought relief, and the ad hoc nature of local government response. Among the most active MPs from Orissa was the Congress party's K. P. Singh Deo, who in a long speech in November 1996 observed:

Our hearts are down with the impoverished, unfortunate, hapless and stoic people of Orissa who are braving the vagaries of the monsoon with tears in their eyes and stark famine staring before their eyes, awaiting help and succour . . . There was a time when Junagarh in Dharamgarh sub-division of Kalahandi was the granary of Western Orissa which could match the production of paddy with that of Balasore and Bhadrak districts. But today, we see mass migration, starvation and of course, in this very House, we have discussed the sale of children.[6]

He argued that Kalahandi, despite being rich in minerals and producing large quantities of foodgrains, had become 'a kingdom of silence', resembling a 'desert' even after five decades of development. Similarly, an MP from West Bengal spoke of how the development process, instead of improving the lives of the poor, appeared to have the opposite effect in Kalahandi:

development is a continuous process and that is an upward process. Similarly, decadence is also a continuous process and that is a downward process. This downward process in respect of decadence of the KBK districts in the Western part of Orissa was a scene during the British period and is still a scene which is continuing after the Independence.[7]

The mention of starvation deaths in Kalahandi was invariably linked to the severity and frequency of drought. Non-Congress MPs were particularly severe in their criticism of successive state governments in Orissa for not formulating long-term drought-proofing strategies. As one MP put it, although a catalyst, drought could not be solely blamed for the suffering in Kalahandi:

Inadequate rainfall or uneven rainfall may be the first reason of drought . . . Deforestation or the felling of trees is the important factor contributing to add poison to the patient. But the most important factor . . . is the failure of the government to tackle the situation. This government could not apply their mind, could not apply their heart and could not apply their conscious efforts to combat the situation.[8]

A good deal of time in the Lok Sabha proceedings was spent in analysing both the 'process' and the 'event' of drought and the fact that, in contrast to other natural calamities like cyclones and floods, droughts actually provide the authorities with early warning information and time to react. There were also questions regarding how the bureaucracy – despite being in possession of advance technological equipment – was not able to foresee the adverse impact of drought.

It is amazing, it is astonishing that we are living in the age of science and technology and we could not utilise the resources . . . for the purpose of irrigation system or for the purpose of drinking water supply. Here is the failure of the government. It is amazing today to remind all these things . . . What do we see? We see the plight of the people and we see the migration of the people . . . A horrible picture I see.[9]

Another MP, representing the Congress party from Assam, was more willing to accept that it was not possible for a government to be in possession of early warning information of all calamities. Indirectly criticising his own party's record in Orissa, he noted that the state government appeared unprepared to tackle the severity of the drought:

> earnestness of the government is proved from what action the government takes before these calamities occur, by way of giving a warning to the people or taking precautions so that people do not suffer much. In the case of drought, it has not happened overnight. The spell is spread over months. The water resources were going to be dried up, it was in the newspapers and was also raised by the Members of the Parliament also, both on the floor of the House and outside.[10]

Several MPs also criticised administrative procedures in place for declaring a drought, arguing that the procedures were cumbersome and contributed to frequent delays in providing an adequate response. The articulate and active Congress MP from Orissa claimed that drought relief funds were made available only several months after the start of suffering since the procedures for declaring drought at the district and state levels involved too many officials:

> [The State government cannot] declare these [areas] as drought-affected because of the red tape and the famine code and the entire gamut of the official line where it has to come through the Collector. Then, it has to come to the Divisional Commissioner, Revenue. It has to come to the Special Relief Commissioner. Then, the Chief Secretary will send it here. Then, there will be crop cuttings in autumn. Then, there will be crop cuttings in December. Then, only in January, we – Hon. Members – will wake up that there is a drought.[11]

During the entire Lok Sabha period, MPs made several references to specific newspaper articles on starvation in Kalahandi and grilled central government ministers on the issue. In general, information provided in such news reports was a very important source of supplementary material used by MPs, and it also appeared that such information was primarily used by those who did not represent the state being discussed. For example, a MP from Rajasthan noted that he had read about the Orissa drought in newspapers and argued that 'We should really be very much concerned about it and we should do the needful and something concrete there'.[12] The central government was also asked on several occasions whether it was aware of newspaper stories of large-scale migration and starvation deaths and what measures it had planned to undertake in light of these reports. MPs generally took media reports seriously, especially those containing details which provided ammunition with which they could criticise the governments for neglect of long-term planning and the failure to adequately implement short-term drought failure.

No explicit definitions of starvation were articulated in the Lok Sabha despite frequent references to phrases such as 'starvation deaths' and 'famine-like situation', and almost all MPs appeared united in the belief that Kalahandi epitomised starvation. As one MP put it:

> It is painful on my part to mention that Kalahandi today is a black spot of hunger and starvation death in the map of India. Kalahandi and Bolangir both are the twin sisters of miseries and sufferings in Orissa and in the broader sense, the whole of India.[13]

Interestingly, whereas the Orissa (Congress) government consistently denied starvation deaths within its territory, several Congress MPs from Orissa appeared to admit that such deaths were indeed taking place. However, refusing to blame the state government, they targeted the central government for its failure to provide emergency assistance to Orissa and for its inability to ensure the successful implementation of the Long Term Action Plan (LTAP) in the KBK region.

> Sir, I wish to invite the attention of this August House to the poverty-stricken and starvation-ridden tribal pockets in Kalahandi–Bolangir–Koraput areas of Orissa. Poverty is so deep-rooted there, that every year a number of starvation deaths are reported from this area. For months together, the people have no foodgrains to eat, and they have to depend on crushed mango seeds . . . Action plan was to be implemented with resources from the Central government, State government, centrally sponsored schemes and Special Central Assistance. According to government's own admission . . . the implementation is highly unsatisfactory and to say the least, is tardy. I would, therefore, request the government to see to it that the Action Plan be implemented as per a time bound scheme.[14]

Two Congress MPs – one from Orissa and the other from Assam – were of the view that media attention on starvation deaths was causing 'panic' as disease-related deaths were being branded as 'starvation deaths'. While the MP from Orissa tried to defend the Orissa government, he simultaneously appeared to let the cat out of the bag by observing that no government in India would ever admit the occurrence of starvation deaths:

> There was some mention about starvation deaths. In fact, I would like to appeal here to the Hon. House that although the Press should be alert to these things, it should not cause panic by converting diarrhoea deaths and gastro-

enteritis deaths into starvation deaths because no Chief Minister or no State government is ever going to admit starvation deaths. It only creates panic and we know that many times we have raised it here in Parliament, but no State government will ever admit.[15]

While these debates were being held in the Lok Sabha, a group of opposition legislators from the Orissa Legislative Assembly requested the central government's agriculture minister to enquire into starvation deaths in Kalahandi and neighbouring districts. The minister subsequently publicly announced that he had asked the NHCR to investigate the matter. Fearing impending embarrassment of the sitting Orissa government, a Congress MP expressed his displeasure:

I understand that the Minister said that he would send the memorandum given by some people on starvation deaths to the Human Rights Commission. If it is a fact, I think, it is not very much justified to do so. It will create more problems. You should not politicise this problem. It should be above politics.[16]

It appeared quite strange that the representative was against an investigation by an impartial committee when he openly agreed that the problem should not be politicised. This was thus an example of a political party – in this case the Congress – resisting any outside scrutiny of its performance. Instead, Congress MPs from the state preferred to consistently highlight the need to treat their state – and areas like Kalahandi – as a 'special case' requiring extraordinary and urgent attention from the centre. In doing so, they defended the Orissa government by placing the entire blame on the centre's reluctance to provide additional funds. For example, towards the end of November 1996, an MP argued:

We have spent fifty years since our Independence and I would like to request the government not to display such a callous and negligent attitude. It is a criminal attitude on the part of the Centre – it is a calculated attempt to destroy the Eastern region. Now it is the time to come forward and take a pledge that we would not allow a single person to die, as is happening every year, in Orissa. This is what we have to do.[17]

A fortnight later the same MP claimed on the floor of the House that a relief package of Rs 500 million announced with much fanfare by the PM was yet to reach the coffers of the Orissa government. He further accused the centre of a 'stepmotherly attitude' for falsely claiming that it had allocated extra funds of over Rs 2 billion for drought relief, since most funds allocated to Orissa were normal plan allocations that had nothing to do with calamity relief.[18] Similar allegations, that no extra funds for drought relief had reached the Orissa government, were made by Congress MPs throughout 1997.

The central government's response in the Lok Sabha – delivered by successive prime ministers in 1996 and 1997 – was to criticise Orissa for its failure to properly utilise available funds. In a Lok Sabha debate in November 1996, the then Prime Minister, Deve Gowda, stated that, instead of clamouring for 'temporary relief, the Orissa government ought to develop permanent measures to manage drought.[19] Similarly, I. K. Gujral, who succeeded Deve Gowda as Prime Minister, accused the Orissa government in May 1997 for its failure to utilise available funds although he subsequently admitted that only a fraction of the total central allocations for drought relief sanctioned in November 1996 had reached Orissa.[20] However, he did not specify the reasons for this delay and insisted that MPs ought not to 'politicise' the issue of calamity relief. Throughout 1997, central government ministers and MPs from Orissa traded charges on the floor of the House on the exact amount of so-called 'extra funds' sanctioned by New Delhi for drought relief, and how much of it had actually made its way to Orissa.

Debates in the Lok Sabha also covered the need to put an end to ad hoc measures to manage drought and instead concentrate on formulating long-term or 'permanent' policies. As one Orissa MP put it:

> We should make a Master Plan. The Planning Commission should make a separate Plan for all these KBK districts and the districts of Palamau, Raipur and some other districts. There are, maybe, some 15–20 districts in our country which are perpetual victims of starvation due to drought conditions.[21]

Despite such appeals, there were no concrete suggestions of which criteria the central government should employ in formulating a long-term strategy. Rather, throughout 1997, several MPs individually suggested very similar and general proposals for immediate action with reference to the following: improvement of agriculture, increased food production and storage facilities; development of irrigation facilities in chronically drought-prone areas and the provision of safe drinking water; increase in labour-intensive works under the EAS; the need to control deforestation; increased monitoring of both development programmes and relief operations to check corruption and mismanagement. Some MPs from Orissa also demanded increased coordination of central and state government-funded programmes, arguing that too many schemes had lead to conflicting objectives and additional administrative burden on district-level officials. Interestingly, no one spoke of measures to improve health services or the need to improve the low purchasing power of the residents of areas like Kalahandi.

Perspectives on drought and starvation deaths, 1999–2002

Kalahandi did not figure as prominently in Lok Sabha debates in 1999–2002 as in 1996–97. In fact, there were no major debates exclusively focusing on drought and starvation in Orissa and most short-duration discussions were on general issues relating to loss of lives following natural calamities in various parts of India. However, it was during these general discussions that the Kalahandi MP and a handful of others representing Orissa raised matters related to drought and poverty in Kalahandi. Barring the Kalahandi MP, the general lack of interest among Orissa MPs in voicing their concerns on drought was matched by MPs from other states. Table 8.7 provides an overview of debates in the thirteenth Lok Sabha in which the issues of drought and starvation deaths in Kalahandi were highlighted.

The 'royal gentleman' from Kalahandi

Bikram Keshari Deo represented Kalahandi in the Lok Sabha for the first time in 1998–99 and was subsequently re-elected to the thirteenth Lok Sabha in 1999. Unlike his predecessor, Bhakta Charan Das – who belonged to the Scheduled Caste group – Keshari Deo belonged to the erstwhile royal family of the Kalahandi princely state with a long history of Lok Sabha representation. His grandfather was Kalahandi's first MP to the Lok Sabha (1952–56); his father took over in 1957

Table 8.7 Chronological sequence of debates on Kalahandi, September 1999–March 2002

Date	Type of debate	Topic
9 March 2000	Matters under rule 377	The need to release funds for early completion of Indravati project in Kalahandi
24 April 2000	Short duration discussion	Drought in various parts of the country
28 April 2000	Special mention	Drinking water shortage and water pollution in Kalahandi
19 December 2000	Matters under rule 377	The need to sanction pending projects of KBK districts in Orissa for all-round development of the region
24 April 2001	Matters under rule 377	Acute water crisis in Kalahandi and the need to start drinking water schemes
24 July 2001	Special mention	Demand to control starvation deaths in several states by supplying free foodgrains
9 August 2001	Short duration discussion	Loss of lives and property due to natural calamities in various parts of India
16 August 2001	Special mention	Urging the central government to approve the Revised LTAP for KBK districts of Orissa against the background of starvation deaths
29 August 2001	Special mention	The need for proper grain distribution mechanism in India
30 August 2001	Short duration discussion	Acute problems faced by the poor due to non-availability of foodgrains
26 November 2001	Matters under rule 377	The need for expeditious environment clearance of pending irrigation projects in Kalahandi
11 March 2002	Matters under rule 377	The need to set up bauxite mining and aluminium refinery complex in Kalahandi

Source: Compiled from reports on thirteenth Lok Sabha proceedings (various years).

and represented the district for two decades from 1957 to 1977. Often described in Kalahandi as a 'polite royal gentleman,' Keshari Deo was not as sensation-oriented or aggressive as his predecessor in Lok Sabha debates; hence, his ability to sell Kalahandi's poverty was somewhat limited. Nonetheless, in comparison with the inactivity of most Orissa MPs, he was relatively active and figured in 11 out of the 12 discussions in which Kalahandi was mentioned, even though most of these discussions fell in the categories of 'special mention' and 'matters under rule 377' where it is customary for a single MP to raise an issue of national importance without there being any follow-up debates.

Keshari Deo's interventions were focused on drought, particularly in relation to the speedy completion of ongoing irrigation projects, increased financial allocation to the KBK region, and the acute drinking water crisis that affected Kalahandi in 2000–01. For example, in early March 2000, he requested the central government to ensure that the Indravati irrigation project was completed at the earliest so that farmers in Kalahandi could enjoy improved irrigation facilities. In April of the same year, he highlighted the acute drinking water crisis in Kalahandi. Criticising the central government for not mentioning Kalahandi during a Rajya Sabha (upper house of Parliament) debate on water crises in India, he referred to information received from press reports in various national newspapers and from the Collector of Kalahandi that confirmed the severity of water shortage in the district. The MP also argued for improved implementation of government programmes at the grassroots level highlighting the 'total failure' of the PDS and the ineffectiveness of the EAS:

> There are lots of programmes to mitigate drought. The present as well as the previous Central Governments have initiated the programmes to mitigate drought under the Drought Prone Area Programme, EAS and DRDA. But, I am sorry to state that in Orissa, in places like Kalahandi, Bolangir and Koraput, the EAS card which is given to labourers for one hundred days is being utilised only for seventeen days . . . So, how can we expect that the objective will be met?[22]

On the matter of starvation deaths, Keshari Deo held an interesting position. On the one hand he was willing to accept that starvation deaths did take place in Kalahandi; on the other hand he was not willing to blame the sitting Orissa government for its inability to prevent such deaths. Rather, he argued that the previous (Congress) regime in Orissa was responsible for the continuation of starvation deaths since it could not implement long-term welfare programmes. When interviewed in February 1999, he observed:

> Yes, starvation deaths do take place and the problem is lack of proper nourishment. In our democratic society, people should not be allowed to die of starvation. Despite many government schemes like Gratuitous Relief, PDS,

etc. people continue to die ... And this is even stranger if you look at the procurement of over one lakh tonnes of paddy from Kalahandi every year.[23]

In the Lok Sabha he highlighted cases of alleged starvation deaths which appeared in the media, insisting that such instances had to be 'seriously looked into and steps should be taken so that incidents of starvation deaths are not repeated'.[24] He also urged the centre to 'take immediate steps to approve the Revised Long Term Action Plan for KBK so that starvation deaths could be avoided in future' in these districts. Defending the Orissa government, he argued that it would take considerable time for his government to undo the mistakes of the previous government and noted: 'We have just come to power three years back.' Profusely praising the central government for its willingness to provide all possible help to Orissa, he repeatedly claimed that Orissa's problems were the fault of the previous government. He bolstered his claim by citing the rulings of the Supreme Court and the Orissa High Court which had indicted the Congress government in Orissa in the 1980s and 1990s for its failure to prevent starvation deaths:

> Sir, a news item appeared in the *Times of India* today saying that people have died of starvation or by eating mango kernel or because of malnutrition. It is a matter of serious concern and I definitely share the view of the Leader of the Opposition, Shrimati Sonia Gandhi on this ... Our Government is committed to eradicate starvation and poverty in these areas and programmes have been prepared. However, at the same time, I am sorry to say that the previous governments never looked into the problems of these areas where 80 per cent of the people live below the poverty line. The previous governments, which ruled Orissa, I would like to categorically name the Congress government, did nothing. When a writ petition was filed in the Supreme Court, it gave a direction. The High Court also gave a direction. It was pointed out that the starvation deaths had taken place due to the neglect of the then government.[25]

In addition to Orissa, the Kalahandi MP further cited cases of starvation deaths in Madhya Pradesh, Rajasthan and Maharashtra in 2000, during which the Congress held power in these states:

> Who are the governments there? There is the Congress government ruled by the Congress Party there. I would say it has been a general habit. When the Congress Party was ruling in Orissa, that time also starvation deaths had taken place in Kalahandi and other regions.[26]

When asked about his performance in the Lok Sabha, Keshari Deo observed – much like his predecessor – that although 'all MPs from Orissa are united in Parliament for the welfare of the people', he was willing to clamour for benefits for Kalahandi even if this meant going against his party. He was, however, quick to add that it was pointless to constantly criticise the state government in the Lok Sabha since 'you cannot strengthen anything by first weakening it and vice-versa'.[27]

General participation of MPs in debates

Given that 19 of the 21 MPs from Orissa in the thirteenth Lok Sabha belonged to the BJP–BJD alliance (holding power in New Delhi and Bhubaneswar), there was a general reluctance to engage in debates on sensitive topics like starvation since this would invariably amount to criticising the performance of the sitting governments at the centre and in Orissa. Among the two opposition (Congress) MPs from Orissa, one deserves special mention as he was active both in 1996–97 and in 1999–2002. Indeed, K. P. Singh Deo raised the issue of starvation deaths on numerous occasions. During the thirteenth Lok Sabha period, the political situation in Orissa had changed considerably and the Congress had been routed in both the state assembly and Lok Sabha elections. In contrast to 1996–97, Singh Deo felt free to air his views on starvation, being the sole representative from Orissa who actively opposed state government policies. For example, he repeatedly criticised the Orissa government for failing to hold anyone accountable when starvation deaths did take place or whenever policy failures were highlighted in the media:

> On the 24th of July, the Supreme Court, the highest court of India, has directed the Centre that they cannot allow any person to die of starvation within the Indian Union . . . In spite of that, why are we feeling so helpless? Is no one accountable or responsible for acts of omission or commission? . . . If there is misappropriation, nobody's head rolls. I have got a paper cutting which states that in my own State, there is a nexus between the mill owner, the civil supply officer, the bureaucrat and maybe sometimes the politician. There is a food mafia. We are trading charges here in Parliament. We will be trading charges in the State Assembly also. They are not held responsible and accountable. Their heads won't roll and people will be dying.[28]

Virtually every year, the Lok Sabha is witness to debates on drought and starvation similar to those of previous years and some MPs even recycle old speeches, often using the same quotations. Highlighting such matters, Singh Deo expressed disappointment with the influence that MPs actually exercise to make fundamental changes in the system:

> it is with a great sense of responsibility and a deep sense of anguish that I am participating in this discussion . . . knowing fully well that this is the highest legislative forum in our country, the largest democracy of the world where the supreme will of the people is manifested. Sir, for 34 years I have had the occasion to speak about cyclone, floods and drought, right from 1967 when I first entered this House. My first, maiden speech was on drought of Orissa. I am pained that 750 of us, Members of both the Houses of Parliament raise

159

this issue and nothing happens . . . Whatever we have been saying, cutting across party lines, is falling on deaf ears.[29]

By late August 2001, several national and local dailies began reporting the starvation-related deaths of 25 people in western Orissa who, facing starvation, had resorted to eating mango kernels. Most reports made a connection between prolonged periods of undernutrition and the consumption of inedible items like mango kernels. Newspapers also had a field day when the highest ranked bureaucrat in the Orissa government – the Chief Secretary – was quoted in a report claiming that mango kernels were a routine part of the diet of local tribal groups and that such diet was actually nutritious. Nutritionists dismissed such claims, pointing out that there was no evidence to indicate that mango kernels had nutritional value. On the floor of the Lok Sabha, however, one Orissa MP – representing Sambalpur, which borders Kalahandi – passionately defended his state government and vehemently denied the occurrence of any starvation deaths. The MP went on to allege that media reports on starvation were intended to malign the sitting Orissa government and his party, the BJD:

Sir, my apprehension or my feeling is that a systematic attempt is being made to present a very bad picture of the State, to defame the State government which has been, during the last 15 months after assuming the power in the State, trying its best to deal with the very crucial situation in the State that has been inherited by this government from the earlier one . . . I confidently and stoutly deny that there has been any starvation deaths in that area. People have died. People have died the day before yesterday and also some fifteen–twenty people have died a few days back. The State government, in the mean time, has sent a high level official team to the area. Proper verifications have been made and the deaths that have occurred in the few villages in the Kashipur block are not owing to starvation.[30]

The MP went on to allege that tribal groups in Orissa had 'peculiar food habits' and that the deaths were 'purely accidental' – the result of food poisoning as the mango kernels had become poisonous. He also claimed that several VIPs who visited Kalahandi – including Indira Gandhi in 1966 and Rajiv Gandhi in 1987 – had eaten traditional tribal food and had received considerable political mileage when these events were reported in the media. However, despite many promises by the central government, 'nothing happened':

I do not deny that there is misery in that area of Orissa. Orissa as such is a backward State. As there is misery in Chattisgarh, in major parts of Madhya Pradesh, and in other parts of the country, there is misery in the State of Orissa. There is no denying the fact that there is poverty in the State. But this poverty has not crept in overnight.[31]

Thus, the real fault, he argued, could be traced back to the Congress party for doing little to improve the conditions of tribal groups during the several decades it held power at both central and state levels. Similar arguments were articulated by other BJP and BJD MPs from Orissa. Apart from the Kalahandi MP – who at least tried to be objective – there was little interest among his colleagues in even remotely admitting that current government policy was inadequate. Indeed, the oft-cited response to Orissa's travails was inevitably to blame the previous government.

Lok Sabha questions on starvation

The chronology and subject matter of questions on starvation in the period 1999–2002 is provided in Table 8.8. Most questions on starvation in Orissa were asked in the period November–March which roughly corresponds to the period when the impact of drought is most severe in places like Kalahandi. All questions had a standard format and usually sought information on three broad sets of issues. First, whether starvation deaths reported in the media were true and, if so, how many individuals (of a particular group, such as tribals) had died and whether the central government was aware of these events. Second, whether immediate and long-term measures were being undertaken by the state and central governments to combat the incidence of starvation deaths. Third, whether financial assistance from the centre had been requested by the state government (and details of amount) in order to undertake relief works. The answers provided by central government ministers were usually presented in an equally standard format. Although details were readily given on measures to combat the adverse effects of drought and the amount of financial assistance provided, the central government consistently refused to admit that starvation deaths had occurred in any part of the country. In most instances, the allegations were categorically and immediately denied, and in a small number of cases the centre responded by claiming that it had asked the state governments in question to inquire into the allegations and submit a report at the earliest. However, state governments on their part – and irrespective of the type of party in power – invariably submitted reports categorically denying starvation deaths. Thus, the role of parliamentary questions appeared to be simply a process whereby an opposition MP alleged the occurrence of starvation deaths in a particular part of the country while the central government either denied it immediately or requested some additional time before eventually issuing a categorical denial.

All questions on starvation deaths in Orissa were directed towards at least one of the following three ministries: agriculture; consumer affairs, food and public distribution; tribal affairs. A question by an MP from Orissa in November 2000 (Box 8.1) illustrates the typical nature and format of parliamentary questions and answers.

The nature and timing of the above question was particularly interesting since the MP belonged to the BJD party, which held power in Orissa. It was a rare

Table 8.8 Questions on starvation deaths in the thirteenth Lok Sabha, 1999–2002

Date	State and party affiliations of MP(s)	Subject
25 February 2000	Assam (INC)	Starvation deaths in tea estates in Assam
25 July 2000	Kerala (INC)	Whether starvation deaths have occurred in tribal areas of Indian states
9 August 2000	Kerala (INC)	Number of starvation deaths in the country in 1999–2000, by state
20 November 2000	Andhra Pradesh (TDP)	Whether starvation deaths are still occurring in Orissa and other places*
28 November 2000	Orissa (BJD)	Sale of children and starvation deaths in Orissa*
9 March 2001	Andhra Pradesh (TDP)	Food shortage in drought-stricken states and starvation deaths*
14 March 2001	West Bengal (CPI(M))	Whether newspaper reports of starvation deaths in Orissa are true*
24 July 2001	Maharashtra (SS)	Starvation deaths in tribal areas of India, particularly Maharashtra
26 July 2001	Orissa (BJP), Andhra Pradesh (AIMIM)	Drought and starvation deaths in Indian states
31 July 2001	Maharashtra (BJP)	Setting up grain banks to prevent starvation deaths
7 August 2001	Uttar Pradesh (SP), Maharashtra (PWPI)	Impact of poverty alleviation programmes on starvation deaths in India
10 August 2001	Punjab (INC), Andhra Pradesh (INC), Bihar (CPI(M) + BJP), West Bengal (CPI(M)), Karnataka (BJP)	Surplus food stocks in India and reports of starvation deaths in Orissa, Rajasthan, Bihar and other states of India*
19 November 2001	Orissa (INC), Maharashtra (INC)	Starvation deaths in many states of India, particularly Orissa*
14 December 2001	Andhra Pradesh (TDP)	Starvation deaths among weavers in Andhra Pradesh
1 March 2002	Rajasthan (INC), Bihar (RJD), Karnataka (INC)	Starvation deaths in six states of India and government efforts to identify Below Poverty Line (BPL) households for targeted intervention*
8 March 2002	Bihar (BJP)	Surplus food stocks and reports of starvation deaths in Orissa, Rajasthan, Bihar and other Indian states
16 April 2002	Madhya Pradesh (INC)	Preventing starvation by setting up grain banks at the village level

Source: Compiled from Reports on thirteenth Lok Sabha proceedings (various years).

Note
Questions relating specifically to Orissa are marked with an asterisk in the subject column.

Box 8.1 A typical question and answer session on starvation deaths in the Lok Sabha

Lok Sabha question No. 126, dated 28.11.2000 by Bhartruhari Mahtab, BJD party, Cuttack, Orissa

Will the Minister of TRIBAL AFFAIRS be pleased to state: (a) whether the Union government have received any report from Orissa about the sale of children and starvation deaths in the tribal areas; (b) if so, the details thereof; and (c) the steps taken by the Union government to avoid starvation deaths and sale of tribal children in the State?

Answer by Jual Oram (BJP party, Minister of Tribal Affairs)

(a) No, Sir.
(b) Does not arise.
(c) This Ministry provides funds under Central/Centrally Sponsored Schemes to the State governments for implementation of various socio-economic developmental programmes for the welfare and development of Scheduled Tribes. A separate Central Sector scheme namely Village Grain Bank Scheme was launched in 1996–97. The scheme was started on a pilot basis in selected areas out of the areas identified by Central Planning Committee for preventive measures against death of tribal in general and children in particular in remote and backward tribal areas by providing a safeguard against fall in nutritional standard of Scheduled Tribes living in remote rural areas.

---

example of the issue of starvation deaths being raised by a ruling-party MP at the risk of embarrassing his own party. Incidentally, the Village Grain Bank Scheme mentioned by the Minister of Tribal Affairs in his reply to the question was unheard of in the study villages of Kalahandi. In order to identify the main characteristic patterns of such question and answer sessions, I will briefly examine some of the questions marked with an asterisk in Table 8.8.

In March 2001, two CPI(M) MPs from West Bengal asked the minister of agriculture whether he was aware of a news report published in the *Hindustan Times* in December 2000 which provided early warning information of impending drought and starvation in Orissa. To this, the minister replied, 'No reports on deaths due to starvation have been received from the Government of Orissa'. Similarly, in August 2001, six MPs from five different states jointly asked the minister of consumer affairs, food and public distribution whether starvation deaths had occurred specifically in Rajasthan, Orissa and Bihar and whether the Food Corporation of Indian had failed to provide foodgrains in 'drought-hit and famine-hit areas, despite record buffer stock of foodgrains'. Responding to the question, the minister replied, 'The information is being collected from the State governments concerned and will be laid on the table of the House.' Indeed, such replies by central government ministers appeared to be the preferred response in the Lok Sabha whenever questions on controversial topics such as starvation were raised. The alternative response, of outright government denial, ran the risk of opposition attack for being premature and not based on empirical evidence. Hence, there was often a preference among central government ministers to simply postpone answering a question by claiming that the government was trying to gather information from state governments. For example, with regard to the above question, no answer was presented in the House, prompting one of the MPs – who had originally raised the question in August 2001 with several colleagues – to re-submit the question in March 2002. However, Lok Sabha records indicate that even this question remained unanswered.

After the Supreme Court ordered all states to radically improve the functioning of the PDS in July 2001 (discussed in Chapter 5), the issue was raised in the Lok Sabha in November of the same year. A Congress MP from Orissa, together with a party colleague from Maharashtra, asked the minister of agriculture whether the central government was aware of starvation deaths in Orissa, Andhra Pradesh and Maharashtra.[32] They further enquired whether the government had sent study teams to these states to investigate the alleged deaths and whether the Supreme Court's directives were being implemented. In an oral response to this question, the agriculture minister provided the following answer:

The Government of Orissa have strongly denied allegations of 'starvation deaths'. This subject is currently sub-judice in a Public Interest Litigation . . . wherein such allegations have been denied by the States. The Department of Food and Public Distribution which is representing the Union of India in the said case has already filed a Statement indicating compliance with the Interim Directions of the Honourable Court.[33]

Table 8.8 also confirms the general passivity of MPs from Orissa as they only asked three questions – two of which were specifically on Orissa and the third related to starvation deaths generally in India. Questions specifically on Kalahandi were, however, raised on several occasions by MPs from Orissa's neighbours – Andhra Pradesh, Bihar and West Bengal. Moreover, the nature of questions on starvation did not appear to differ from questions on other topics. In fact, although most questions were designed to force the central government to acknowledge that starvation deaths were taking place, they generally failed to do so since the central government – like all its predecessors – categorically refused to accept the validity of media reports on starvation. Parliamentary questions were thus a useful way of soliciting information on specific issues which were not available to MPs in debates and other discussions in the Lok Sabha. The most useful information arrived in the form of statistics on drought relief and other central government allocations together with the amount of money that states were actually able to spend. The questions also provided an opportunity for the MPs to encourage the government to reinvestigate its response to drought and starvation while at the same sending the message that its activities would continue to be closely monitored. For the major part, however, all parliamentary questions on starvation resulted in standard replies. And since there is seldom a debate following answers provided by ministers, these Q & A sessions have become what Mathur and Jayal (1993: 109) term 'ritualistic', providing MPs with a sense of contentment at having at least tried to raise an important matter.

Concluding remarks

The above discussion on Lok Sabha debates and questions reveals several interesting features. The issue of starvation deaths figured prominently mainly thanks to the efforts of MPs belonging to opposition parties in Orissa and those from other states who opposed both the central and Orissa governments. The status of Kalahandi as the 'starvation capital' of India was borne out quite clearly from the analysis of Lok Sabha proceedings since the district was mentioned in almost all debates on drought in Orissa and in over half of the parliamentary questions on starvation. Not only was the Kalahandi MP active, but the Kalahandi story was also often used as a benchmark by MPs to criticise general policy failure elsewhere in India. That an area could be termed another 'Kalahandi' in the making was an effective way of drawing attention to a problem. MPs also frequently quoted from news reports alleging starvation, child sale and large-scale migration in various parts of the country and it appeared that the press played a key role in keeping the country's top legislators informed on drought and deprivation.

Although most MPs agreed that deaths from malnutrition and disease continued to take place, there were differences on whether they could be labelled as 'starvation deaths'. Ruling-party MPs were more likely to argue that opposition parties were politicising the issue and that deaths from other causes were being described as starvation-related. The discussions in the Lok Sabha also suggested that MPs were well aware that, despite their efforts, no state government would ever admit to starvation deaths within its territory. All parliamentary questions invariably met the same fate – the centre and the state in question categorical denied that such deaths were starvation-related.

The nature and level of adversarial politics and criticism of state governments in the Lok Sabha was directly correlated with the number of ruling-party MPs from the state – the larger the number of opposition MPs the more the criticism of the state government. Since elections to the state legislative assembly and the Lok Sabha often throw up similar results, the ruling party/coalition at the state level invariably also has the largest delegation of MPs from the state to the Lok Sabha. This was the story of Orissa in both Lok Sabha periods, when an overwhelming majority of MPs belonged to the ruling party/alliance in Orissa – 17 of 21 MPs in 1996–97 belonged to the ruling Congress party whereas 19 of 21 MPs in 1999–2002 belonged to the BJD–BJP coalition. Thus, a large majority of MPs in both periods were able to defend the Orissa government against charges of starvation deaths levelled in the Lok Sabha by opposition MPs. When its own drought relief policy was criticised, the central government usually responded by claiming that it was doing everything possible to provide assistance to Orissa. Particularly in the 1996–97 period – when different political parties held power at the centre and in Orissa – the central government's major strategy in the Lok Sabha was to blame the Orissa government for its failure to utilise available funds at its disposal.

Finally, there were instances when MPs provided some form of early warning information, urging the central government to take action. For example, the MP from Kalahandi warned of drought-related distress in Kalahandi in July–August 1996 and subsequently argued in November 1996 that, despite his warnings, the central and state governments were slow to react. In general, however, it does not appear that early warning was provided on a regular basis, and the fact that the Lok Sabha is only in session for only a few months every year makes it difficult for MPs to raise issues on the floor of the House in time. Overall, and considering the wide array of topics and regions discussed in the Lok Sabha, Kalahandi appears to have received more than its fair share of attention, having figured prominently in several Lok Sabha debates and questions.

9

PURULIA'S ACHIEVEMENT

In order to better understand the conditions under which democracy and public action work to prevent starvation deaths, this chapter briefly examines the case of Purulia (sometimes also spelt Puruliya)[1] district in West Bengal, which is very similar to Kalahandi in many respects. For example, Purulia has a high percentage of SC and ST groups, low levels of literacy, and large groups of children and adults suffering from chronic undernutrition, and is among the most 'backward' districts in West Bengal. Like Kalahandi, Purulia is chronically drought-prone. Apart from the district capital, Purulia town, most of the villages suffer from food shortages and water scarcity during drought years when the monsoon rains are erratic and unevenly distributed. However, despite recurrent drought episodes, high population density, undeveloped agricultural potential, stagnation in industry and high levels of undernutrition, no starvation deaths have ever been reported in Purulia. Although radical improvements in the condition of the poor have not occurred, the district's apparent success in preventing starvation deaths against great odds warrants a closer look. Against the background of a particularly severe drought in 1998–99, this chapter examines the nature and impact of public action in combating drought and preventing loss of lives.

Poverty, drought and government interventions

Purulia is among the poorest of West Bengal's 18 districts; of the estimated total population of 2.4 million in 2000, 48 per cent were classified as living below the poverty line (BPL).[2] SC and ST groups constitute 19.35 per cent and 19.22 per cent of the population, respectively.[3] The district's literacy rate is low (45.6 per cent) and even lower among women (13.3 per cent) (Government of West Bengal 1999b).[4] Over 90 per cent of the population live in rural areas, and although agriculture is the main source of livelihood, the average size of operational landholdings in the district in 1991 was 0.99 hectares – far less than the 1.94 hectares in Kalahandi (Government of West Bengal 1999c). Rainfall (annual average 1,300 mm) is unevenly distributed and invariably erratic in nature, with the soil having poor water-retention capacity. Moreover, the rapidly diminishing underground water supply in recent years had been a major source of concern among district officials, and the impact of a drought was normally further aggravated by the poor state of irrigation facilities in the district.[5] Thus, whereas only 6 of 13 blocks in Kalahandi were classified as drought-prone (DPAP), all 20 blocks of Purulia fell under this category. The frequency and adverse impact of drought in Purulia was further borne out by the fact that, of the 34 blocks that were covered under the DPAP in West Bengal, Purulia alone accounted for 20.

Land in Purulia is divided into three categories – *bahal* (lowland), *kanali* (medium land) and *baid* (uplands). Small and marginal farmers usually cultivate *kanali* and *baid* land, which are less fertile and have less water-retention capacity than *bahal*. The district has rich but fast depleting resources, with low intensity of cultivation, and over two thirds of those involved in agriculture are marginal farmers. A major difference between Purulia and Kalahandi, however, related to the implementation of land reforms, which have been extensively implemented in West Bengal[6] but largely neglected in Orissa. Thus, marginal, small and semi-medium farmers in Purulia each control, on average, 30 per cent of the cultivated area whereas the corresponding figure for medium and large farmers is around 9 per cent and 0.22 per cent, respectively. However, although land redistribution has resulted in a more egalitarian peasantry – the beneficiaries of the state's land redistribution efforts have included almost equal numbers of SC, ST and other groups – the large group of marginal farmers in Purulia (constituting two thirds of all cultivators) are particularly vulnerable to recurrent episodes of drought. The large number of fragmented plots under their control also adversely affects total agricultural productivity in the district, and several NGOs and opposition parties in West Bengal alleged that a considerable share of the land actually redistributed in the district was land unfit for agricultural activity.

From short field visits to villages located in remote blocks of Purulia, it appeared that, like Kalahandi, the nutritional status of SC and ST households was more vulnerable than other groups. Moreover, moderate levels of child malnutrition were clearly visible in most villages. Rice was the main diet for the majority of the population; vegetables, meat and fish remained beyond the reach of the poor, and local doctors and NGOs claimed that the consumption of wild fruits and roots together with country-made alcohol had increased the incidence of malnutrition and the risk of disease, particularly among ST households. Poor nutritional habits including diets with little protein and vitamin content also contributed to a variety of nutritional deficiency diseases among large sections of the rural poor. For example, an important factor affecting nutrition was the consumption of husked mill rice, which local doctors argued contained little carbohydrates, hence providing less nutritional value than other rice types. Similarly, the widespread presence of contaminated water in the district was a major problem. Although the water did not generally contain arsenic as in many other districts of West Bengal, it was often so polluted that the risk of water-borne diseases was high. In addition to malaria, there was widespread presence of diarrhoea, filaria, tuberculosis, viral hepatitis, acute respiratory infections, acute gastroenteritis, pneumonia, measles and whooping cough.

Local health officials openly admitted that more than 40 per cent of rural women were anaemic and that undernutrition among pregnant women was responsible for low birth weight particularly in tribal areas of the district. A survey conducted by the department of health in July 2001 found that 28 per cent of all births were premature and that 40 per cent of children under 5 suffered from mild malnutrition, 30 per cent from moderate malnutrition and approximately 1 per cent from severe malnutrition.[7] Although the health system in Purulia did not appear to work significantly better than in Kalahandi, two features deserve special mention. First, Public Health Centres (PHCs) regularly sent detailed monthly reports to the district health department on the incidence of disease, the number of patients treated and the total number of deaths. Further, when the outbreak of diarrhoea or mass epidemics was imminent, village-level extension workers provided crucial early warning to the local PHC, which subsequently contacted district health authorities for further instructions and assistance. In Kalahandi such a health and disease surveillance system, although in place, was not equally effective. Second, major hospitals and PHCs did not face a shortage of doctors, nurses and administrative personnel as was the case in Kalahandi. Although Purulia was not an attractive posting in comparison to other districts of West Bengal that were closer to Calcutta, most doctors appeared to enjoy working in the district. In addition, many young doctors found it easier to get much-needed practical experience in Purulia than other districts, where the competition for government jobs was much stiffer. In general, a combination of altruistic motives, positive incentives for young doctors and the relatively good train and road communications connecting Purulia to Calcutta and other major cities of West Bengal helped Purulia avoid understaffing in its health services.

Like Kalahandi, Purulia had a range of social security and anti-poverty programmes in place, including ITDP, JRY, IAY, SGSY, and pension and benefit schemes. Although the workings of these programmes were not studied in detail, there was little evidence to suggest that they functioned any better or any worse than in Kalahandi. However, Purulia differed significantly in the manner in which the programmes were targeted at selected groups of beneficiaries. Not only did the ruling CPI(M) party heavily influence the compilation of BPL lists, but in certain areas large groups of deserving beneficiaries – who supported opposition parties like the Trinamul Congress and the Congress – were excluded from programme benefits. District officials also complained that, in addition to limited funds for the maintenance of social security services, there were frequent delays in the allocation of funds from Calcutta and the subsequent receipt of the same in Purulia. This, for example, meant that pensioners often had to wait for several months in order to receive their cash allowances which exacerbated their poverty. The district relief officer also complained that an increasing number of defunct tube wells had become a problem and that no drilling machines were available in the district that could dig below 30 m in order to access new underground water supplies.[8]

As in Kalahandi, the PDS, ICDS and NMMP were the main nutritional interventions in Purulia. Although information on the ICDS and NMMP was unavailable,[9] field visits to select blocks of the district revealed that the coverage of these programmes was patchy and several areas with poor road communication (e.g. many villages in the Ayodhya Hills region) did not have any Aganwadi centres. There were also frequent allegations of corruption in the ICDS and NMMP and numerous allegations were made by NGOs and villagers of food rations being sold in the open market. Information on the PDS was, however, available and according to the district civil supplies officer, around 800 Fair Price Shops were in operation, covering 1.7 million ration card holders. Of these, 48.08 per cent belonged to the BPL category and were hence entitled to subsidised rice, wheat and sugar rations. Four features of the PDS in Purulia were interesting in relation to the Kalahandi experience. First, targeting the programme to include the poorest of the poor was a problem, although for very different reasons from in Kalahandi. As briefly mentioned earlier, the process of selecting beneficiaries was largely controlled by the ruling party, and the civil supplies officer complained that Panchayat representatives regularly added and deleted households from BPL lists depending on political affiliation and irrespective of economic need.[10] Adding to the problem was the continued use of an outdated BPL list (compiled in 1994–95), which meant that the PDS did not reach out to all deserving BPL households. Second, the general cost of living in Purulia was low as the prices of locally produced rice and vegetables were cheaper than in other districts of West Bengal. Hence, the average purchasing power of rural households in Purulia appeared to be better than in Kalahandi. Third, monitoring systems in place to check leakage of PDS stocks also appeared to be more effective than in Kalahandi. An innovative scheme in Purulia was the formation of block-level monitoring committees consisting of three members (the sub-inspector of food supplies, a Panchayat representative and a social worker) that monitored the transport and arrival of PDS stocks from Purulia town. Fourth, and most importantly, Purulia had far better storage capacity than Kalahandi for foodgrains procured by the FCI. Not only was there in excess of 100,000 tonnes of storage space, but government-managed godowns were also better maintained than in Kalahandi, preventing damage to foodgrains. Thus, the overall impression from Purulia was that, although the PDS faced some of the same problems as in Kalahandi, it nonetheless functioned relatively well in areas covered by the programme.

Administrative response to drought in 1998–99

Although Purulia received 1,210 mm of rainfall in 1998, the erratic nature and uneven distribution of the rains led to a severe drought starting in October 1998. By November the drought had affected 87 per cent of revenue villages (*mouzas*) spread across 170 GPs in all of Purulia's 20 blocks and 67 per cent of the villages experienced more than 50 per cent crop loss. After a quick official declaration of drought in late November 1998, administrative response was mainly directed at repairing wells and tube wells, providing drinking water to scarcity areas by means of hired water tankers, and the provision of cattle fodder. Land revenue collection was waived and labour-intensive works were started all over the district with a minimum daily wage rate of Rs 48. Emergency gratuitous relief was provided to the elderly and the destitute in the form of rice, wheat and clothing (dhotis, lungis, saris, cotton blankets, etc.). This form of assistance was subsequently extended to cover approximately 2 per cent of the total population of the district and – compared with Kalahandi – appeared more capable of identifying potentially vulnerable individuals and households. This was primarily thanks to alert Panchayat representatives who feared loss of political support if they ignored the plight of people close to destitution within their areas.

By February 1999, a major drinking water crisis had erupted following a sustained period of heatwave and the district administration sent repeated requests to the West Bengal government for increased financial resources to fight the drought. Interviews with the District Magistrate[11] and other district officials revealed that, despite their pleas, the state government in Calcutta was particularly unsuccessful in securing allocations from the Calamity Relief Fund and the National Fund for Calamity Relief. For example, district officials had submitted, in January 1999, a detailed proposal requesting additional grants from various state government ministries, totalling Rs 1.05 billion of which Rs 0.9 billion constituted wages to agricultural labourers. As of May 1999, however, the district had received only Rs 39 million for the provision of GR, emergency drinking water and cash relief to the distressed and for the purchase of clothing, blankets and tarpaulins. This adversely affected the district administration's ability to purchase foodgrains from neighbouring districts and extra Fair Price Shops for the distribution of emergency PDS rations could not be opened. The shortage of drought relief funds invariably also had consequences for the provision of wage labour through labour-intensive programmes. Interviews in some of the severe drought-affected blocks of Purulia revealed that, on average, an individual received between 17 and 20 days of employment instead of the promised 100 days a year. Nonetheless, this figure was three times higher than in Kalahandi. Although agricultural loans to farmers were not provided, officials distributed so-called 'mini-kits' to farmers which included seeds for vegetable and pulse cultivation.

Being traditionally drought-prone, the coping strategies of the rural poor in Purulia were similar to their counterparts in Kalahandi. The forests provided alternative food items and minor forest products like seeds, herbs, roots, etc., which tribal households sold in the market. Whereas there was some distress sale of assets during the 1998 drought, the role of moneylenders in Purulia was virtually negligible and, despite several queries, it was not possible to locate a single moneylender in the areas I visited nor did people complain about the exploitative practices of outside traders. On these aspects, Purulia fared much better than Kalahandi and it appeared that the high level of political consciousness in the district made it difficult for outside traders and moneylenders to operate unchecked. A further difference between the two districts was that there was no evidence of an increase in large-scale 'distress-induced' out-migration from Purulia. Although 'seasonal migration' to agriculturally prosperous districts within West Bengal (e.g.

Burdwan and Midnapore) and major cities like Ranchi, Dhanbad and Jamshedpur has been commonly practised for several decades, there was no evidence of an increase in 'distress migration' during the 1998 drought. The social security system functioned reasonably well throughout the drought period and the administration was triggered into high alert during the initial stages of a food and water crisis. Thus, despite a shortage of financial resources, the Purulia district administration's record in managing the drought and preventing starvation deaths and major epidemics appears to be a creditable one. As a senior doctor described it, despite widespread suffering not once was the situation in the district allowed to deteriorate to become one of 'severe undernutrition' – not even during the 1998 drought. This, he argued, explained Purulia's success in preventing starvation deaths.[12]

Public action and the prevention of starvation deaths

In this section I will briefly discuss the role of public action in preventing starvation deaths in Purulia. Except for the sensational arms-drop case in the early 1990s,[13] the district was seldom mentioned in Parliament. The West Bengal government's allegations of New Delhi's discrimination in the politics of calamity relief have already been discussed in Chapter 7. Rather, the following sections briefly highlight certain key differences between Kalahandi and Purulia with a focus on the role of political parties, Panchayats, bureaucracy, judiciary and the press in the prevention of starvation deaths.

Politics and the dominance of the Left Front

Whereas there has been a change in government almost every five years in Orissa since the mid-1980s, the political situation in West Bengal is a picture of stability with 30 years of Left Front rule. The main opposition party for a considerable number of years was the Congress, although internal feuds between various factions gradually weakened the party's influence. Subsequently, the Trinamul Congress – a breakaway faction of the Congress party – donned the role of the main opposition party. However, none of these parties enjoy the kind of mass support that the CPI(M) does in West Bengal. In Purulia, the CPI(M) and its allies thoroughly dominated the political landscape. Indeed, an important feature of the CPI(M)'s dominance in West Bengal politics in recent decades has been the overwhelming support it enjoys in rural areas. Voter turnout at 82.94 per cent during the 1996 State Assembly elections was extremely high by Indian standards and over 80 per cent of the rural votes were captured by the Left Front alliance. Thus, throughout the state, the Left Front government relies heavily on village-level voter banks and there is a conscious effort not to antagonise these groups. This was also the case in Purulia where over 85 per cent of the rural vote was captured by the CPI(M)[14] whereas the two major opposition parties enjoyed some support among middle-class groups residing in urban centres like Purulia town. Consequently, the opposition was hardly visible in rural Purulia.

On the issue of defining 'starvation' and 'starvation deaths', politicians in West Bengal appeared just as vague as their colleagues in Orissa. The few that were willing to elaborate on the issue, including a major opposition leader in Purulia, operated with a very strict definition of starvation. For example, they argued that starvation deaths could only occur when individuals were not in a position to consume minimum caloric needs for 10–15 consecutive days. Politicians across parties were united in their assertion that, although Purulia was poor and highly illiterate, no starvation deaths had taken place since the mid-1970s. For example, the leader of the Congress party in Purulia, who was also a doctor by profession, remarked: 'There are no starvation deaths but people face difficulty during the lean agricultural season . . . besides, there is considerable drought-related distress and during severe droughts the nutritional situation becomes precarious'.[15] Similarly, the West Bengal government's minister of relief – a long-time resident of Purulia belonging to the Forward Block party (a Left Front partner) – agreed that starvation deaths in the district were a matter of history although he pointed to the continued existence of high levels of chronic undernutrition, particularly in tribal blocks.[16] But, most interestingly, he was critical of his own government's record in developing the district and claimed that Purulia was not considered politically important by the CPI(M) and that other areas of the state received preferential treatment in allocation of resources for development.

Senior members of the ruling CPI(M), not surprisingly, emphasised the party's achievements in implementing decentralised governance and land reforms which, they argued, strengthened the overall food security situation in the state. As the minister for Panchayati Raj and Land Reform observed, 'When the poor get land, they are interested in food production, and as such food security is crucially dependent on the successful implementation of land reforms'.[17] The government's claims of complete success in this area were disputed not only by opposition parties but also by NGOs working in the agriculture sector who claimed the bulk of the land redistributed in Purulia was actually wasteland that was unfit for cultivation. On a similar note, the minister of relief claimed that several landlords in Purulia had repeatedly avoided confiscation of their land since they have financially and politically supported the CPI(M). Thus, the general impression on land reforms was that, although West Bengal indeed had an impressive record at redistributing land, this factor alone did not explain Purulia's success at preventing starvation deaths. Rather, a major factor could be traced to the comparatively high level of political consciousness in rural Purulia which was reflected not only in terms of high voter turnout during elections but also in the continued support that the CPI(M) and its allies continued to receive in rural areas despite having been in power for several decades. Indeed, the anti-incumbency factor – which contributed to the downfall of successive governments in Orissa – appeared notably absent in West Bengal.

The high level of voter mobilisation meant that villagers frequently complained to local party workers whenever something went wrong or when drought-related distress appeared on the village map. Hence, the local organisation and presence of the CPI(M) cadre in virtually all villages of Purulia was important as party workers regularly provided early warning information on crises – drought, food shortage and major epidemics – directly to both the district administration and the party leadership in Purulia town. The CPI(M) cadre in Purulia generally argued that they particularly gave priority to the monitoring of the drinking water situation (undertaken by keeping a close watch on the conditions of tube wells and ponds) and the local price of foodgrains and essential commodities. The CPI(M)'s district unit subsequently informed its leaders, ministers and senior bureaucrats in Calcutta. It was during such communication between district and state politicians and civil servants that requests for additional personnel, equipment and financial assistance were made. Thus, the widespread presence and relative efficiency of the CPI(M) cadre at the block and district levels meant that the party hierarchy often received information even before the district administration or the state government. Villagers in Purulia also appeared more demanding of their elected representatives than in Kalahandi. As a minister (elected from Purulia) put it, 'The CPI(M) does not have a magic wand . . . People just feel and know we can do a good job.'[18] Her colleague, the minister for tribal welfare, similarly argued that the problems faced by Purulia's tribal groups were extremely well articulated by local CPI(M) party workers, since 'Tribals are always an important support base for CPI(M) and will be our supporters even if we are voted out of power'.[19]

Opposition parties in Purulia – in particular the Trinamul – were quick to highlight that the CPI(M)'s role in responding to drought and acute deprivation was generally characterised by a 'fire-fighting approach' and that there was no evidence to suggest that vulnerable groups were prioritised in drought relief. Rather, they alleged that drought relief was undertaken in an ad hoc manner and that most benefits usually went to those who supported the CPI(M).[20] In a similar vein the district police chief noted 'The CPI(M) is a good manager of the vote bank . . . They have fine-tuned the art of sharing benefits with the last supporter.'[21] The district civil supplies officer alleged that the CPI(M) had 'brainwashed the people of the district and that the party's supporters blindly followed whatever party workers told them to do'. However, with regard to the distribution of benefits to loyal supporters, the same officer added that opposition parties did exactly the same thing and similarly favoured their own supporters in terms of the distribution of goods and services in the areas they controlled.

Thus, a general conclusion from Purulia was that the CPI(M) and its Left Front allies were extremely preoccupied with avoiding the embarrassment of news of starvation deaths from the district. As a result, the district administration was pressured into ensuring that major food crises were kept from snowballing and that sensational starvation deaths were prevented. However, not all was well in the district and large sections of the population suffered from chronic undernutrition, which, unlike starvation, was not politicised. Opposition parties in Purulia – given their weak support in rural areas – appeared not to be interested in politicising chronic hunger. And since the CPI(M) ruled supreme in rural Purulia, it faced little pressure to address the issue, which was, in any case, generally understood to be far more difficult to eradicate – involving greater allocation of financial resources – than isolated cases of starvation. Indeed, from the CPI(M)'s point of view, it would be foolish to put undernutrition on the political agenda when it can claim success on the starvation death front. Thus, the political trigger to do something about a problem is only used in situations when the government is completely convinced that things are bad. In other words, it is only when a situation meets the definition of a 'crisis' as understood by the political authorities that a political trigger may be applied to mount an impressive crisis-induced response. The occurrence of starvation deaths is one such crisis that the ruling CPI(M) party in West Bengal has actively tried to prevent.

Empowered and pro-active Panchayats

Unlike Kalahandi, the Panchayat system in Purulia not only has been functioning for several decades but also appeared to be immensely active. One of the first policy initiatives of the Left Front government, after coming to power in 1977, was to initiate land reforms through Operation Barga, which sought to secure *bargadars* (share-croppers) hereditary rights to cultivate leased land. Following this, the CPI(M) party aimed at promoting rural development through a revitalisation of the system of decentralised government, and Panchayat bodies were actively involved in registering *bargadars*, a process which further helped the party to mobilise the rural peasantry. The actual process of decentralised development planning in West Bengal, however, started in 1985, when Panchayats were assigned the responsibility for rural development. Since then, the district bureaucracies in West Bengal have been under the overall control of Panchayats.[22] Indeed, the bureaucrat–politician relationship in Purulia was very different from that of Kalahandi. For example, the Chairman of the Zilla Parishad (*Sabhadhipati*) was the most powerful official in Purulia and not only controlled the functioning of Panchayat institutions but also had a stakeholder function in the formulation and implementation of the district's development policy. The District Magistrate functioned as Member-Secretary for the Zilla Parishad, and as such was placed under the overall control of the Sabhadhipati on most matters relating to rural development. Similarly, at the block level, the PS Chairman (*Sabhapati*) was formally more powerful than the BDO. As a result, elected representatives in Purulia enjoyed total control of district level policy-making in comparison to Kalahandi where bureaucrats ruled supreme.

The practice of an elected Panchayat representative dominating a career civil servant was, however, not without problems, and the efficient functioning of the district administration was more often than not dependent on personal chemistry. Purulia had witnessed several bitter feuds involving successive District Magistrates and a Sabhadhipati who had been in power for several years. Upon close inspection it appeared that District Magistrate–Sabhadhipati clashes were more likely when young IAS officers were posted to Purulia as compared with older, Bengali and so-called 'promotee' officers from the West Bengal Civil Service

(WBCS).[23] The IAS is an elite service and its officers nationally recruited and posted to the most important posts in the state and the district. The WBCS is the state-level civil service corresponding to the IAS although it enjoys less prestige and importance. After many decades of loyal and distinguished service, a WBCS could be eligible for 'promotion' to the IAS, hence the term 'promotee'. In Purulia, such promotee officers were usually appointed to the post of District Magistrate a few years before their retirement and were, in many senses, extremely grateful to the Left Front government for the elevation to such a coveted post. Therefore, there was a general feeling in Purulia that promotee WBCS officers seldom undertook bold initiatives of their own, preferring largely to toe the party line, and hence were more willing to be subordinated under the Sabhadhipati than their 'direct' IAS counterparts.[24] The Sabhadhipati defended the appointment of successive promotee officers in Purulia arguing that young officers recruited directly from the IAS were often hot-headed and stubborn and did not have adequate 'rural experience'. In contrast, he argued that 'promotee' officers – by virtue of their previous work in rural areas of the state – were better qualified for the post and generally easier to cooperate with.[25]

Several opposition-party politicians and district officials complained that a major problem in Purulia was that all Panchayat institutions were dominated by the CPI(M) and that there was generally very little transparency in the workings of these institutions. Arguing that little concrete information was available to the public on the government policy, these leaders also complained that the rural population did not really have a forum to vent their true feelings as the CPI(M) dictated every aspect of village life. In addition, some accused Panchayats of corruption, mismanagement and dereliction of duty. Despite such allegations, the most important feature of the Panchayat system in Purulia, in terms of preventing starvation deaths, was its ability to provide early warning of distress with predictive significance. In this task, the Panchayats supplemented the work of CPI(M) party workers at the village level, working to resolve conflicts, distributing goods and services and generally functioning as intermediaries between the government and the people. Not only were Panchayats highly empowered, but in Purulia they were accustomed to routinely 'interfering' in administrative matters. Regular meetings were held at all three levels of the Panchayat system, and the Zilla Parishad – headed by the Sabhadhipati in Purulia town – provided detailed instructions and advice to Panchayat Samities (block level) and GPs (village level) on the type of development activity they ought to undertake. Most Panchayat representatives in Purulia possessed greater experience in preparing budgets and plans in order to spend allocated funds and also appeared to be far more professional and demanding in their interactions with private contractors than was the case in Kalahandi.

Thus, the Panchayat system in Purulia enabled rural populations to assert themselves better than in Kalahandi. When the CPI(M) cadre failed to alert their superiors of impending scarcities, most of Purulia's villages had an alternative channel of political influence via their GP representatives who could pressure the

Panchayat Samity, the Zilla Parishad and the district administration to address lo-cal problems. Although it was common to hear Panchayats complain of the delay in the arrival of drought relief funds, the overall conclusion from Purulia was that Panchayats were first able to clamour for assistance and thereafter generally efficient in quickly distributing available resources while awaiting additional as-sistance from the district and state levels. This ability and sensitiveness to provide assistance to vulnerable individuals and groups in times of acute crisis may also explain Purulia's success at preventing starvation deaths.

Stable but subdued bureaucracy

District officials in Purulia were very proud of the fact that no starvation deaths had been reported from the district since the mid-1970s. As a senior official ob-served, 'Starvation deaths have become very unusual in India . . . There are no starvation deaths in Purulia, unlike Kalahandi where it is still pretty common.'[26] The same official went on to argue that, although there was widespread malnu-trition in Purulia, his administration had excelled at providing an immediate re-sponse to news of acute distress and destitution. Similarly, a junior officer argued that 'In Kalahandi there are no crops at all . . . In Purulia, we at least have some crop . . . and, in contrast to Kalahandi, we manage to at least feed everyone even if their stomachs are half-full.' Purulia's District Magistrate claimed that, given the high level of political consciousness of the villagers in the district, the district administration would quickly be informed if an individual or group were facing starvation.[27]

Uninterrupted Left Front rule since 1977 has also provided political and admin-istrative stability in the civil service. Frequent and mass transfers of bureaucrats based on vindictiveness and on arbitrary grounds – commonly practiced in Orissa and a major cause of demotivation – were unusual in West Bengal. Indeed, there was continuity in the Purulia district administration with civil servants serving long and stable tenures. A major explanation for this was the absence of strong opposition parties in West Bengal with a realistic ability to win an election. In comparison, Orissa had several parties with the ability to come to power, and civil servants routinely aligned themselves with influential politicians from a wide range of political parties with the aim of securing lucrative and/or prestigious postings. Since the main opposition parties in West Bengal – the Trinamul and the Congress – were weak in Purulia, district officials did not have the opportunity to seek favours or alliances with opposition party leaders, and hence they tended to serve the ruling party 'loyally' and were in turn granted stability of tenure. Such stability also gave officials ample time to get accustomed to the particular nature of the problems affecting the district. They were then better able to supervise the implementation of long-term development programmes and better prepared to manage drought-related problems. This, however, came at a price; the District Magistrate argued that excessive political interference (and subordination to the Panchayats) had disillusioned and demotivated a large section of the bureaucracy, making officials generally passive and unwilling to take bold and innovative initiatives.[28] Senior officials claimed that even the slightest hint of disagreement or controversy could land them in trouble with their political masters. Indeed, when fresh young officers proposed radical solutions to the district's problems, the standard response from their seniors was *Ki darkar* ('What's the point?'). Similarly, BDOs complained that the process of relief planning was 'heavy top-down' in nature as all important policy initiatives were formulated by the CPI(M) and its allies at both the state and district levels instead of being formulated with inputs from 'qualified and objective' civil servants. As a result, one BDO remarked, 'We are soldiers without weapons . . . we only do what we are told . . . our proposals for improved implementation of programmes are seldom considered'. Despite this factor, officials did not consider Purulia to be a 'punishment posting'. Most officials did not mind the relatively comfortable six-hour train ride to Calcutta and some even claimed that political interference was comparatively less in Purulia in comparison to other districts of West Bengal that are closer to Calcutta.

A judicial enquiry

Without any reports of starvation deaths originating from Purulia or other districts, the courts in West Bengal neither were petitioned nor intervened specifically on food and nutritional matters. However, a specific case relating to Purulia – which was under judicial review at the time of fieldwork in West Bengal – deserves a brief mention. In 2000, the noted Bengali novelist and social activist, Mahasweta Devi, filed a public interest litigation motion in the Calcutta High Court claiming that government funds earmarked for the development of tribal groups in Purulia – especially in areas with large concentrations of the Shabar tribe – were being misused. The petition also alleged that the Purulia district administration had thoroughly neglected the welfare of tribal groups and that the economic conditions of Shabar villages in particular were precarious. Upon receipt of this petition, the Calcutta High Court instructed the Purulia district judge, Arup Das, to conduct a thorough investigation and submit a report based on field visits in rural Purulia. When interviewed in December 2000, the judge complained that the district administration and CPI(M) members of the Purulia Zilla Parishad had, on numerous occasions, tried to prevent him from visiting 'sensitive' areas of the district where poverty and hunger were widespread. Nonetheless – and after a 17-day-long investigation and visits to numerous tribal villages in rural Purulia – the judge's report arrived at five broad conclusions.[29] First, it noted that little development had taken place in villages far from the district centre and that he frequently came across 'half-naked' men and women living in abject poverty and facing destitution. Second, the district administration's claims regarding the construction of houses under the IAY programme and the provision of water supply, electricity and employment under the Employment Assurance Scheme were grossly inflated. Third, a large portion of funds received by Panchayats in Purulia and earmarked for assistance to the poorest of the poor remained unspent. Fourth, there was rampant racial discrimination against the Shabar tribe, who were accused of being thieves, and on several occasions Shabar males had been lynched by other ethnic groups based simply on rumours and suspicion of theft. Fifth, the report noted that, although the judge observed widespread and chronic undernutrition in the villages he visited, he had not heard of any allegations of starvation deaths in Purulia. Following this report, the Calcutta High Court subpoenaed several officials of the Purulia district administration but no verdict was issued at the time of completion of this study. If the court does indict district officials in Purulia on this matter, it will provide an interesting case to contrast the impact of such a verdict with the legal interventions of the Supreme Court of India and the Orissa High Court on starvation deaths in Kalahandi.

An urbanised and uninterested media

There were two important differences between the press in Orissa and West Bengal which related to newspaper ownership and the impact of urbanisation. First, in contrast to Orissa where politicians owned and edited most newspapers, the situation was quite the opposite in West Bengal with major business houses owning and running influential dailies and the press being free of party political ownership and control. In particular, the two major English-language dailies published from Calcutta – *The Telegraph* and *The Statesman* – had a professed anti-Left Front stance, publishing critical reports against the government on a daily basis. In addition, the most influential Bengali language daily, *Ananda Bazar Patrika*, prided itself on its independence and was frequently critical of the West Bengal government. Indeed, the highly critical nature of press reports in the state prompted a senior leader of the ruling CPI(M) to complain: 'newspapers only publish critical stories of our government's performance . . . there is seldom an attempt to cover the positive achievements.'[30] Similarly, a minister remarked, 'The press is quite unkind to us and do not serve the interests of the rural poor . . . It keeps harping on failures instead of covering our successes and that is why I have no contact with the press.'[31]

Second, in comparison to Orissa which had several small cities spread over the state, West Bengal has traditionally had only one major city – Calcutta – where all major dailies were based. Besides being one of India's four major cities, Calcutta had also traditionally fostered the growth of an active print media independent of political control. The growing popularity of the Indian nationalist movement against British rule was reflected in the growth of the nationalist press, particularly in Bengal, and newspapers published from Calcutta played a crucial role in arousing the political consciousness of Indians in the pre-independence era. In spite of this legendary background, however, the newspapers in West Bengal had a poor record of covering rural news. The main readership of the major dailies consisted of large urban middle-class groups residing in Calcutta and its surrounding areas. By comparison, Orissa had several cities of similar size to its capital (Bhubaneswar), where local editions of various regional newspapers were published. Rural news did not sell newspapers in Calcutta and hence most news reports were Calcutta-centric, catering to the interests of the urban readership. Although there are several Bengali language dailies and periodicals published from the districts of West Bengal, their readership and influence was extremely limited.

The local press in Purulia was, however, very similar to that of Kalahandi, characterised by low circulation rates, unstable finances and irregular publication. There were no dailies published from Purulia except weeklies, fortnightlies and monthlies.[32] The editions of the three main Bengali-language weeklies – *Purulia Darpan* (approximate circulation 10,000), *Manbhum Sambad* (*c.* 7,000) and *Mukti* (*c.* 1,000) – were studied in the period 1998–2000 in terms of their coverage of drought, undernutrition and health-related issues.[33] It was surprising to note that, even during the height of the 1998–99 drought, these papers provided little coverage of drought-related distress. In fact, throughout the study period, the three papers primarily covered news related to crime, scandals, corruption in local government, brief statements by major district-level and visiting state-level political leaders promising funds for development, and local cultural activities. The few drought-related reports in *Purulia Darpan* and *Manbhum Sambad* concerned malaria-related deaths, water scarcity in certain blocks of the district and the poor state of health services. However, even these reports appeared only when villagers or political activists organised protests in Purulia town (often in the form of road blockades and *gherao*) against the district administration. Such reports were, however, not human-interest-related but focused on the violence and disruption of normal life arising out of local protests. Another factor that triggered some reports indirectly related to drought was the visit of VIPs from Calcutta including the Chief Minister, his cabinet colleagues, leaders of opposition parties and visiting teams of MLAs from the West Bengal Legislative Assembly. In contrast to *Purulia Darpan* and *Manbhum Sambad*, the third main weekly, *Mukti*, covered drought-related news somewhat more frequently. These stories concerned shortage of rainfall, drinking water crises and general problems that marginal and small farmers faced during both drought and non-drought years. Occasionally, the paper also published articles advising farmers about farming techniques to be adopted during a drought and their rights to government loans for the purchase of seeds and fertilisers. Nevertheless, *Mukti* appeared to be only slightly more interested in covering drought than its rivals and it was not possible to find even one piece of investigative reporting in these newspapers that dealt with drought, poverty and destitution.

There were several reasons for the generally poor coverage of rural news by Purulia-based papers. As in Kalahandi, these related to the poor working conditions of stringers (not trained in journalism and without fixed salaries), low circulation rates which adversely affected their ability to generate advertisement revenue, and a readership concentrated mainly in the small urban centres of the district. As a result, the local press in Purulia did not enjoy much credibility among district officials and political leaders. Several block and village level officers and

Panchayat representatives complained that reporters seldom visited their areas, even when such areas were not very far from Purulia town. West Bengal's minister of relief also claimed that 'reporters do not bother to visit far-flung areas where deprivation is widespread' and that most reporters were 'not interested in analytical reports'.[34] Similarly, the leader of the Congress party in Purulia argued that 'except for *Mukti*, none of the other papers publish anything worthwhile'. In response to such criticism, newspaper editors in Purulia argued that, although they tried to provide critical reports of government activities in the district, they were considerably dependent on government advertisement which in effect smothered any harsh criticism of the district administration and the CPI(M). They further alleged that, when critical reports against the administration were published, the CPI(M) and its Sabhadhipati instructed the district information department to stop issuing advertisements to their papers.[35] Thus most small papers were able to survive mainly because they did not criticise the ruling party.

Like in Kalahandi, most officials and politicians in the district read the main Calcutta-based dailies, where news from Purulia seldom figured in the reports. The correspondents of two influential regional newspapers – the Bengali-language *Ananda Bazaar Patrika* and the English-language *The Statesman* – lamented that although stories were filed on a wide range of issues, including drought and development-related activity, only one out of 10 reports sent from the district actually appeared in print. The few articles on Purulia that interested their editors were mainly related to crime and sport from the district.[36] This, however, appeared only to be a partial explanation of the poor coverage of drought and related issues from Purulia in the Calcutta press. For example, correspondents of major Calcutta-based newspapers posted to Purulia seldom, if ever, visited remote areas of the district in order to highlight rural problems. The lethargy about actively touring the district was partly due to poor communication facilities and lack of travel funds and partly due to the lack of initiative among correspondents as they believed that such reports stood little chance of being published. Opposition leaders also claimed that, despite representing powerful and independent media houses, these correspondents were very reluctant to openly criticise the district administration and generally did their best to keep the Sabhadhipati and other Left Front politicians in 'good humour' in order to be able to spend a 'peaceful year in the district without threats'. The correspondent for *Ananda Bazaar Patrika* confirmed this when he claimed that 'Politicians often demand an explanation when I publish negative stories on their activities and I have been threatened by unknown persons over the telephone . . . But if I do not publish critical reports my paper will lose credibility . . . This is my dilemma.'[37]

As a result of the combination of the above-mentioned factors, news from Purulia appeared in the pages of Calcutta-based newspapers only when something sensational occured (e.g. crime and political scandals) or when VIPs visited the district (e.g. the Chief Minister or influential national and regional politicians). Thus, in a comparative perspective, reporting on Kalahandi in the national and regional press was far more frequent and investigative in character than the reports on Purulia. In terms of the sheer volume of reports, Kalahandi received far more attention than Purulia. This could be because there were no sensational starvation deaths in Purulia to report, but also because of the relative indifference of Purulia-based and Calcutta-based newspapers to prioritising rural news. Unlike Orissa, political parties and influential leaders in West Bengal did not own or edit major dailies and the press in West Bengal prided itself on its ability to deliver credible news.[38] It was therefore not possible for opposition parties and their leaders to easily influence the publication of sensational reports in order simply to malign the government. Thus, whenever critical reports did appear, the West Bengal government had to react without being able to simply dismiss the reports as being politically biased.

10

CONCLUSION

In the mind of many Indians, Kalahandi symbolises deprivation like no other part of the country. Indeed, undernutrition is widespread and the likelihood of starvation deaths occurring in the district increases in severe drought years. The poor nutritional status of Kalahandi is also reflected in the fact that it has one of the highest infant mortality and maternal morbidity rates in the country and health statistics reveal that over 1,000 people died from various diseases during successive droughts in 1996–2000. Drought – which leaves large sections of the vulnerable population undernourished and starved – cannot be entirely prevented; its impact, however, can be lessened by concerted efforts including those related to reforestation and improvements in irrigation. Drought therefore need not spell doom every other year if long-term efforts at drought-proofing are undertaken together with an improved social security system – backed by reliable sources of funding – which is better able to identify and target groups vulnerable to starvation.

The conventional view in Orissa, and for that matter throughout India, is that Kalahandi's vulnerability to starvation is due to inadequate production of foodgrains. This is incorrect. Overall foodgrain production in the period 1996–2000 actually increased and the Food Corporation of India was consistently able to procure large amounts of rice from the district in both drought and non-drought years. In this respect, Sen's entitlement approach and his subsequent critique of FAD approaches is relevant as the major problem for vulnerable groups is not inadequate foodgrain production, but lack of access to food and weak purchasing capacity following unemployment and ill health. And starvation deaths are more likely when the lost entitlements of vulnerable groups are not successfully recreated by the district administration.

Administrative response to drought and starvation is largely based on the Orissa Relief Code which provides procedural guidelines to the district administration and is important in terms of administrative early warning, declaration of drought and the nature of actions to be undertaken. The general conclusion is that the curative aspect in these guidelines overwhelms the preventive aspect. Government intervention is emphasised only with regard to major calamities, which essentially means that human distress has to be on a sufficiently large scale in order

183

to trigger an official response. The Code also defines drought exclusively in terms of rainfall and crop loss indicators, an aspect which neglects the importance of the timing and uneven distribution of rainfall in districts like Kalahandi. Crop-cutting experiments undertaken are highly unreliable and many villages that experience slightly less than 50 per cent crop loss are not declared to be drought-affected, so vulnerable individuals in such areas are not entitled to 'gratuitous relief'. However, most importantly, the provisions of the Code function only as guidelines, and hence cannot be enforced in a court of law.

The three main nutritional interventions studied – the PDS, ICDS and NMMP – played an important role in promoting food security in the district but faced a set of common problems related to the following: selection and targeting of programme beneficiaries; recruitment and training of programme personnel; minimising corruption and leakage; increased and timely allocation of funds. In order to achieve these goals sustained political commitment on improving nutritional status is required. Such consistent commitment was, unfortunately, lacking in Orissa, borne out from the experience of the NMMP, which was abruptly discontinued in 2000 on the excuse that it was affecting the teaching process in schools. The nature of India's federal system complicates the matter by the disparate administration of various programmes funded (requiring separate reporting procedures) by central and state government. Thus there is little point in implementing ambitious programmes like the EAS without properly established and tested mechanisms for communication and feedback together with a regular flow of resources from central and state levels to the districts which allow the district administration to plan its activities well before a major crisis sets in.

Understanding starvation and famine

The situation in Kalahandi in 1996–2000 was not one of famine as claimed by certain sections of the press. However, owing to a combination of poor dietary practices resulting from poverty, unemployment and drought-related distress, the joint effects of severe undernutrition and infectious disease made the district highly prone to starvation-related deaths. In times of severe hardship, the poorest of the poor went without any form of edible food for several consecutive days, which often resulted in death depending on the prior nutritional status of the individual, climate (very hot summers and cold winters), the level of physical activity and their immunity to infectious disease. Thus, starvation deaths in Kalahandi must not be understood exclusively in terms of lack of food intake but rather as resulting from a combination of undernutrition and disease. Indeed, it is very difficult to identify a starvation death in practice. Disease, in some form or the other, triggers most deaths, but the official focus in Kalahandi has primarily been on the end result (death from disease) while ignoring the process (of chronic and severe undernutrition). District officials, including medical practitioners, were also under intense pressure from the ruling party to deny allegations of starvation deaths and classify all deaths in the district exclusively as disease-related. Interestingly, deaths from preventable disease were deemed acceptable, whereas starvation was not. Related to this was the preference of bureaucrats and ruling-party politicians for a strict definition of starvation – a total lack of food intake for 10 or more consecutive days – which enabled them to dismiss allegations of 'starvation' while accepting the presence of widespread 'malnutrition' in Kalahandi. There are also considerable methodological difficulties involved in investigating alleged cases of starvation death. Since the victim's body is often cremated before a post-mortem can be carried out and most investigating officers rely on hearsay and general observations of whether food was present in the victim's house, it is relatively easy for a government to continue denying the role of starvation in causing deaths.

Within Sen's framework, it is particularly difficult to place the phenomenon of 'starvation deaths' – in which people die from starvation but the situation cannot be described as one of mass starvation that characterises a famine. Thus the discussion on the need to operationalise famine shows that famine cannot be equated with severe undernutrition and that occasional 'starvation deaths' in places like Kalahandi cannot be termed a famine. And, although Sen operates with a dualistic distinction between chronic hunger on the one hand and famine on the other, there is, however, a need to recognise that there is a continuum between these two extremes. In other words, famine must be understood as a long 'process' resulting from a combination of various factors rather than an isolated 'event'. A famine is thus the culmination of a long process starting from a general situation of undernutrition which progresses to severe undernutrition and starvation, gradually weakening the immune system in individuals and making them highly vulnerable to disease.

A crucial stage is reached when a condition of severe undernutrition and starvation further worsens and begins to affect large groups in the population facing destitution. This is what I have termed 'famine threat', a phase characterised by an increase in infant mortality and maternal morbidity rates. Some deaths may occur from a combination of starvation and infectious disease among the general adult population. Depending on the nature and impact of a natural trigger (e.g. drought), the prior nutritional status of the community and the type of local coping strategies adopted, an increasing number of vulnerable individuals may risk premature death. If radical and immediate steps are not taken to combat the situation, a full-blown famine may be imminent. Thus, without distinguishing famine from related terms, it is impossible to assign institutional and political responsibility (or 'culpability') when famines occur. By declaring a famine, the national political leadership risks embarrassment at home and abroad. And without an official declaration international agencies and voluntary organisations cannot mobilise sufficient resources or operate in a concerted manner in the famine-affected regions. In other cases, a hastily declared famine and inflation of the real magnitude of the tragedy may be a ploy to receive international sympathy and assistance and deflect subsequent criticism of the government's own policies. Similarly, aid agencies may be reluctant to use the term 'famine' in order to avoid mounting an appropriate and timely response. Unless it is formally declared, the international community does not appear to react immediately or generously. The simple typology of famine and related terms proposed in Chapter 2 is an attempt at encouraging politicians, administrators, NGOs and international agencies to agree on a platform for correctly diagnosing the problem and thereafter remedying a developing crisis an early stage. However, given the severe weaknesses of the international crisis response system, even this may not be enough unless efforts at reducing poverty and preventing starvation and famines are based on human rights principles which impose corresponding obligations on those with the power and resources to prevent such tragedies.

The democracy and starvation relationship

While Sen's praise of the ability of democracies to prevent famines has received widespread attention among academics and policymakers alike, it has also attracted considerable criticism. I have tried to refine Sen's overall approach by arguing that it should be understood not as a universal theory of the relationship between democracy and famine but rather as an attempt to highlight certain aspects of democracy that make famine prevention possible. It is thus not a demonstration of the truth of a general hypothesis that democracy is always better than non-democracy for coping with famine. Hence, instead of a narrow and rigorous interpretation of Sen's argument – democracy prevents famine under all circumstances – a loose interpretation – democracy increases government responsiveness towards famine prevention – appears more appropriate. In other words, although democracy provides necessary conditions for increased government responsiveness and accountability, these are not sufficient conditions to prevent famine. Thus, it is possible for weak and young/non-consolidated electoral democracies to experience famine as societal and political institutions are unable to ensure the guarantee and protection of basic economic rights and freedoms. By comparison, certain 'non-democracies' may enjoy considerable success in preventing famine as long as certain basic freedoms are protected, allowing for effective public action.

Sen accepts that, although public action successfully combats famines in India, it fails to address problems of acute poverty and chronic malnutrition. However, he does not explain why this is so. This book has argued that, in addition to the role of political parties and a free press, it is necessary and important to study the actual interactions and relations between a whole set of actors and institutions at various levels, including the courts, voluntary organisations, the bureaucracy, Panchayati Raj institutions and national and regional legislative organs. The focus has been on understanding the conditions under which public action is effective or ineffective in preventing starvation deaths. In Kalahandi, a set of conditions – mainly related to disagreements over the magnitude of the problem and the required remedy – has limited the role and scope of public action in preventing starvation and in reducing the overall incidence of undernutrition in the district. Public and private actors disagree not only over definitions of undernutrition and starvation, but also with regard to the magnitude of drought-related distress and the nature and type of interventions required by vulnerable groups. The proposed typology of famine and related terms is important in this context since democratic governments may refuse to accept the persistence of 'severe undernutrition' or a condition of 'famine threat' in certain areas within their territories, as the ruling party fears losing the next (imminent) elections or simply giving the opposition a credible weapon to attack government policy. Thus, although the ability of Indian democracy to prevent major crises like famine is commendable, this study has identified the following seven conditions under which democracy and public action in the country are far less successful in preventing starvation deaths.

Non-operational administrative procedures and unmotivated bureaucracy

There was no effort by district officials to monitor the nutritional status of vulnerable groups in Kalahandi. Similarly, there was correspondingly little effort to compile information on landlessness, patterns of out-migration, distress sale of assets and the exploitative practices of moneylenders. Hospitals and health centres were preoccupied with filing reports of little use on the number of patients treated and the total number of deaths from various diseases. Even administrative procedures – originally designed to enable the district administration to launch a timely and adequate response to drought – were largely non-operational. One example was the District Natural Calamities Committee, which seldom met and was consequently unable to provide early warning or influence government response. Thus, during the droughts in 1996–2000, the district administration largely functioned in splendid isolation, without valuable inputs from elected representatives and civil society organisations. Moreover, there was a total lack of trust and collaboration between the district administration and NGOs working in Kalahandi. Bureaucrats at all levels in Orissa readily accepted the widespread presence of 'malnutrition' in Kalahandi although they were most reluctant to openly admit to cases of 'starvation death'. This was partly on account of their narrow interpretation of starvation and partly because they feared the wrath of their political masters if they openly made such politically explosive statements. Therefore, from the bureaucratic point of view, all deaths in Kalahandi occurred from natural causes and disease, and the entire administrative response was geared towards denying press reports instead of actively investigating long-term vulnerabilities that can cause starvation.

Many senior district-level officials, especially IAS officers, suffered from demotivation since they were frequently transferred from one post to another and seldom spent enough time in one posting. This adversely affected the implementation of developmental programmes in Kalahandi. Related to this problem was the acute shortage of qualified personnel in most district departments. A large number of doctors, nurses, teachers and administrative officials from coastal districts of Orissa refused to work in Kalahandi. The large numbers of vacant posts in the district administration placed additional pressure on those already overburdened with numerous other responsibilities. There was also little contact between policy formulators and policy implementers, which made the provision of regular feedback difficult, if not impossible. Thus, despite detailed – and often meticulously specified – administrative guidelines, successfully implementing public policy in India, no matter how well-intended it may be – remains a major challenge.

Judicial and quasi-judicial interventions lack teeth

Starting from the late 1980s, the Supreme Court, the Orissa High Court and the NHRC conducted several investigations and repeatedly confirmed the occurrence of starvation deaths in Kalahandi. All three actors were also firm in their communication to the Orissa government that, unless the nature of government response was radically altered, the spectre of starvation deaths would not only continue to haunt Orissa but further escalate beyond control. The ensuing investigative reports and court rulings helped to focus considerable media attention on Kalahandi and put the Orissa government on the defensive. In this sense such actions not only had symbolic value but also managed to place the issue of starvation deaths firmly on the regional and national political agenda. However, successive governments and senior administrators in Orissa paid little attention to court rulings, repeatedly questioning the credibility of the empirical evidence and the impartiality of the investigating agencies. There was therefore very little political and administrative commitment to implementing the recommendations. Although some cosmetic changes to the Orissa Relief Code were made in the mid-1990s, these related mainly to how district officials should 'react' to reports of starvation deaths rather than preventing them in the first place. No fundamental changes were made in the way drought relief and nutritional programmes are implemented in areas vulnerable to starvation.

The general conclusion is that in order for judicial interventions to have a major impact, the actions and recommendations of the courts must be taken seriously by the political and administrative leadership. There must be stricter sanctions (e.g. jail) for non-compliance. State governments in India are habitual violators of court orders; not just the controversial ones but also orders relating to routine state offences related to discrimination against certain groups and individuals. Politicians in Orissa are no different and have simply dismissed legal and quasi-legal findings, and the courts, in turn, have had neither the capacity nor the power to enforce their directives and extract accountability from those in responsible positions. In any case, the courts do not intervene on their own unless petitions and PILs are filed by concerned individuals or civil society organisations. Since the mid-1990s, such civil society activism has declined. This also points to the relative inactivity and lack of influence of NGOs in Orissa in the area of food and nutritional security. By comparison, as discussed in Chapter 5, there has been an increase in NGO efforts at seeking judicial redress on the right to food in other Indian states.

Highly vocal press, but news reports lack credibility

Although India has a free press, it does not mean that newspapers are necessarily interested in covering the plight of those starving in an objective manner.
The influence of the press is also highly dependent on the working conditions of
journalists. Further, the political ownership of newspapers poses a major problem
of credibility, and critical reports can be dismissed by the government as being
politically biased. News reports of starvation deaths in Kalahandi appeared in
national, regional and local dailies with remarkable frequency. In most reports,
however, the term 'starvation death' was used broadly and generally included all
deaths resulting from undernutrition and disease. These reports were often based
on hearsay and guesses, although some appeared to be more credible than others,
particularly those with an investigative twist and written by professional journalists. And only a handful of cases of death from starvation end up being highlighted
in the press. Because of high levels of illiteracy, poor communication facilities
and the lack of resources available to journalists for travel, many deaths in remote and often inaccessible areas are never reported. It is only when a voluntary
organisation or political party workers hear of an incident that the case receives
publicity. At the same time – and for purposes of sensationalism and criticism of
ruling-party efforts – journalists, NGOs and opposition-party politicians willingly
pass off certain 'natural' deaths as being the result of starvation. These factors
have contributed to a loss of credibility among both those alleging a starvation
death and those denying it.

Owing to low levels of literacy and a small middle-class group in the population, the circulation rates of local newspapers in Kalahandi were very low. Consequently, the local press had little influence, suffering from a weak economic
base and struggling to attract public and private advertisements. And although
state-level or regional Oriya dailies actively highlighted drought and starvation
deaths in Kalahandi, they were seldom able to provide credible early warning to
the authorities given the poor working conditions of their reporters and stringers.
The political affiliation of owners and editors further limited their ability to hold
the district administration and the ruling party to account for possible lapses since
a critical report could be dismissed on the grounds of being baseless and politically motivated. The English-language/national press generally lacked the ability
to provide early warning as all correspondents were based in the state capital
– Bhubaneswar – and not in the districts. Only occasionally did these correspondents visit Kalahandi, so most of their reports were based on information gathered
from a network of politicians and bureaucrats. The one exception was the *Indian
Express*'s correspondent based in Kalahandi, who was consistently able to provide
a string of hard-hitting and critical reports on the district's problems. Although the
ability of the English-language press to provide early warning was limited, once
a story was published in a major national daily, its impact was substantial as the
English-language press is generally regarded to be politically neutral and more

influential than the Oriya-language press. Thus, although the press is highly vocal and consistently highlights problems of starvation, its general ability to influence public policy – and change established practice on controversial issues such as starvation – is severely compromised by the credibility factor related to poor working conditions of journalists, the absence of investigative reporting and the political ownership of regional newspapers.

A change in government does not result in radical changes in public policy

Political parties in Orissa were not strongly organised at the district, block and village levels in Kalahandi, and were seldom in a position to provide any form of early warning. Nonetheless, the district was more fortunate than many other poor districts of Orissa in that it had a few vocal leaders (e.g. the MP from Kalahandi in 1996–97). These leaders enjoyed a good rapport with the press and were able to articulate Kalahandi's needs at both state and national levels. The opposition in Orissa, despite being traditionally fragmented, managed to unite on drought and starvation. Apart from being highly critical of the government's policies in the Orissa Assembly, opposition parties also managed, on a few occasions, to launch joint campaigns aimed at ousting the ruling party from power.

Drought alone did not trigger political activity to the same extent as when it was combined with sensational reports of starvation deaths. Allegations of starvation deaths were used by the opposition to exemplify the incompetence and callousness of the sitting government. Although Kalahandi received much publicity from such efforts, several cases of unsubstantiated claims of starvation deaths, when disproven, became a liability for the opposition and diminished its overall credibility on the issue. The Orissa government could thereby consistently accuse the opposition of fabricating stories. Finally, as soon as one or more of these opposition parties came to power in Orissa, they were equally quick to deny allegations of starvation deaths similar to the ones they had made only a few months before coming to office. Thus, despite regular shifts in government, the party in power largely inherits and adopts the development policies of its predecessor. Indeed, one can question what a new political leadership brings to the table and the major changes it manages to implement in terms of reducing vulnerability to drought and starvation. The general tendency is to react only when the situation crosses a threshold of sensational proportions, and even then the reaction may simply be to refuse to accept the magnitude of the problem or to blame the policies of the previous state government or the stinginess of the current central government about providing calamity relief.

Weak Panchayats and the limits of public action by the poor

Implementation of the Panchayati Raj system of decentralised government in India has been tardy in most states, and Orissa is no exception. Politicians from virtually all parties are reluctant to share financial and other decision-making powers with Panchayat representatives at the district and block levels. In Orissa, the complete implementation of the Panchayat system was postponed for over three decades and it is still not perceived as an important institution that can play a crucial role in furthering all-round development. Rather, politicians continue to consider Panchayats as rivals instead of partners. This is borne out by the fact that, despite the functioning of the full three-tier Panchayat system in Orissa since 1997, the Zilla Parishad, the highest Panchayat body, was not empowered fully in accordance with the provisions of the 73rd and 74th amendments of the Indian Constitution.

Although Panchayats in Kalahandi had the potential to play an important role in managing drought-related distress and cases of starvation, they were unable to function effectively for several interrelated reasons which included low literacy levels, lack of training in administrative routines, poor salaries and lack of adequate (and timely) funding for planned activities. Furthermore, given their relative inexperience, Panchayat representatives were largely under the control of the district bureaucracy. As a result, villagers seldom considered their Panchayats capable of initiating radical change independent of officialdom. Without a representative channel to articulate local demands – and with most NGOs uninterested in food and nutritional security – the extent of public action that the poor themselves were capable of was limited. In such situations, public action becomes synonymous with top-down state action, based on the principles of charity and benevolence of political leaders and administrators rather than concerted and more bottom-up efforts at promoting development based on individual and group rights and claims.

Size of the opposition in parliament and the character of MPs

Not surprisingly, given the flurry of news reports on Kalahandi, the Indian Parliament actively debated issues related to drought and starvation. Indeed, Kalahandi was often used as a yardstick by MPs to measure and compare deprivation in other parts of India. Opposition-party MPs from Orissa and other states actively criticised both the Orissa and central governments whenever newspapers reported alleged starvation deaths in various parts of the country. Like their colleagues at the state legislative level, Lok Sabha MPs appeared to have conflicting understandings of famine, undernutrition and starvation, and used these concepts interchangeably, causing much confusion in the debates.

The general trend in the Lok Sabha was that MPs belonging to the opposition camp in Orissa argued that it was a national shame that starvation deaths continued to take place in Kalahandi, while MPs from the ruling-party/coalition in Orissa did their best to argue that such deaths had not taken place. Since the ruling party/coalition in Orissa usually also has the greatest share of MPs from the state in the Lok Sabha, criticism of the Orissa government by these MPs was negligible. Thus the extent of adversarial activity by MPs in parliament was strongly correlated with their party affiliations, and the larger the number of opposition-party MPs from Orissa, the more likely the criticism of the Orissa government. In comparison, it was relatively safe and easy for all MPs from Orissa – irrespective of political ties – to make the central government the scapegoat and criticise it for its failure to allocate sufficient money to their state for long-term development programmes and short-term calamity relief. On a few occasions, however, parliamentary debates assumed particular significance when MPs cutting across party lines were united in venting their anger and frustration. For example, it was particularly advantageous for Kalahandi that, during the 1996–97 drought, its MP was not only the sole voice of opposition from Orissa in the Lok Sabha but also a vocal critic of the Orissa government's efforts in drought management. His dynamic personality appealed to many legislators and enabled him to receive support across party lines. Such cases are, however, rare. Moreover, it is of little use for parliamentarians to involve themselves in heated debates without being in a position to exert influence on policy implementation. Even when specific questions on controversial topics are tabled in parliament, the replies from state governments are inevitably vaguely formulated and arrive several months late. Thus, although MPs are active in criticising the government, they are not able to exercise much influence in changing or correcting existing policies, particularly at the state level.

Centre–state disputes over calamity relief as an excuse to cover up policy failure

Whenever confronted with criticism of the state government's failure to successfully respond to drought and prevent starvation deaths, successive ruling parties in Orissa blamed New Delhi for not allocating adequate and timely funds for calamity relief. In fact, the excuse of neglect of Orissa by the centre was a recurrent theme in Orissa politics, and bureaucrats and politicians alike used this excuse to deflect criticism from their own failures. Whereas senior bureaucrats mainly complained of lengthy delays in the receipt of funds, politicians – in power and in opposition – frequently accused the central government of gross underfunding despite clearly visible deprivation in many areas of the state. Kalahandi did, on several occasions, suffer from the lack of timely availability of funds and this appeared to be the fault of both the central and Orissa governments. For example, despite highly publicised promises of emergency assistance to Kalahandi by the Prime Minister, the actual transfer of the funds to Orissa was delayed by several months. In turn, the Orissa government was extremely slow to transfer funds it had received from the centre to Kalahandi. It is difficult to establish whether the central government actively discriminated against opposition-party controlled states like Orissa during the 1996–97 drought. There is nevertheless some evidence to indicate that, from a national perspective, state governments formed by the ruling party in Delhi and/or its allies did – on several occasions – receive a larger share of calamity relief funds than those states which had opposition parties in power. Certain state governments were also able to secure large and timely calamity relief allocations by virtue of the influence they wielded in the coalition government in New Delhi. Thus there is an urgent need to revise the existing set of procedures that govern centre–state relations in India's federal set-up. In particular, transparent procedures must be formulated for allocation and disbursement of both long-term development and short-term calamity-relief funds so that allegations and counter-allegations of favouritism and discrimination are minimised and do not impede efforts to provide assistance to starving groups.

The challenge ahead

Developmental efforts in India during the past five decades have not managed to provide improved opportunities for a productive and healthy life to millions of Indians. Increased food availability in the country has not improved the health and nutritional status of large sections of the population. Over 200 million (and rising) men, women and children suffer from a combination of chronic malnutrition and severe undernutrition, and every year more than 2.5 million children in India die before reaching the age of five. This is clearly a major problem that needs to be seen in parallel with Amartya Sen's claim that independent India has successfully avoided famine. But India's record so far has been most impressive whenever 'crisis' has been clearly defined and when there is an unambiguous understanding and consensus on the seriousness of the situation. India has in the past witnessed, and will continue to experience in the future, numerous situations that can best be described as 'famine threats'. Thus far, the country has managed to prevent such famine threats from escalating into famine and there is reason to believe that India will continue to enjoy success on this issue. In this respect, Sen is right that democracy and public action work well towards preventing famine in India. A more mixed picture emerges on India's ability to prevent cases of starvation death. The phenomenon is difficult to define and starvation deaths take place in rural, and often remote, areas – far removed from the seats of power. Given this relative invisibility, chronic malnutrition and severe undernutrition causing starvation deaths is not recognised as a major crisis warranting the same kind of response that is reserved for famine.

The comparison between Kalahandi and Purulia shows that there are differences even within India's democratic political system in terms of the ability to prevent starvation deaths. In Purulia there appears to be a consensus that, despite widespread undernutrition, starvation deaths must never be allowed to take place. The presence of party workers and Panchayat institutions at the village level and their active role in providing information to administrative and political authorities appear to explain Purulia's success at preventing starvation deaths. The role of local politics and the presence of effective structures of decentralised government are crucial. In contrast, public action to prevent people from falling below the 'starvation line' is not forthcoming in Kalahandi. Instead of complementing each other, institutional interactions are here often characterised by mutual suspicion and lack of cooperation among bureaucrats, politicians, voluntary organisations and the press. Political opposition is thus not in itself a guarantee for preventing starvation deaths, especially when politicians are preoccupied with politicising the issue – hurling accusations, which the ruling party conveniently denies – rather than being concerned with deteriorating health and nutritional status which cause death. Indeed, there appears to be a general consensus among successive ruling parties in India that the term 'starvation' must be avoided at all cost. In comparison, 'malnutrition' is a relatively safe term to use, given that it is widespread not just in India but throughout the world. Ruling parties in India are confident that they will not be held politically accountable for failing to tackle malnutrition.

The 'public' is not a homogenous entity and democratic institutions and public action are not always beneficial for all groups. Rather, their success depends on how powerful and vocal the public is in making its demands heard. From a methodological angle, the task of identifying 'democracy' or 'public action' as the explanatory variable in preventing starvation deaths remains a complex one. Indian democracy excels at emergency-type responses and this explains its success in avoiding famine. Although this is a creditable achievement, a concerted effort directed at tackling drought and preventing starvation deaths is urgently needed. The goal of saving lives must be recognised as a major concern and, in addition to starvation deaths, central and state governments in India must view the fight against chronic undernutrition as a high priority.

GLOSSARY

Att	high-lying land ('upland')
Bahal	low-lying land
Bargadar	share-cropper (used in West Bengal)
Berana	medium-height land
Begari	forced labour
Bethi	forced labour
Bhatti	temporary village-level liquor shop
Biri	a type of pulse
Bhogra	land cultivated by village headman (Gountia)
Chas	cultivation
Collector	officer of the Indian Administrative Service in charge of a district (commonly referred to as District Magistrate in West Bengal)
Crore	10 million
Dalit	low caste, Untouchables
Dhoti	men's clothing
Gherao	form of protest, usually 'surrounding' an official and/or office, thus preventing anyone from entering or leaving a building
Gountia	village headman
Gram	village
Gram Panchayat	elected village-level government
Harijan	member of a Scheduled Caste
Kharif	post-monsoon cropping season
Lakh	100,000
Lok Sabha	lower house of Indian parliament
Mal	terraced/sloped land
Marwari	generic term used to describe merchants and land-owners of non-Oriya origin (even though they may not necessarily be of Marwari origin)
Mouza	revenue village (used in West Bengal)

Paisa	monetary unit (100 paisa = 1 Rupee)
Palli Sabha	annual general meeting of villagers within a Gram Panchayat
Panchayati Raj	Panchayat rule, a system of decentralised government
Panchayat Samity	elected block-level local government
Podu	'slash and burn' shifting cultivation
Rabi	winter cropping season
Raj	rule
Raja	king
Rajya Sabha	upper house of Indian parliament
Ragi	a type of millet
Sabhapati	Panchayat Samity Chairman (West Bengal)
Sabhadhipati	Chairman of the Zilla Parishad (West Bengal)
Sahukar	moneylender
Sarpanch	elected president of a Gram Panchayat
Sari	women's clothing
Tehsil	unit of land revenue administration
Tehsildar	land revenue officer in charge of a Tehsil
Varna	refers to Hindu Caste system and has two interrelated meanings: *Colour* (qualities or energies of human nature); *Veil* (four different ways in which the Divine Self is hidden in human beings)
Zamindar	landlord, revenue intermediary
Zilla Parishad	elected district-level local government

NOTES

1 INTRODUCTION

1 Between 1961 and 1997, foodgrain productivity growth exceeded the population growth rate and resulted in an increase in per capita availability of foodgrains from 469 grams per day in 1961 to 512 grams per day in 1997 (World Bank 2001: 1).

2 For further details, see Planning Commission (2000: Table 6.3.2.1).

3 These include the Ministry of Agriculture, Ministry of Consumer Affairs and Public Distribution, Ministry of Health and Family Welfare, Ministry of Labour, Ministry of Rural Development, Ministry of Social Justice and Empowerment, Ministry of Tribal Affairs and the Department of Women and Children in the Ministry of Human Resource Development.

4 This particular famine has greatly influenced local culture in Kalahandi. For example, when a child hankers for food the mother responds by asking the child, 'Why are you hankering like a famine-affected child of Chappan Sal?' (M. K. Mishra, http://www.geocites.com/bororissa/dro.html).

5 The list was compiled by the Central Planning Committee constituted by the central government after receiving reports of starvation deaths among tribal children in Amaravati district of Maharashtra in 1993 ('41 districts prone to starvation deaths', *Times of India*, 2 December 1996).

6 To respect, protect and fulfil the right to food are three levels of government obligations defined by the UN's Committee on Economic, Social and Cultural Rights in its general comment no. 12 on the right to adequate food (E/C.12/1999/5), 12 May 1999.

7 Panchayati Raj is a three-tier system (district, block, village levels) of decentralised government in India.

8 'Scheduled Caste' is an administrative term introduced by the British to denote communities (castes) outside the *Varna* system. Historically 'outcast' or 'pariah', they have been the object of blatant discrimination throughout India. Their social emancipation came partly with Mahatma Gandhi, who introduced the term *Harijans* (Children of God), and partly with the political activity of B. R. Ambedkar, who called them *Dalits* (the Oppressed). The term continues to be used in connection with affirmative action programmes. 'Scheduled Tribes' is an administrative term that denotes 255 ethnic communities that were among the earliest inhabitants of India. Tribal communities are traditionally self-contained and in many respects distinct culturally and ethnically from mainstream communities.

2 DEMOCRACY AND STARVATION

1 The successful relief efforts launched to prevent famine during drought and ensuing food crises in Bihar (1965–67) and Maharashtra (1971–73) have also been extensively covered in Scarfe and Scarfe (1969), Berg (1971), Ramalingaswami *et al.* (1971), Mundle (1974), Mathur and Bhattacharya (1975), Subramaniam (1975), Brass (1986), Echeverri-Gent (1988), and Dyson and Maharatna (1992). For further details on the Bengal famine, see Sen (1981), Greenough (1982) and Chattopadhyay (1987).

2 Some policy failures included the popularisation of new breeds and seeds and new methods of deep ploughing and high-density planting with wheat, cotton, sorghum, etc. Major setbacks were also suffered when China tried to mass-produce heavy machinery based on impractical designs and major irrigation schemes failed to work. For further details see Becker (1996: 59–82).

3 Sen also argues that even 'fairly authoritarian political leaders have, to a great extent, to accept the discipline of public criticism and social opposition' (Drèze and Sen 1989: 19). He points to the examples of South Korea and Pinochet's Chile and argues that 'Many of the social programs that served these countries well were at least partly aimed at reducing the appeal of the opposition, and in this way, the opposition had some effectiveness even before coming to office' (Sen 2000: 154).

4 Also see Sen's reply to these (Sen 1986a, 1993).

5 Parts of this section have benefited from discussions with participants at the conference, 'Famine in the 21st Century', organised by the Institute of Development Studies, University of Sussex, Brighton, February–March 2002.

6 Dan Maxwell, CARE International, Nairobi (personal communication).

7 For further details, see http://www.fews.net/alerts/?pageID=alertLevelsDefined.

8 I am grateful to Amartya Sen for several interesting discussions. In addition, this section has benefited enormously from the inputs of Luka Biong Deng, Stephen Devereux and Paul Howe, all from the Institute for Development Studies, University of Sussex.

9 This figure builds on a classification provided by FAO (1999: 11). FAO, however, uses the term 'undernourishment', which is defined as 'chronic food insecurity, in which food intake is insufficient to meet basic energy requirements on a continuing basis'. This is very different from 'starvation'. Further, the FAO classification does not include linkages with famine.

10 Excess deaths can be caused directly, as a result of starvation, and/or indirectly, as a result of famine-related diseases.

11 Such an attempt, although similar to a recent study which proposes famine scales based on the criteria of intensity and magnitude (Howe and Devereux 2004), is also noticeably different in terms of the classifications proposed.

12 Elsewhere, de Waal (1996) refers to this as a 'social contract'.

13 Author's emphasis in italics.

14 Amartya Sen, interview, Oslo, December 2001 and March 2002; Sen's speech on globalization, Harvard University, 13 April 2002.

15 This follows Beetham (1999: 2), who argues that one of the most common mistakes in defining democracy involves confusing 'the question of the definition of democracy with the separate question of whether it is a good, or how much of it is a good'.

3 KALAHANDI'S POVERTY

1 'Kalahandi' was used for the first time in the Dadhibaman Temple Inscription in Junagarh, issued by Maharaja Juga Shahi Deo from his capital, Kalahandi Nagar, around AD 1718 (Kalahandi Gazetteer 1980: 2).

2 The princely state of Kalahandi was merged with Orissa on 1 January 1948. Subse-

quently, the Zamindari of Khariar was added to Kalahandi in November 1949, and in 1962 the Kashipur Police Station area was taken out of Kalahandi and merged with Koraput district. Finally, in April 1993, the Nawapara sub-division was made into a separate (Nuapada) district. It is still common in Orissa to refer to 'undivided' Kalahandi district as comprising present-day Kalahandi and Nuapada districts. This study, however, focuses exclusively on Kalahandi.

3 The elite IAS comprises around 5,000 officers, who not only occupy the highest administrative positions at the policy-making level but also serve as administrative heads of ministries, departments and public sector enterprises. Freshly recruited officers are posted in the districts and, after a period of training, appointed as District Collector.

4 Financial allocations to the districts are made in three or more instalments. Utilisation certificates had to be sent by the district administration in order to receive fresh instalments under most central and state government programmes.

5 Dr Gopal Patnaik, interview, Department of Health, Bhubaneswar, 30 January 2001.

6 The cited data is adapted from a nutritional survey conducted in Kalahandi by the Nutrition Section of the Orissa government's Department of Health and Family Welfare, January 1997.

7 This method differs slightly from the categories used currently by the ICDS programme, which classifies malnutrition into four grades. In practice, however, the difference relates only to the categories of 'mild' and 'moderate' malnutrition. Both methods use less than 60 per cent of the mean annual weight for age to measure 'severe' malnutrition among children.

8 Such strategies are also common in sub-Saharan Africa. For details see Maxwell (1995).

9 Quoted in M. K. Mishra (http://www.geocities.com/bororissa/dro.html).

10 'Mass Migration from Kalahandi', *New Indian Express*, 18 October 2000.

11 Cited in Mishra (1989: 42). A slightly different version of this folksong is the following: *Dalkhaire; desare kala akala, Ghara duara chhadi bidese ghara, Dalkhaire peta kaje harabara* (O leaf eater, drought occurred in the country, Sent us abroad, beyond homeland, Unrest for belly, O leaf eater).

4   DROUGHT AND STATE ACTION

1 The departments involved in relief operations include the following: Agriculture, Panchayati Raj, Works, Women and Child Development, Health and Family Welfare, Food and Consumer Welfare, Water Resources, Planning and Co-ordination, Rural Development, Forest and Environment, Fishery and Animal Resources, Harijans and Tribal Welfare, Higher Education and Youth Services, Mass Education, Home, Housing and Urban Development, Revenue and Excise.

2 Protective irrigation includes attempts to save standing crops by constructing *cross bandhs* and repairing minor irrigation projects and lift irrigation points in addition to providing diesel pumps to farmers.

3 District Collector's report to the Orissa government's Chief Secretary, 6 January 2001

4 Shiva Patnaik, interview, Bhawanipatna, 23 January 2001.

5 Hemant Sharma, interview, Dharamgarh, 7 February 1999.

6 According to a report by the Office of the Comptroller and Auditor General of India (CAG 2001), the reasons behind the delay included defective planning, frequent changes in the scope of work during execution, incorrect procedures followed in the allocation of contracts to private corporations, corruption, lack of qualified personnel and lack of adequate number of project staff.

7 The survey was commissioned by the Kalahandi District Natural Calamity Committee (cited in 'Farming delayed in Kalahandi', *Indian Express*, 3 September 1997).

8 The main storage facilities in Kalahandi included the FCI godown in Kesinga and the State Warehousing Corporation and Central Warehousing Corporation godowns in Junagarh.

9 G. Mishra, interview, Bhawanipatna, 17 January 2001.

10 'Government fails to achieve rice procurement target', *New Indian Express*, 29 November 2000.

11 'Farmers fail to get returns', *New Indian Express*, 13 May 2000.

12 There were two categories of ration card households: approximately 176,000 households with an annual income less than Rs 6,000, and approximately 114,000 households with an annual income between Rs 6,001 and Rs 11,000. Of the 845 fair price shops operating in Kalahandi in 2000, 726 were privately owned, 39 were run by cooperative societies, 48 by women's self-help groups, 19 by Gram Panchayats, 12 by voluntary organisations and 1 by the Orissa State Civil Supplies Corporation.

13 'Mid-day meal programme to be closed', *Dharitri*, 21 April 2000.

5 LEGAL INTERVENTIONS AND ADMINISTRATIVE RESPONSE TO STARVATION

1 http://www.indiancourts.nic.in/indian_jud.htm

2 PIL Writ Petition (Civil) No. 12847 of 1985, *Kishan Pattnayak and Another* vs. *the state of Orissa*, Paragraph 1 (quoted in Currie 1998: 423).

3 Writ Petition (Civil) No. 1081 of 1987, *the Indian People's Front through its Chairman, Nagbhushan Patnaik* vs. *State of Orissa*.

4 Kapil Narayan Tiwari, interview, Khariar, 9 February 1999.

5 Case No. 3517/88 filed on 17 October 1988, *Bhawani Mund* vs. *state of Orissa*.

6 Case No. 525/89 filed in 1989, *A. C. Pradhan* vs. *state of Orissa*.

7 The sum awarded was Rs 25,000 to four families and Rs 40,000 to one family. Interviews with villagers of Udeypur village, where two starvation deaths had occurred, revealed that the compensation provided was of little help to the households of the victim as the authorities placed the money in a fixed deposit account for seven years.

8 Orissa Chief Minister's letter dated 11 December 1996, quoted in 'NHRC probe into starvation deaths: Patnaik irked over move', *Hindustan Times*, 19 December 1996.

9 Cited in 'Secrecy over starvation deaths in Orissa?', *Hindustan Times*, 20 May 1997.

10 Cited in 'Orissa faults hunger death report', *Indian Express*, 30 March 1997.

11 Cited in 'Secrecy over starvation deaths in Orissa?', *Hindustan Times*, 20 May 1997.

12 'Orissa HC asks Centre, State to prove "starvation deaths"', *The Statesman*, 22 November 1998; 'Probe starvation deaths: HC', *Indian Express*, 22 November 1998; 'HC asks government to probe starvation deaths', *Asian Age*, 22 November 1998.

13 Quoted in an article in *Utkal Age*, 18 January 2001.

14 Writ Petition (civil) 196 of 2001, submitted in April 2001.

15 'PUCL petitions Supreme Court on starvation deaths', *PUCL Bulletin*, July 2001 (http://www.pucl.org/reports/Rajasthan/2001/starvation_death.htm).

16 Cited in 'NHRC issues notice to Orissa government on starvation deaths', 29 August 2001 (http://www.nhrc.nic.in); 'NHRC notice to Orissa govt on hunger deaths', *Times of India*, 10 September 2001.

17 Satyabrata Sahu, interview, Bhawanipatna, 10 February 1999.

18 Hemant Sharma, interview, Dharamgarh, 7 February 1999.

19 Ibid.

20 Dr Dasarath Biswal, additional district medical officer, interview, Bhawanipatna, 25 January 2001.

21 Fakir Mohan Pradhan, interview, Bhawanipatna, 10 February 1999.
22 B. Panigrahi, Additional Relief Commissioner, Bhubaneswar, 30 January 2001.
23 Dr Gopal Patnaik, interview, Bhubaneswar, 30 January 2001.
24 Meena Gupta, interview, Bhubaneswar, 29 December 1998.
25 This section is based on interviews with a large number of district officials. Particularly informative were two interviews with the additional district magistrate, Fakir Mohan Pradhan, in February 1999 and January 2001.
26 P. K. Sahoo, district forest officer, interview, Bhawanipatna, 17 January 2001.
27 Fakir Mohan Pradhan, interview, Bhawanipatna, 11 January 2001.
28 Meena Gupta, health department, interview, Bhubaneswar, 29 December 1998.
29 Chinmay Basu, Panchayati Raj Department, interview, Bhubaneswar, 28 December 1998.
30 'Cracked land and parched throats spell doom in Kalahandi', *Indian Express*, 16 April 1997.
31 Ibid.; 'SC guidelines given a go-by', *Indian Express*, 1 June 1998.
32 Letter from S. R. Pal, Principal Secretary, to Collectors, 18 November 1992, referring to Revenue Department letters No. 12307/R dated 7 March 1992 and No. 17763 dated 3 April 1992 (Appendix – VI A, Orissa Relief Code).
33 Dr Behera, Additional District Medical Officer, interview, Bhawanipatna, 19 January 2001.
34 Dr Rabi Ranjan Mishra, interview, Thuamul Rampur, 8 February 1999.
35 Hemant Sharma, interview, Bhawanipatna, 18 January 2001.
36 Pradeep Kumar Jena, department of agriculture, interview, Bhubaneswar, 10 February 1999.
37 Dr Dasarath Biswal, interview, Bhawanipatna, 25 January 2001.
38 B. Panigrahi, interview, Bhubaneswar, 30 January 2001.

6 THE VOCAL PRESS

1 Passing judgements in several cases, the Supreme Court has held that the right to propagate one's ideas is inherent in the freedom of speech and expression as guaranteed under Article 19(1).
2 In the period between 1976 and 1981, the circulation of daily newspapers in all languages increased from 9.3 million copies daily to 15.3 million, an increase of 65 per cent. By comparison, the corresponding increase in the period 1971–76 was only 2.5 per cent (Jeffrey 1987: 607).
3 It later turned out that these reports were highly inaccurate as it was not exactly a sale but rather a traditional local marriage and the bridegroom was not very old and not totally blind (he had a sight impairment) (Sainath 1996: 325–338).
4 Uma Shankar Kar, interview, Bhawanipatna, 6 February 1999.
5 'Orissa Dal, Left seek session on drought', *The Hindu*, 19 September 1996.
6 'Aid for drought-hit Orissa districts sought', *The Hindu*, 19 October 1996.
7 'Plan shelved, drought stays', *The Hindu*, 18 November 1996.
8 'Noisy scenes in Orissa Assembly over drought', *The Hindu*, 22 November 1996.
9 'Orissa's travails', editorial, *The Hindu*, 22 November 1996.
10 'Orissa's tale of woe', *The Hindu*, 24 November 1996.
11 'India's Africa: Orissa – Chasing virtual food', *The Hindu*, 27 November 1996.
12 'BJP demands inquiry into drought relief in Orissa', *The Hindu*, 11 November 1996.
13 'Spectre of hunger deaths again', *The Hindu*, 16 December 1996.
14 Ibid.
15 'P.M. faults Orissa's handling of drought', *The Hindu*, 24 December 1996.
16 'Only pious words, no relief', *The Hindu*, 30 December 1996.

17 'Orissa House flays Centre's apathy', *The Hindu*, 31 December 1996.
18 'Steps to tackle drought in Orissa', *The Hindu*, 1 March 1997.
19 'Drought-hit Kalahandi awaits Central funds', *The Hindu*, 23 March 1997.
20 'Orissa Opposition to observe "hunger week"', *The Hindu*, 15 April 1997.
21 'Drought in Kalahandi man-made, says Oxfam', *The Hindu*, 30 May 1997.
22 'Steps to check migration: BDOs asked to create more man-days', *Indian Express*, 11 October 1996.
23 *Indian Express*, 8 November 1996.
24 *Indian Express*, 10 November 1996.
25 'They wait in vain for money orders', *Indian Express*, 19 December 1996.
26 'The tragedy is unfolding again', *Indian Express*, 24 March 1997.
27 'Cracked land and parched throats spell doom in Kalahandi', *Indian Express*, 16 April 1997.
28 'Heat dries up water sources in Kalahandi', *Indian Express*, 26 April 1997.
29 'Erratic rainfall dampens hopes', *Indian Express*, 10 July 1997.
30 'Making wrong use of benefits', *Indian Express*, 15 July 1997.
31 'Poor progress of group finance scheme, claims Nabard study', *Indian Express*, 23 July 1997.
32 'A wet desert: Kalahandi's thirst for water continues', *Times of India*, 27 June 1997.
33 'The Kalahandi syndrome: Poverty amid foodgrain surplus', *Times of India*, 28 June 1997.
34 'Everybody loves a good drought', *The Hindu*, 19 January 1997. Also see Sainath (1996).
35 K. Ravi, interview, Bhubaneswar, 12 February 1999.
36 N. Ramdas, interview, Bhubaneswar, 3 February 1999.
37 Uma Shankar Kar, interview, Bhawanipatna, 6 February 1999.
38 Estimates are based on ABC (Audited Bureau of Circulations) figures for 1996, provided in Jeffrey (1997: 512).
39 Gopal Mahapatra, interview, Bhubaneswar, 2 February 1999; Sanjib Biswal, interview, Bhawanipatna, 7 February 1999.
40 Except for *Samaj*, which is run by a public trust fund, the remaining three dailies are owned by active politicians. The proprietor–editor of *Dharitri*, Tathagata Satpathy, is a Lok Sabha MP from the BJD party. *Prajatantra* is run by Bhartruhari Mahtab, also a Lok Sabha MP from the BJD party. *Sambad* is owned and edited by Souma Ranjan Patnaik, the son-in-law of the Chief Minister of Orissa.
41 Mr U. S. Kar provided research assistance for parts of this section.
42 I am grateful to Dr Amareswar Mishra (Utkal University) and a group of his students who provided a broad overview of reports published in these four Oriya newspapers during the period under study.
43 This is a form of protest where important officials and their offices are surrounded by a large group of people who prevent anyone from entering or leaving a building unless their demands are met.
44 I do not claim that these figures are entirely accurate. They were compiled from daily editions of the paper, and deviations and overlap in the total number of starvation deaths reported are likely.
45 Interviews in Bhubaneswar with Gopal Mahapatra (*Dharitri*), 2 February 1999, and Ratikant Satpathy (*Sambad* and *Sun Times*), 4 February 1999.
46 S. Hota, interview, Bhubaneswar, 29 December 1999.
47 Bhartruhari Mahtab, interview, Bhubaneswar, 28 December 1998.
48 In their study, Besley and Burgess (2002) rank 16 Indian States in terms of responsiveness to media coverage. Kerala is ranked number 1 (highest responsiveness) while Orissa is ranked 12.
49 Tathagata Satpathy, interview, Bhubaneswar, 2 February 1999.

7 THE POLITICS OF STARVATION AND CALAMITY RELIEF

1 J. B. Patnaik, interview, Bhubaneswar, 30 December 1998.
2 Hemananda Biswal, interview, Bhubaneswar, 28 December 1998.
3 Nandini Satpathy, interview, Bhubaneswar, 3 February 1999.
4 Naveen Patnaik, interview, Bhubaneswar, 28 December 1998.
5 Bikram Kesari Deo, interview, Bhawanipatna, 10 February 1999.
6 Janardan Pati, interview, Bhubaneswar, 4 February 1999.
7 'Orissa parties for special House meet on drought', *Hindustan Times*, 10 September 1998.
8 Bhakta Charan Das, interview, Bhawanipatna, 23 January 2001.
9 Janardan Pati, interview, Bhubaneswar, 4 February 1999.
10 Bhakta Charan Das, interview, Bhawanipatna, 23 January 2001.
11 Naba Patnaik, CPI(M) party worker, interview, Bhawaniptana, 6 February 1999.
12 Shiva Patnaik, interview, Bhawanipatna, 23 January 2001.
13 Chinmay Basu, interview, Bhubaneswar, 30 January 2001 and 1 February 2001.
14 U. N. Pradhan, L. Bhoi and N. Biswal, representing Sahabhagi Vikash Abhiyan, interview, Bhawanipatna, 10 February 1999.
15 'Plan shelved, drought stays', *The Hindu*, 18 November 1996; 'New action plan for Orissa's KBK districts', *The Hindu*, 8 July 1998. For further details of the RLTAP, visit: http://kbk.nic.in/RLATP.htm
16 'Orissa drought situation grim, relief issue being politicised', *Economic Times*, 24 November 1996.
17 'Funds not constraint for Orissa relief', *The Hindu*, 23 November 1996.
18 'P.M. faults Orissa's handling of drought', *The Hindu*, 24 December 1996.
19 Chief Minister, J. B. Patnaik, and Revenue Minister, K. C. Lenka, quoted in 'Only pious words, no relief', *The Hindu*, 30 December 1996.
20 'Orissa House flays Centre's apathy', *The Hindu*, 31 December 1996.
21 'Orissa drought-hit areas: Panel to look into "starvation deaths"', *Hindustan Times*, 14 March 1997.
22 'Gujral to Orissa's rescue', *Indian Express*, 2 May 1997.
23 'P.M. to visit Orissa drought-hit areas', *Hindustan Times*, 6 May 1997.
24 Once a block is classified under the DPAP, a number of subsequent development schemes (e.g. employment assurance scheme, projects for the provision of drinking water, soil conservation and watershed management schemes) provide the state government with increased resources.
25 For example, in the months following a major cyclone disaster, the Chief Minister of Andhra Pradesh repeatedly criticised the centre for failing to provide aid despite the PM's public statements according to which funds had already been sent to the state ('AP has not received any aid so far, says Naidu', *The Hindu*, 20 November 1996).
26 The Chief Minister of West Bengal accused the centre of neglecting acute deprivation in his state while the ruling party in Bihar accused the central government of playing politics with flood relief ('75 for Bengal, 550 for Uttar Pradesh', *The Telegraph*, 12 September 1998).
27 'Way the crore flies: Proper use of relief funds is for the birds', Editorial, *The Statesman*, 14 September 1998.
28 'National calamity of rare severity: Sonia', *The Statesman*, 2 November 1999.
29 Bhaskar Barua quoted in, 'Calamity by name, not national', *The Telegraph*, 2 November 1999.
30 Ibid.
31 Atal Bihari Vajpayee quoted in 'Consensus on crisis, not calamity', *The Telegraph*, 26 April 2000.

8 PARLIAMENTARY ACTIVISM

1 The maximum strength of the Lok Sabha is 552 of which up to 530 members represent states, up to 20 members represent 'union territories' and two members are nominated from the Anglo-Indian community by the President.
2 These studies are cited in Jain (1985b) and Mathur and Jayal (1993).
3 B. C. Das, speech in the Lok Sabha, 27 November 1996.
4 Ibid.
5 Short duration discussion, 28 November 1996.
6 K. P. Singh Deo, Congress, speech in the Lok Sabha, 28 November 1996.
7 P. Mukherjee, RSP, speech in the Lok Sabha, 28 November 1996.
8 Ibid.
9 Ibid.
10 S. M. Dev, Congress, speech in the Lok Sabha, 29 November 1996.
11 K. P. Singh Deo, Congress, speech in the Lok Sabha, 28 November 1996.
12 S. R. Choudhary, Congress, speech in the Lok Sabha, 28 November 1996.
13 P. Mukherjee, RSS, speech in the Lok Sabha, 28 November 1996.
14 P. Mishra, Congress, speech in the Lok Sabha, 9 September 1996.
15 K. P. Singh Deo, Congress, speech in the Lok Sabha, 28 November 1996.
16 S. M. Dev, Congress, speech in the Lok Sabha, 29 December 1996.
17 S. Panigrahi, Congress, speech in the Lok Sabha, 28 November 1996
18 S. Panigrahi, speech in the Lok Sabha, 11 December 1996.
19 Prime Minister, Deve Gowda, speech in the Lok Sabha, 29 November 1996.
20 Prime Minister, I. K. Gujral, speech in the Lok Sabha, 16 May 1997.
21 S. Panigrahi, Congress, speech in the Lok Sabha, 28 November 1996.
22 B. K. Deo, BJP, speech in the Lok Sabha, 24 April 2000.
23 B. K. Deo, interview, Bhawanipatna, 10 February 1999.
24 B. K. Deo, BJP, speech in the Lok Sabha, 19 December 2000.
25 B. K. Deo, BJP, speech in the Lok Sabha, 29 August 2001.
26 Ibid.
27 B. K. Deo, Interview, Bhawanipatna, 10 February 1999.
28 K. P. Singh Deo, Congress, speech in the Lok Sabha, 30 August 2001.
29 K. P. Singh Deo, Congress, speech in the Lok Sabha, 9 August 2001.
30 P. Acharya, BJD, speech in the Lok Sabha, 30 August 2001.
31 Ibid.
32 'Starvation deaths', Lok Sabha question no. 11 dated 19 November 2001, by K. P. Singh Deo (Congress, Orissa) and S. K. Shinde (Congress, Maharashtra).
33 Ajit Singh, Union Minister of Agriculture, statement in the Lok Sabha, 19 November 2001.

9 PURULIA'S ACHIEVEMENT

1 The district owes its name to Purulia village, now a town, which grew in importance as the headquarters of the erstwhile Manbhum district in 1838. The name was retained when the district was separated from Bihar and merged with West Bengal in 1956 (Purulia Gazetteer 1985: 1).
2 Statistics provided by the Office of the District Controller, Food and Supplies, Purulia.
3 Figures are based on the 1991 Census (Government of West Bengal 1999a). The main SC groups in Purulia are Bauri, Mahato, Rajwar, Dom and Goala. The major ST groups are Santhal, Bhumij, Munda, Kora and Oraon (Purulia Gazetteer 1985: 140–154).
4 The exact figures for SC and ST categories were surprisingly unavailable but were

generally expected to be even lower. The average literacy rate in rural Purulia was approximately 35 per cent and in most areas was below 10 per cent for women (Government of West Bengal 1999c).

5   Senior district officials admitted that most river lift irrigation projects were normally defunct in drought years and that the construction of large-scale dams was urgently required. In addition, irrigation department officials complained that since farmers of the district preferred cultivating four crops annually – on the same piece of land – the provision of continuous irrigation facilities was necessary and particularly challenging since this did not give much opportunity to the irrigation department to repair and maintain existing irrigation structures. Irrigation engineers further pointed out that, if an irrigation project was temporarily stopped, farmers would complain to Panchayat representatives and the ruling CPI (M) party would intervene to pressure the irrigation department to make the project operational immediately.

6   For details, see Boyce (1987), Webster (1990), Lieten (1992), Mallick (1993) and Sengupta and Gazdar (1996).

7   Information made available from the Natural Resources Data Management System Centre, Purulia.

8   Anondo Rajowar, interview, Purulia, 8 December 2000.

9   The District Social Welfare Officer appeared particularly suspicious of my requests to study ICDS survey data on child malnutrition. It appeared that he was worried that, if the high rates of malnutrition borne out in the survey were made public, it would reduce CARE funding of ICDS projects in Purulia. Similarly, there was limited available information on the NMMP and several district officials claimed that not even the District Magistrate knew the details related to the implementation of the programme and that reports documenting NMMP activities and expenditures had not been submitted by the district to the state and central governments for several years.

10   S. K. Sarkar, interview, Purulia, 9 December 2000.

11   In West Bengal, the Collector is usually referred to as the District Magistrate.

12   Dr Amiya Kumar Sengupta, interview, Purulia, 20 December 2000.

13   In the early 1990s, a group of foreigners were arrested for having supplied arms and ammunitions to a religious sect in Purulia.

14   Field visits confirmed the overwhelming support enjoyed by the CPI(M) in rural areas of Purulia. Almost every village had a few mud walls painted with the symbols of the CPI(M) party, and in larger villages there was usually a very visible 'party office'.

15   Sukumar Roy, interview, Purulia, 9 December 2000.

16   Satya Ranjan Mahato, interview, Purulia, 18 December 2000.

17   Surya Kanta Mishra, interview, Calcutta, 24 November 1998.

18   Bilasi Bala Sahis, interview, Calcutta, 24 November 1998.

19   Upen Kishku, interview, Calcutta, 24 November 1998.

20   K. Singh Deo, President of the Trinamul Congress – Purulia, interview, Purulia, 20 January 1999.

21   Arun Sharma, interview, Purulia, 11 December 2000.

22   For an overview of the Panchayat system and decentralised government in West Bengal, see Kumar and Ghosh (1996) and Ghatak and Ghatak (2000).

23   Half of the IAS cadre in each state must be recruited from other states. In addition, at least one fifth of the cadre must be recruited ('promoted') from within the state's own civil service. Those who are promoted from the state civil service to IAS ranks are popularly referred to as 'promotees' and enjoy the same rank and status as that of IAS officers.

24   A promotee District Magistrate of Purulia argued that promotees in general were better aware of ground-level realities than young IAS officers and that thepersonal dynamism of a young IAS officer does not matter much in West Bengal (A. Das, interview, Purulia, 8 December 2000).

25 Swapan Banerjee, interview, Purulia, 20 January 1999.
26 Mr Dasgupta, Additional District Magistrate, interview, Purulia, 14 December 2000.
27 Debasish Basu, interview, Purulia, 18 January 1999.
28 A. Das, interview, Purulia, 8 December 2000.
29 Arup Das, interview, Purulia, 10 December 2000 and 12 December 2000. Since the matter was still under consideration in the Calcutta High Court and thus *sub judice*, the judge's report was not available to the public at the time of the study. The main conclusions are based on two interviews with the judge in December 2000.
30 Biman Bose, interview, Calcutta, 2 November 1998.
31 Surya Kanta Mishra, Minister of Panchayati Raj and Land Reform, Government of West Bengal, interview, Calcutta, 24 November 1998.
32 Mr K. Chakrabarty provided research assistance for parts of this section.
33 According to the District Information Office, a total of 27 newspapers were published from Purulia as of December 2000.
34 Satya Ranjan Mahato, Minister of Relief, Government of West Bengal, interview, Purulia, 18 December 2000.
35 Interviews with Ujjal Kumar Mishra (*Purulia Darpan*), 22 January 1998 and Asit Kumar Basu (*Manbhum Sambad*) 11 February 2001.
36 Interviews with Kishore Saha (*Ananda Bazaar Patrika*, 20 January 1999), Kanchan Chakrabarty (*Ananda Bazaar Patrika*, 19 December 2000) and Noni Gopal Pal (*The Statesman*, 21 December 2000).
37 Kishore Saha, interview, Purulia, 20 January 1999.
38 In a recent study Besley and Burgess (2002) ranked 16 Indian states in terms of government responsiveness to media coverage. West Bengal was third on the list, far higher than Orissa, which was placed at 12.

BIBLIOGRAPHY

Alamgir, M. (1978) *Bangladesh: A Case of Below Poverty Level Equilibrium Trap*, Dhaka: Bangladesh Institute of Development Studies.

Alamgir, M. (1980) *Famine in South Asia*, Cambridge, MA: Oelgeschlager, Gunn & Hain.

Arnold, D. (1979) 'Looting, Grain Riots and Government Policy in South India 1918', *Past and Present*, 84:111–145.

Ashton, B., Hill, K., Piazza, A. and Zeitz, R. (1984) 'Famine in China, 1958–61', *Population and Development Review*, 10 (4):613–646.

Atkinson, A. B. (1993) 'Capabilities, Exclusion, and the Supply of Goods', Welfare State Programme Discussion Paper WSP97, London School of Economics.

Atkinson, A. B. (1998) 'The Contribution of Amartya Sen to Welfare Economics', unpublished paper, Nuffield College, Oxford.

Aykroyd, W. R. (1971) 'Definition of Different Degrees of Starvation', in G. Blix *et al.* (eds), *Famine: A Symposium Dealing With Nutrition and Relief Operations in Times of Disaster*, Uppsala: Almquist and Wiksell.

Aykroyd, W. R. (1974) *The Conquest of Famine*, London: Chatto and Windus.

Banik, D. (2001) 'The Transfer Raj: Indian Civil Servants on the Move', *European Journal of Development Research*, 13 (1):104–132.

Banik, D. and Brekke, K. A. (2004) 'Politicians as Saviours: The Incentive to Preserve Poverty', unpublished paper, Centre for Development and the Environment, University of Oslo.

Bathla, S. (1998) *Women, Democracy and the Media: Cultural and Political Representations in the Indian Press*, New Delhi: Sage Publications.

Becker, J. (1996) *Hungry Ghosts: China's Secret Famine*, London: John Murray.

Beetham, D. (1999) *Democracy and Human Rights*, Cambridge: Polity Press.

Behura, N. K. and Das, P. K. (1991) 'Effect of Drought on Health Condition and Nutritional Status of People', in P. K. Nayak and A. Mahajan (eds), *Human Encounter with Drought*, New Delhi: Reliance Publishing House.

Berg, A. (1971) 'Famine Contained: Notes and Lessons From the Bihar Experience', in G. Blix *et al.* (eds), *Famine: A Symposium Dealing with Nutrition and Relief Operations in Times of Disaster*, Uppsala: Almquist and Wiksell.

Berg, A. (1987) *Malnutrition: What Can Be Done?*, Washington, DC: The World Bank/ Johns Hopkins University Press.

Besley, T. and Burgess, R. (2002) 'The Political Economy of Government Responsiveness:

Theory and Evidence from India', discussion paper, London School of Economics (http://econ.lse.ac.uk/~rburgess/wp/media.pdf).

Bhagwati, J. (1995) 'The New Thinking on Development', *Journal of Democracy*, 6 (4):50–64.

Bhalla, S. S. and Bandyopadhyay, S. (1992) 'The Politics and Economics of Drought in India', in K. Basu and P. Nayak (eds), *Development Policy and Economic Theory*, New Delhi: Oxford University Press.

Bhaskar, M. (1989) *Press and Working Class Consciousness in Developing Societies: A Case Study of an Indian State – Kerala*, New Delhi: Gian Publishing House.

Bhatia, B. M. (1993) 'The "Entitlement Approach" to Famine Analysis: A Critique', in J. Floud and A. Rangasami (eds), *Famine and Society*, New Delhi: The Indian Law Institute.

Blix, G., Hofvander, Y. and Vahiquist, B. (eds) (1971) *Famine: A Symposium Dealing with Nutrition and Relief Operations in Times of Disaster*, Uppsala: Almquist and Wiksell.

Bova, R. (1997) 'Democracy and Liberty: The Cultural Connection', *Journal of Democracy*, 8 (1):112–126.

Bowbrick, P. (1986) 'The Causes of Famine: A Refutation of Sen Theory', *Food Policy*, 11 (2):105–124.

Bowbrick, P. (1987) 'Rejoinder: An Untenable Hypothesis on the Causes of Famine', *Food Policy*, 12 (1):5–9.

Boyce, J. (1987) *Agrarian Impasse in Bengal: Institutional Constraints to Technological Change*, Oxford: Oxford University Press.

Brass, P. (1986) 'The Political Uses of Crisis: The Bihar Famine of 1966–1967', *Journal of Asian Studies*, 45 (2):245–267.

Brennan, L. (1984) 'The Development of the Indian Famine Codes' in B. Currey and G. Hugo (eds), *Famine as a Geographical Phenomenon*, Riedel: Dordrecht.

Buch, N. and Baboo, B. (1997) 'Drought in Kalahandi, Nuapada and Bolangir: Action Plan for Mitigation and Rehabilitation', unpublished paper, April 1997.

CAG (1999) *Report of the CAG on the Union Government for the Year ended March 1998*, Delhi: Office of the Comptroller and Auditor General, Government of India (http://www.cagindia.org/reports/civil/1999_book3/).

CAG (2001) *Audit Reports on the State Governments – Orissa: Report (Commercial) for the Year ended 31 March 2000*, Delhi: Office of the Comptroller and Auditor General, Government of India (http://www.cagindia.org/states/orissa/2001_comm/index.htm).

Chatterjee, M. (1996) *Lessons Learned from 20 Years of ICDS*, New Delhi: World Bank.

Chattopadhyay, B. (1987) 'Understanding the Bengal Famine of 1943', in B. Chattopadhyay and P. Spitz (eds), *Food Systems and Society in Eastern India: Selected Readings*, Geneva: United Nations Research Institute for Social Development.

Cox, G. W. (1981) 'The Ecology of Famine: An Overview', in J. R. K. Robson (ed.), *Famine: Its Causes, Effects, and Management*, New York: Gordon and Breach Science Publishers.

Currey, B. (1978) 'The Famine Syndrome: Its Definition for Preparedness and Prevention in Bangladesh', *Ecology of Food and Nutrition*, 7 (2):87–98.

Currey, B. and Hugo, G. (1984) *Famine as a Geographical Phenomenon*, Riedel: Dordrecht.

Currie, B. (1998) 'Laws for the Rich and Flaws for the Poor? Legal Action and Food Insecurity in the Kalahandi Case', in H. O'Neill and J. Toye (eds), *A World without Famine? New Approaches to Aid and Development*, Basingstoke: Macmillan.

Currie, B. (2000) *The Politics of Hunger in India: A Study of Democracy, Governance and Kalahandi's Poverty*, Basingstoke: Macmillan.

Dahl, R. A. (1992) 'Democracy and Human Rights Under Different Conditions of Development', in A. Eide and B. Hagtvet (eds), *Human Rights in Perspective: A Global Assessment*, Oxford: Blackwell Publishers.

Devereux, S. (1993) *Theories of Famine*, London: Harvester Wheatsheaf.

Devereux, S. (2000) 'Famine in the Twentieth Century', IDS Working Paper 105, Brighton: Institute for Development Studies.

Diamond, L. (1996) 'Is the Third Wave Over?' *Journal of Democracy*, 7 (3):20–37.

Dirks, R. (1993) 'Starvation and Famine: Cross-Cultural Codes and some Hypothesis Tests', *Cross-Cultural Research*, 27 (1, 2):28–70.

Drèze, J. (1990) 'Famine Prevention in India', in J. Drèze and A. Sen (eds), *The Political Economy of Hunger: Famine Prevention*, Oxford: Clarendon Press.

Drèze, J. and Sen, A. (1989) *Hunger and Public Action*, Oxford: Clarendon Press.

Drèze, J. and Sen, A. (1995) *India: Economic Development and Social Opportunity*, Delhi: Oxford University Press.

Dubashi, P. R. (1992) 'Drought and Development', *Economic and Political Weekly*, 27 (13):A27–A36.

Dubashi, P. R. (1994) 'Strategies to Counter Drought', *Economic and Political Weekly*, 29 (40):2602.

Dunnett, P. J. S. (1988) *The World Newspaper Industry*, London: Croom Helm.

Dyson, T. and Maharatna, A. (1992) 'Bihar Famine, 1966–67 and Maharashtra Drought, 1970–73: The Demographic Consequences', *Economic and Political Weekly*, 27 (26):1325–1331.

Echeverri-Gent, J. (1988) 'Guaranteed Employment in an Indian State: The Maharashtra Experience', *Asian Survey*, 28 (12):1294–1310.

Edkins, J. (2000) *Whose Hunger? Concepts of Famine, Practices of Aid*, Minneapolis: University of Minnesota Press.

Edkins, J. (2002) 'Mass Starvation and the Limitations of Famine Theorising', paper presented at the conference, *Ending Famine in the 21st Century*, organised by the Institute for Development Studies, University of Sussex, Brighton, 27 February–1 March 2002.

FAO (1999) 'Food Insecurity: When People Must Live with Hunger and Fear Starvation', *The State of Food Insecurity in the World 1999*, Rome: Food and Agricultural Organization.

Fine, B. (1997) 'Entitlement Failure?' *Development and Change*, 28 (4):617–647.

Fischer, H. W. (1994) *Response to Disaster: Fact versus Fiction & Its Perpetuation – The Sociology of Disaster*, New York: University Press of America.

Foege, W. H. (1971) 'Famine, Infections, and Epidemics' in G. Blix *et al.* (eds), *Famine: A Symposium Dealing With Nutrition and Relief Operations in Times of Disaster*, Uppsala: Almquist and Wiksell.

de Gaay Fortman, B. (1990) 'Entitlement and Development: An Institutional Approach to the Acquirement Problem', ISS Working Paper No. 87, The Hague: Institute of Social Studies.

Ghatak, M. and Ghatak, M. (2000) 'Grassroots Democracy: A Study of the Panchayat System in West Bengal', paper presented at the conference on *Experiments in Empowered Deliberative Democracy*, Madison, WI, January 2000.

Gore, C. (1993) 'Entitlement Relations and "Unruly" Social Practices: A Comment on the Work of Amartya Sen', *Journal of Development Studies*, 29 (3):429–60.

Government of Orissa (2000) 'White Paper on Drought in Orissa', Cuttack: Revenue Department.

Government of Orissa (2001) *Economic Survey, 2000–2001*, Bhubaneswar: Finance Department.

Government of West Bengal (1999a) *Key Statistics: Purulia 1998*, Purulia: Bureau of Applied Economics and Statistics.

Government of West Bengal (1999b) *Statistical Abstract, 1997–1998*, Calcutta: Bureau of Applied Economics and Statistics.

Government of West Bengal (1999c) *District Statistical Handbook 1998: Purulia*, Calcutta: Bureau of Applied Economics and Statistics.

Greenough, P. (1982) *Prosperity and Misery in Modern Bengal: The Famine of 1943–1944*, New York: Oxford University Press.

Habermas, J. (1989) *The Structural Transformation of the Public Sphere: An Inquiry into a Category of Bourgeois Society*, Cambridge: Polity Press.

Haque, M. and Narag, S. (1983) 'The Coverage of Two Indian Elections by Three Prestigious Indian Dailies', *Media Asia*, 10 (1):35–43.

Harriss, B. (1988) 'Limitations of the "Lessons from India"', in D. Curtis *et al.* (eds), *Preventing Famine: Policies and Prospects for Africa*, London: Routledge.

Harriss, J. (2000) 'How Much Difference Does Politics Make? Regime Differences across Indian States and Rural Poverty Reduction', working paper, LSE Development Studies Institute, No. 00-01.

High Court of Orissa (1992) 'O.J.C. No. 3517 of 1988, O.J.C. No. 525 of 1989', Cuttack: High Court of Orissa.

Howe, P. and Devereux, S. (2004) 'Famine Intensity and Magnitude Scales: A Proposal for an Instrumental Definition of Famine', *Disasters*, 28 (4): 353–372.

Hubbard, M. (1988) 'Drought Relief and Drought-Proofing in the State of Gujarat, India', in D. Curtis *et al.* (eds), *Preventing Famine: Policies and Prospects for Africa*, London: Routledge.

Jain, R. B. (1985a) 'Electronics Policy and Indian Parliament', *Indian Journal of Public Administration*, April–June 1985.

Jain, R. B. (ed.) (1985b) *The Legislative Process in Development*, New Delhi: Gitanjali Publishing House.

Jeffrey, R. (1987) 'Culture of Daily Newspapers in India: How It's Grown, What It Means', *Economic and Political Weekly*, 22 (4):607–611.

Jeffrey, R. (1993) 'Indian Language Newspapers and Why They Grow', *Economic and Political Weekly*, 28 (38):2004–2011.

Jeffrey, R. (1997) 'Oriya: Identifying . . . with Newspapers: Indian Language Newspapers 3', *Economic and Political Weekly*, 32 (11):511–514.

Jeffrey, R. (2000) *India's Newspaper Revolution: Capitalism, Politics and the Indian-Language Press, 1977–99*, London: Hurst & Co.

Jelliffe, D. B. and Jelliffe, E. F. P. (1971) 'The Effects of Starvation on the Function of the Family and of Society', in G. Blix *et al.* (eds), *Famine: A Symposium Dealing with Nutrition and Relief Operations in Times of Disaster*. Uppsala: Almquist and Wiksell.

Joseph, A. and Sharma, K. (eds) (1994) *Whose News? The Media and Women's Issues*, New Delhi: Sage Publications.

Kalahandi District Statistical Handbook (1997) Bhawanipatna: District Statistical Department, Government of Orissa.

Kalahandi Gazetteer (1980) *Orissa District Gazetteers: Kalahandi*, by N. Senapati and D. C. Kuanr, Cuttack: Gazetteers Unit, Department of Revenue, Government of Orissa.

Katiyar, V. S. (1993) *Human Dimensions and Drought Management in India*, Jaipur: Pointer Publishers.

Keen, D. (1994) *The Benefits of Famines: A Political Economy of Famine Relief in South-Western Sudan, 1983–1989*, Princeton, NJ: Princeton University Press.

Keys, A. *et al.* (1950) *The Biology of Human Starvation*, Minneapolis: The University of Minnesota Press.

Kumar, G. and Ghosh, B. (1996) *West Bengal Panchayat Elections 1993: A Study in Participation*, New Delhi: Institute of Social Sciences.

Lal, A. B. (ed.) (1956) *Indian Parliament*, Allahabad: Chaitanya Publishing.

Lieten, G. K. (1992) *Continuity and Change in Rural West Bengal*, New Delhi: Sage Publications.

Mahapatra, R. (1994) *Food Crises in Kalahandi: 1960/61–1992/93*, M.Phil. dissertation submitted to the Centre for Economic Studies and Planning, School of Social Sciences, Jawaharlal Nehru University.

Mallick, R. (1993) *Development Policy of a Communist Government: West Bengal since 1977*, Cambridge: Cambridge University Press.

Martorell, R. (1999) 'The Nature of Child Malnutrition and its Long-Term Implications', *Food and Nutrition Bulletin*, 20 (3):288–292.

Mathur, K. and Bhattacharya, M. (1975) *Administrative Response to Emergency: Scarcity Administration in Maharashtra*, Delhi: Concept Publishing.

Mathur, K. and Jayal, N. (1992) 'Drought Management in India: The Long Term Perspective', *Disasters*, 16 (1):60–65.

Mathur, K. and Jayal, N. (1993) *Drought, Policy and Politics in India: The Need for a Long-Term Perspective*, New Delhi: Sage Publications.

Maxwell, D. G. (1995) 'Measuring Food Insecurity: The Frequency and Severity of Coping Strategies', FCND Discussion Paper No. 8, Washington, DC: International Food Policy Research Institute.

Measham, A. R. and Chatterjee, M. (1999) *Wasting Away: The Crisis of Malnutrition in India*, Washington, DC: World Bank.

Mishra Commission (1990) 'Report on Inquiry in O.J.C.'s No. 3517/88 and No. 525/89', Cuttack: Orissa High Court.

Mishra, M. K. (1989) *Folksongs of Kalahandi*, Bhubaneswar: Mayur Publications.

Mitra, S. (1992) *Power, Protest and Participation: Local Elites and the Politics of Development in India*, London: Routledge.

Mohanty, M. (1990) 'Class, Caste and Dominance in a Backward State: Orissa', in F. Frankel and M. S. A. Rao (eds), *Dominance and State Power in Modern India: Decline of a Social Order*, Vol. 2, Delhi: Oxford University Press.

Mohanty, M. and Mishra, L. N. (1976) 'Orissa: Patterns of Political Stagnation', in I. Narain (ed.), *State Politics in India*, Meerut: Meenakshi Prakashan.

Mooley, D. A. (1994) 'Origin, Incidence and Impact of Droughts over Indian and Remedial Measures for their Mitigation', *Sadhana*, 19 (August):597–608.

Morris-Jones, W. H. (1957) *Parliament in India*, Philadelphia: University of Pennsylvania Press.

Mundle, S. (1974) 'Relief Planning in Maharashtra', *Indian Journal of Public Administration*, 20.

Narayana, G. (1980) 'Rule Making for Scheduled Castes: Analysis of Lok Sabha Debates, 1962–71', *Economic and Political Weekly*, 15 (8): 433–440.

NHRC (1996) 'Report of the Visit of the Official Team (11–12–96 to 17–12–96) of the National Human Rights Commission to the Scarcity Affected Areas of Orissa', New Delhi: National Human Rights Commission.

Nolan, P. (1993) 'The Causation and Prevention of Famines: A Critique of A. K. Sen', *Journal of Peasant Studies*, 21 (1):1–28.

Orissa Relief Code (1996) *The Orissa Relief Code (Corrected up to 31/12/1996)*, by Board of Revenue (Special Relief), Cuttack: Revenue Department, Government of Orissa.

Osmani, S. (1995) 'The Entitlement Approach to Famine: An Assessment', in K. Basu, P. Pattanaik and K. Suzumura (eds), *Choice, Welfare and Development*, Oxford: Oxford University Press.

Pacey, A. and Payne, P. (eds) (1985) *Agricultural Development and Nutrition*, London: Hutchinson.

Panda Commission (1988) 'Report of the Panda Commission Inquiry in the Matter of Writ Petition No. 12847 of 1985', New Delhi: Supreme Court of India.

Payne, P. (1994) 'Not Enough Food: Malnutrition and Famine', in B. Harris-White and Sir R. Hoffenberg (eds), *Food: Multidisciplinary Perspectives*, Oxford: Blackwell Publishers.

Planning Commission (2000) 'Nutrition', Chapter 6.3.2 in *Annual Plan 2000–2001*, New Delhi: Planning Commission, Government of India. (http://planningcommission.nic.in/plans/annualplan/ap2021pdf/ap2021ch6–3.pdf).

Prasad, N. (1992) *A Pressing Matter: Women in Press*, Delhi: Friedrich Ebert Stiftung.

Przeworski, A., Alvarez, M. E., Cheibub, J. A. and Limongi, F. (2000) *Democracy and Development*, Cambridge: Cambridge University Press.

Purulia Gazetteer (1985) *Gazetteer of India: West Bengal – Puruliya*, Calcutta: West Bengal District Gazetteers, Government of West Bengal.

Rahman, A. and Haritash, N. (1985) *The Role of Parliament in the Formulation of National Science and Technology Policy*, New Delhi: National Institute of Science, Technology and Development Studies.

Ram, N. (1990) 'An Independent Press and Anti-hunger Strategies: The Indian Experience', in J. Drèze and A. Sen (eds), *The Political Economy of Hunger, Vol. 1: Entitlement and Well-Being*, Oxford: Clarendon Press.

Ramalingaswami, V., Deo, M. G., Guleria, J. S., Malhotra, K. K., Sood, S. K., Prakash, O., and Sinha, R. V. N. (1971) 'Studies of the Bihar Famine of 1966–67', in G. Blix *et al.* (eds), *Famine: A Symposium Dealing with Nutrition and Relief Operations in Times of Disaster*, Uppsala: Almquist and Wiksell.

Ramalingaswami, V., Jonsson, U. and Rohde, J. (1996) 'Nutrition Commentary: The Asian Enigma', *The Progress of Nations 1996*, New York: UNICEF (http://www.unicef.org).

Rangasami, A. (1985) 'Failure of Exchange Entitlements Theory of Famine', *Economic and Political Weekly*, 20 (41, 42):1747–1752, 1797–1801.

Rangasami, A. (1994) 'The "Limits" of Drought', in R. K. Gurjar (ed.), *Drought Planning in India*, Jaipur: Printwell.

Ravallion, M. (1996) 'Famines and Economics', Policy Research Working Paper 1693, Washington, DC: World Bank.

Reddy, S. (1988) 'An Independent Press Working Against Famine: The Nigerian Experience', *The Journal of Modern African Studies*, 26 (2):337–345.

Report of the Eleventh Finance Commission (2000) (http://ndmindia.nic.in/management/efc.html).

Rivers, J., Holt, J., Seaman, J. and Bowden, M. (1976) 'Lessons for Epidemiology from the Ethiopian Famines', *Annales Sociéte Belge de Médecine Tropicale*, 56 (4–5): 345–360.

Robson, J. R. K. (1972) *Malnutrition: Its Causation and Control*, Vol. 1, New York: Gordon and Breach.

Rubin, O. (2001) *Entitlements, Employment Programmes and Democracy: An Assessment of Amartya Sen's Famine Contributions*, M.A. thesis submitted to the Department of Political Science, University of Copenhagen.

Sainath, P. (1996) *Everybody Loves a Good Drought: Stories from India's Poorest Districts*, New Delhi: Penguin Books.

Saxena Commission (2003): 'The Right to Food, Two Years on' (http://www.righttofoodindia.org/data/comm3.pdf).

Scarfe, W. and Scarfe, A. (1969) *Tiger on a Rein: Report on the Bihar Famine*, London: Geoffrey Chapman.

Schumpeter, J. (1947) *Capitalism, Socialism and Democracy*, 2nd edn, New York: Harper.

Scrimshaw, N. S., Taylor, C. E. and Gordon, J. E. (1968) 'Interactions of Nutrition and Infection', WHO Monograph Series, No. 57, Geneva: World Health Organization.

Sen, A. (1981) *Poverty and Famines: An Essay on Entitlement and Deprivation*, Oxford: Clarendon Press.

Sen, A. (1983a) 'Development: Which Way Now?', *The Economic Journal*, 93:745–762.

Sen, A. (1983b) 'Poor, Relatively Speaking', *Oxford Economic Papers*, 35:135–169.

Sen, A. (1984) 'Food Battles: Conflicts in the Access to Food', *Food and Nutrition*, 10:81–89.

Sen, A. (1986a) 'The Causes of Famine: A Reply', *Food Policy*, 11 (2):125–132.

Sen, A. (1986b) 'How is India Doing?' in D. Basu and R. Sisson (eds), *Social and Economic Development in India: A Reassessment*, New Delhi: Sage Publications.

Sen, A. (1987) 'Hunger and Entitlements', Helsinki: World Institute for Development Economics Research.

Sen, A. (1990a) 'Food, Economics, and Entitlements', in J. Drèze and A. Sen (eds), *The Political Economy of Hunger, Vol. 1: Entitlement and Well-Being*, Oxford: Clarendon Press.

Sen, A. (1990b) 'Public Action to Remedy Hunger', The Arturo Tanco Memorial Lecture, August 1990, London: The Hunger Project and CAB International, in association with The Commonwealth Trust and The Royal Institute of International Affairs (http://www.thp.org/reports/sen/sen890.htm).

Sen, A. (1991) 'Public Action to Remedy Hunger', *Interdisciplinary Science Reviews*, 16 (4): 324–336.

Sen, A. (1992) *Inequality Reexamined*, New York: Oxford University Press.

Sen, A. (1993) 'The Causation and Prevention of Famines: A Reply', *Journal of Peasant Studies*, 21 (1):29–40.

Sen, A. (2000) *Development as Freedom*, New York: Anchor Books.

Sengupta, S. and Gazdar, H. (1996) 'Agrarian Politics and Rural Development in West Bengal', in J. Drèze and A. Sen (eds), *Indian Development: Selected Regional Perspectives*, Oxford: Oxford University Press.

Srivastava, H. S. (1968) *History of Indian Famines and Development of Famine Policy 1858–1918*, Agra: Sri Ram Nehra & Co.

Subramaniam, V. (1975) *Parched Earth: The Maharashtra Drought 1970–73*, Bombay: Orient Longman.

Supreme Court of India (1989) '1989 Supp (1) Supreme Court Cases 258: Writ Petition (Civil) No. 12847 of 1985 *Kishan Pattnayak and Another* versus *The State of Orissa*; Writ Petition (Civil) No. 1081 of 1987 *Indian People's Front* versus *The State of Orissa and others*', New Delhi: Supreme Court of India.

Swaminathan Research Foundation (2000) 'Ending Undernutrition in India by 2020', *Food and Nutrition Bulletin*, 21 (3): 70–73.

Törnquist, O. (2002) *Popular Development and Democracy: Case Studies with Rural Dimensions in the Philippines, Indonesia, and Kerala*, Oslo: Centre for Development and the Environment, University of Oslo in cooperation with UNRISD.

Verghese, G. (1978) 'Press Censorship under Indira Gandhi', in P. C. Horton (ed.), *The Third World and Press Freedom*, New York: Praeger Publishers.

de Waal, A. (1989) *Famine That Kills: Darfur, Sudan, 1984–85*, Oxford: Clarendon Press.

de Waal, A. (1990) 'Reassessment of Entitlement Theory in the Light of Recent Famines in Africa', *Development and Change*, 21 (3): 474–478.

de Waal, A. (1996) 'Social Contract and Deterring Famine: First Thoughts', *Disasters*, 20 (3):194–205.

de Waal, A. (1997) *Famine Crimes: Politics and the Disaster Relief Industry in Africa*, Oxford: James Curry.

de Waal, A. (2000) 'Democratic Political Process and the Fight against Famine', IDS Working Paper 107, Brighton: Institute for Development Studies.

Walker, P. (1989) *Famine Early Warning Systems: Victims and Destitution*, London: Earthscan Publications.

Webster, N. (1990) *Panchayati Raj and the Decentralisation of Development Planning in West Bengal: A Case Study*, Copenhagen: Centre for Development Research.

Woldemariam, M. (1984) *Rural Vulnerability to Famine in Ethiopia: 1958–1977*, Addis Ababa: Vikas.

World Bank (2001) *India – Improving Household Food and Nutrition Security: Achievements and Challenges Ahead*, Volume 1, Main Report, Washington, DC: The World Bank.

Young, H. and Jaspars, S. (1995) *Nutrition Matters: People, Food and Famine*, London: Intermediate Technology Publications.

INDEX